The Municipal
Year Book
2011

The authoritative source book of local government data and developments

The Municipal
Year Book
2011

Washington, DC

ICMA advances professional local government worldwide. Its mission is to create excellence in local governance by developing and advancing professional management of local government. ICMA, the International City/County Management Association, provides member support; publications, data, and information; peer and results-oriented assistance; and training and professional development to more than 9,000 city, town, and county experts and other individuals and organizations throughout the world. The management decisions made by ICMA's members affect 185 million individuals living in thousands of communities, from small villages and towns to large metropolitan areas.

Volume 78, 2011

ISBN: 978-0-87326-766-3

ISSN: 0077-2186

43640

Library of Congress Catalog Card Number:

34-27121

The views expressed in this *Year Book* are those of individual authors and are not necessarily those of ICMA.

Suggested citation for use of material in this *Year Book*: Jane S. Author [and John N. Other], "Title of Article," in *The Municipal Year Book 2011* (Washington, D.C.: ICMA, 2011), 00–000.

Design and composition: Charles E. Mountain

Contents

Directories

A Note to Our Readers

In focus groups held at ICMA's annual conference two years ago, we asked participants to tell us what they valued in the *Municipal Year Book*. Periodically touching base with readers is an essential step to maintaining relevancy. The *Year Book* has served its constituency well over the years, but we were aware that the Internet had begun to change how and where people look for information. And, like any publisher, we need to make the best use of our limited resources. With these realities in mind, we have refashioned the *Year Book*, creating a leaner and more relevant publication that focuses primarily on issues that readers have identified as priority content areas—issues such as leadership, ethics, citizen engagement, professional development, and sustainability.

One omission in this edition is worth noting: the absence of the municipal and county officials' salaries (formerly, C1 and C2). This omission is temporary. Although the Waters Consulting Group's salary survey tool provided an excellent online resource, the number of local governments reporting was so small that the survey findings were not usable. Especially in light of situations like that in Bell, California, we are acutely aware of how important salary data can be. The ICMA board determined at its October 2010 meeting that, as the professional association of appointed officials, ICMA needs to resume responsibility for collecting and reporting salary and compensation information. Accordingly, we will again be conducting our own salary and compensation surveys for chief appointed officials and will report summary data in future editions of the *Year Book*.

This new edition of the *Year Book* retains the essential elements of previous editions while eliminating information that can easily be found elsewhere or has been deemed to be of limited value to readers. And in keeping with its new streamlined approach, it has also been redesigned for an easier reading experience.

We hope you like these changes and welcome your feedback. Please send your comments or questions to me at jcotnoir@icma.org.

Jane C. Cotnoir
Editor, *Municipal Year Book*
ICMA

Acknowledgments

The Municipal Year Book, which provides local government officials with information on local government management, represents an important part of ICMA's extensive research program. Each year, ICMA surveys local officials on a variety of topics, and the data derived from their responses constitute the primary information source for the *Year Book*. Authors from local, state, and federal government agencies; universities; and public interest groups as well as ICMA staff prepare articles that describe the data collected and examine trends and developments affecting local government.

We would like to express our appreciation to the thousands of city and county managers, clerks, finance officers, personnel directors, police chiefs, fire chiefs, and other officials who patiently and conscientiously responded to ICMA questionnaires. It is only because of their time-consuming efforts that we are able to provide the information in this volume.

In addition, I would like to thank the ICMA staff who have devoted countless hours to making the *Year Book* so valuable. Ann I. Mahoney is the director of publishing and Jane C. Cotnoir is the *Year Book* editor. Other ICMA staff members who contributed to this publication are Evelina Moulder, director of survey research and information management; Valerie Hepler, director of publications production; Charles Mountain, senior graphic designer; Sebia Clark, program analyst; and Nedra James, editorial assistant.

Robert J. O'Neill Jr.
Executive Director
ICMA

Inside the *Year Book*

Local government concerns are increasingly complex and sophisticated, and the need for familiarity with a broad range of issues is unsurpassed. Furthering the knowledge base needed to better manage local government is one of ICMA's top goals.

Management Trends and Survey Research

1 Reflections on the First Decade of the 21st Century: Leadership Implications for Local Government

Local governments will face a host of challenges in the coming decade—natural, human, and technological threats; uneven economic recovery; and persistent social inequity. Across these areas local governments can assert vision and self-determination, yet there will always be elements that are beyond their control and beyond prediction. This article reflects on the past decade, on the lessons we have learned, and on the implications for local government leadership in 2011 and beyond. It addresses the need for sustainability, which encompasses the environment, the economy, and social equity, and for the effective management of two compelling forces that affect sustainability: disaster response and rapidly changing technologies. The premise is that the achievement of these societal objectives requires leadership, especially from professional local government managers, working together with all sectors of the community to build communities of intent—places to which residents feel connected and in which they want to live.

2 Second-Order Devolution? What City Managers Have to Say

For all the debates about the nature of federalism in the United States and the evolving relationships among the national, state, and local governments, the reality remains that, legally, local governments are "creatures of the state," subject to state statutory and constitutional grants of authority and discretion. The powers of counties, municipalities, towns, townships, and other general-purpose local governments are to be granted expressly by the states through laws, charters, or broad home rule provisions—that is, "second-order devolution." And the states have granted them to various degrees, resulting in extensive interstate variance in local discretionary powers. This article reports the results of a survey asking city managers, whose jobs are defined and actions bounded, in part, by the scope and degree of the decision-making authority they hold under state law, about their experiences with and perceptions of devolution at the local level.

3 Alternative Notions of Community: Understanding Local Government Responses to Immigrants

Immigration policy is widely understood to be the responsibility of the national government, but local governments across the country have been frustrated with Washington's inaction and ineffectiveness. With growing numbers of immigrants challenging their service delivery and financial resource capacities, many communities have imposed their own policies—the most notable being Arizona's SB 1070, widely characterized as one of the broadest and most stringent laws against illegal immigration in recent decades. As this article explains, these wide-ranging local ordinances, programs, and practices could affect the experiences of immigrants more directly and immediately than any policy changes at the national level. Moreover, they reflect broader notions of how to define community and of whether local government responsibilities for creating and maintaining community are primarily for the benefit of long-term residents or extend equally to new and diverse populations. Given these issues, a careful review of local government policies and practices is warranted, as is an effort to understand the factors influencing the selection of a particular local policy response.

4 Economic Development Strategies for Recessionary Times: Survey Results from 2009

ICMA has been tracking the use of economic development strategies among local municipalities every five years. Business attraction strategies—namely, firm-specific incentives and subsidies—have been the most common strategies reported. Over the decade of 1994–2004, local governments complemented this approach with strategies to promote business retention and expansion as well as small-business and community development; to these they added increased attention to the importance of accountability measures and the use of written business attraction plans. By the time that ICMA conducted its *Economic Development Survey 2009*, the financial crisis and meltdown on Wall Street had engulfed local governments in great economic uncertainty. This article reports the findings of that survey, shedding light on how local governments have responded to this turmoil and what actions they have taken to further develop their economies.

5 The Early Stage of Local Government Action to Promote Sustainability

Sustainability is a comprehensive concept that captures many of the major problems facing society today, problems that can be summarized by the three "e's": environment, economy, and social equity. Specifically, these are problems that have arisen from practices that will eventually deplete resources, lower quality of life, and fragment societies if they are not modified. Accordingly, the path toward addressing these problems requires attention to long-term interests through a broad range of actions in which all levels of government, all sectors of the economy, and all citizens must participate. This article reports on findings from ICMA's *Local Government Sustainability Policies and Programs, 2010* survey, a major effort

undertaken to examine what local elected officials and administrators have done so far to address the sustainability challenge and how they are working with citizens as partners to advance shared goals and change behaviors to advance sustainability.

6 Achieving Greater Accountability in Social Programs

The goal of prevention programs is to sustain and improve the lives of children, families, and communities. But there is little evidence of their success in addressing serious social problems, from crime to substance abuse to dropout rates. Most of the approaches now in use have never been rigorously evaluated, and some of the most widely used interventions have proved to be ineffective or harmful. Lacking reliable, research-based information about best practices, many communities invest in untested programs that are based on questionable assumptions, delivered with little quality control, and subject to little or no evaluation. This article describes an accountability system that is designed to improve the well-being of children and families while making the best use of limited public resources, enabling policy makers to accurately determine how well taxpayer dollars are being spent, whether the activities being supported justify the investment, and how the job might be done better.

7 The Hurt Dividend: Residents' Appreciation for Local Government Services in Tough Times

Although word on the street is that the recession is over, most pundits argue that government will remain sickly for months to come. In 2001, National Research Center, Inc. (NRC) partnered with ICMA to offer The National Citizen Survey™ to local governments, enabling them to garner residents' opinions about scores of local government services and many characteristics of community quality and thus identify current trends in resident opinions. In 2008, researchers at NRC sought to determine resident reactions to government services and their communities in the wake of the steep economic decline. Expectations were that the country's fall off the economic cliff would be reflected in a drop in ratings by those who had enjoyed local government services back when the economy was strong. This article reports on their somewhat surprising findings.

8 How Local Governments Are Navigating the Fiscal Crisis: Taking Stock and Looking Forward

The fiscal crisis that has engulfed local governments in the United States has the potential to fundamentally reshape local governance. For the most part, change is unavoidable because the decline in resources means that the government cannot maintain the status quo. Pressing need can unleash the creativity of participants in the local government to come up with innovative possibilities. This article reports on the results of an ICMA survey of city and county administrators about the effects of the fiscal crisis on their communities. With a special focus on 11 local governments that the Alliance for Innovation has been monitoring since the early months of 2009, it examines how the budget crisis has been affecting communities across the country, what approaches have been taken to handle budget retrenchment, and the extent to which forward-looking governments have made the commitment to long-term change.

9 Police and Fire Personnel, Salaries, and Expenditures for 2010

Unlike 2009, when it appeared that police and fire departments were shielded from budget cuts, 2010 brought financial challenges of such severity to local governments that police and fire departments saw their budgets reduced just like those of other local government departments. This article, which has long been a staple of the *Municipal Year Book*, is based on the results of an annual survey that is meant to provide a general picture of police and fire personnel and expenditures for each year. It presents the following information for both police and fire departments in tabular form: total personnel, the number of uniformed personnel, minimum crew per fire apparatus, entrance and maximum salaries, information on longevity pay, and a breakdown of departmental expenditures. Data from the 2010 survey are compared with those from 2009.

Directories

Directory 1 consists of eight lists providing the names and websites of U.S. state municipal leagues; provincial and territorial associations and unions in Canada; state agencies for community affairs; provincial and territorial agencies for local affairs in Canada; U.S. municipal management associations; international municipal management associations; state associations of counties; and U.S. councils of governments recognized by ICMA.

Directory 2 presents "Professional, Special Assistance, and Educational Organizations Serving Local and State Governments." The 81 organizations that are included provide educational and research services to members and others, strengthening professionalism in government administration.

Organization of Data

Most of the tabular data for *The Municipal Year Book 2011* were obtained from public officials through questionnaires developed and administered by ICMA. ICMA maintains databases with the result of these surveys. All survey responses are reviewed for errors. Extreme values are identified and investigated; logic checks are applied in the analysis of the results.

Government Definitions

A municipality, by census definition, is a "political subdivision within which a municipal corporation has been established to provide general local government for a specific population concentration in a defined area." This definition includes all active governmental units officially designated as cities, boroughs (except in Alaska), villages, or towns (except in Minnesota, New York, Wisconsin, and New England), and it generally includes all places incorporated under the procedures established by the several states.

Counties are the primary political administrative divisions of the state. In Louisiana these units are called parishes. Alaska has county-type governments called boroughs. There are certain unorganized areas of some states that are not included in the *Year Book* database and that have a county designation from the Census Bureau for strictly administrative purposes. These comprise 11 areas in Alaska, 5 areas in Rhode Island, 8 areas in Connecticut, and 7 areas in Massachusetts.[1]

According to the U.S. Bureau of the Census, in January 2007 there were 89,476 governments in the United States (Table 1).

Municipality Classification

Table 2 details the distribution of all municipalities of 2,500 and over in population by population, geographic region and division, metro status, and form of government.

Population This edition of the *Year Book* generally uses the 2000 Census Bureau figures for placing local governments in the United States into population

Table 1 U.S. Local Governments, 2007

Local governments	89,476
County	3,033
Municipal	19,492
Town or township	16,519
School district	13,051
Special district	37,381

Table 2 Cumulative Distribution of U.S. Municipalities with a Population of 2,500 and Over

Classification	Population								
	2,500 and over	5,000 and over	10,000 and over	25,000 and over	50,000 and over	100,000 and over	250,000 and over	500,000 and over	Over 1,000,000
Total, all cities	7,483	5,233	3,299	1,452	666	247	68	32	9
Population group									
Over 1,000,000	9	9	9	9	9	9	9	9	9
500,000-1,000,000	23	23	23	23	23	23	23	23	...[1]
250,000-499,999	36	36	36	36	36	36	36	...	...
100,000-249,999	179	179	179	179	179	179	...	...	...
50,000-99,999	419	419	419	419	419	...	...	...	...
25,000-49,999	786	786	786	786	...	...	...	...	...
10,000-24,999	1,847	1,847	1,847	...	...	...	...	...	...
5,000-9,999	1,934	1,934	...	...	...	...	...	...	...
2,500-4,999	2,250	...	...	...	...	...	...	...	...
Geographic region									
Northeast	2,012	1,471	897	326	114	33	8	4	2
North-Central	2,170	1,474	926	373	148	44	14	5	1
South	2,181	1,407	847	357	178	77	23	13	3
West	1,120	881	629	396	226	93	23	10	3
Geographic division									
New England	750	555	352	138	46	12	1	1	...
Mid-Atlantic	1,262	916	545	188	68	21	7	3	2
East North-Central	1,452	1,043	679	268	104	30	8	5	1
West North-Central	720	432	248	105	44	14	6	...	...
South Atlantic	937	608	387	170	86	34	9	4	...
East South-Central	468	310	169	56	23	12	3	2	...
West South-Central	777	488	290	131	69	31	11	7	3
Mountain	410	281	163	94	52	27	8	3	1
Pacific Coast	707	600	466	302	174	66	15	7	2
Metro status									
Central	540	539	539	504	361	175	65	31	9
Suburban	4,517	3,319	2,140	824	298	72	3	1	...
Independent	2,426	1,375	620	124	7	...	...	...	...
Form of government									
Mayor-council	3,280	2,042	1,195	491	240	99	40	21	6
Council-manager	3,647	2,791	1,882	910	412	143	26	10	3
Commission	143	110	70	25	9	5	2	1	...
Town meeting	349	235	106	5	7	...	...	...	...
Rep. town meeting	64	55	46	21	5	...	...	...	...

Note: This table comprises *only* city-type local governments with populations of 2,500 and above.

1   (...) indicates data not applicable or not reported.

groups for tabular presentation. The population categories are self-explanatory.

Geographic Classification Nine geographic divisions and four regions are used by the Bureau

of the Census (Figure 1). The nine divisions are *New England:* Connecticut, Maine, Massachusetts, New Hampshire, Rhode Island, and Vermont; *Mid-Atlantic:* New Jersey, New York, and Pennsylvania; *East North-Central:* Illinois, Indiana, Michigan, Ohio, and

Figure 1 U.S. Bureau of the Census Geographic Regions and Divisions

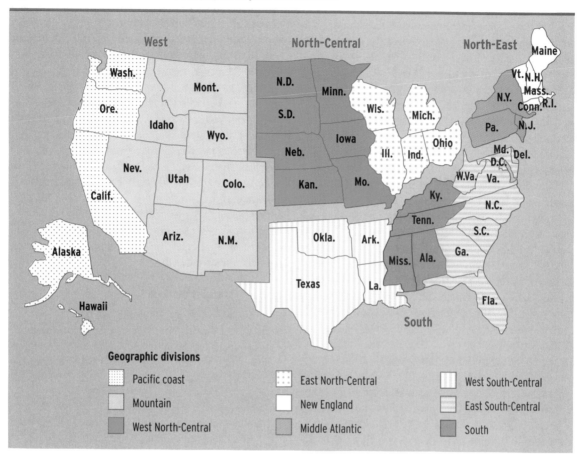

Wisconsin; *West North-Central:* Iowa, Kansas, Minnesota, Missouri, Nebraska, North Dakota, and South Dakota; *South Atlantic:* Delaware, the District of Columbia, Florida, Georgia, Maryland, North Carolina, South Carolina, Virginia, and West Virginia; *East South-Central:* Alabama, Kentucky, Mississippi, and Tennessee; *West South-Central:* Arkansas, Louisiana, Oklahoma, and Texas; *Mountain:* Arizona, Colorado, Idaho, Montana, Nevada, New Mexico, Utah, and Wyoming; and *Pacific Coast:* Alaska, California, Hawaii, Oregon, and Washington.

The geographic regions are consolidations of states in divisions: *Northeast:* Connecticut, Maine, Massachusetts, New Hampshire, New Jersey, New York, Pennsylvania, Rhode Island, and Vermont; *North-Central:* Illinois, Indiana, Iowa, Kansas, Michigan, Minnesota, Missouri, Nebraska, North Dakota, Ohio, South Dakota, and Wisconsin; *South:* Alabama, Arkansas, Delaware, the District of Columbia, Florida, Georgia, Kentucky, Louisiana, Maryland, Mississippi, North Carolina, Oklahoma, South Carolina, Tennessee, Texas, Virginia, and West Virginia; and *West:* Alaska, Arizona, California,

Colorado, Hawaii, Idaho, Montana, Nevada, New Mexico, Oregon, Utah, Washington, and Wyoming.

Metro Status Metro status refers to the status of a municipality within the context of the U.S. Office of Management and Budget (OMB) definition of a metropolitan area. A metropolitan area is typically "a core area containing a large population nucleus, together with adjacent communities having a high degree of economic and social integration with that core."[2] There are three levels of classification: metropolitan statistical areas, consolidated metropolitan statistical areas, and primary metropolitan statistical areas.

The current standards require that each newly qualifying *metropolitan statistical area* (MSA) must include *either* at least one city with a population of 50,000 or more, *or* a Census Bureau—defined urbanized area of at least 50,000 *and* a total metropolitan population of at least 100,000 (75,000 in New England).[3] The county (or counties) that contains the largest city becomes the central county (counties), along with any adjacent counties that have at least 50% of their population in the urbanized area surrounding the largest city in the MSA. Additional outlying counties are included in the MSA if they meet the specified requirement of commuting to the central counties and other selected requirements of metropolitan character (such as population density and percentage urban). In New England, the MSAs are defined in terms of cities and towns rather than counties.

An area that meets the requirements for an MSA and has a population of 1,000,000 or more may be recognized as a *consolidated metropolitan statistical area* (CMSA) if separate component areas can be identified within the entire area as meeting statistical criteria specified in the standards and if local opinion indicates support for the component areas. If recognized, the component areas are designated *primary metropolitan statistical areas* (PMSAs). Like the CMSAs that contain them, PMSAs comprise entire counties, except in New England, where they comprise cities and towns. If no PMSAs are recognized, the entire area is designated an MSA.

As of June 30, 1999, there were 258 MSAs and 18 CMSAs, comprising 73 PMSAs in the United States.

The largest city in each MSA/CMSA is designated a *central city*. Additional cities qualify *if specified requirements are met for population size* and commuting patterns. The title of each MSA consists of the names of up to three of its central cities and the name of each state into which the MSA extends. However, the name of a central city with fewer than 250,000 in population and less than one-third of the population of the area's largest city is not included in the MSA title unless local opinion supports its inclusion. Titles of PMSAs are also typically based on central city names but may consist of county names.

Form of Government Form of government relates primarily to the organization of the legislative and executive branches of municipalities and townships.

In the *mayor-council* form, an elected council or board serves as the legislative body. The head of government is the chief elected official, who is generally elected separately from the council and has significant administrative authority.

Many cities with a mayor-council form of government have a city administrator who is appointed by the elected representatives (council) and/or the chief elected official and is responsible to the elected officials. Appointed city administrators in mayor-council governments have limited administrative authority: they often do not directly appoint department heads or other key city personnel, and their responsibility for budget preparation and administration, although significant, is subordinate to that of the elected officials.

Under the *council-manager* form, the elected council or board and chief elected official (e.g., the mayor) are responsible for making policy. A professional administrator appointed by the council or board has full responsibility for the day-to-day operations of the government.

The *commission* form of government operates with an elected commission performing both legislative and executive functions, generally with departmental administration divided among the commissioners.

The *town meeting* form of government is a system in which all qualified voters of a municipality meet to make basic policy and elect officials to carry out the policies.

Under the *representative town meeting* form of government, the voters select a large number of citizens to represent them at the town meeting(s). All citizens can participate in the meeting(s), but only the representatives may vote.

County Classification

Counties are the primary political administrative divisions of the states. The county-type governments in Alaska are called boroughs. Table 3 details the distribution of counties throughout the nation, using the same geographic and population categories as Table 2.

Metro Status For counties, metro status refers to the status of a county within the context of the OMB definition of an MSA. "Metro" means that a county is located within an MSA; "nonmetro" indicates that it is located outside the boundaries of an MSA.

Counties that are located in an MSA are classified in a way similar to that for cities. *Central* counties are those in which central cities are located. *Suburban* counties are the other counties located within an MSA. Counties not located in an MSA are considered *independent*.

Form of Government For counties, form of government relates to the structural organization of the legislative and executive branches of counties; counties are classified as being with or without an administrator. There are three basic forms of county government: commission, council-administrator, and council–elected executive.

The *commission* form of government is characterized by a governing board that shares the administrative and, to an extent, legislative responsibilities with several independently elected functional officials.

In counties with the *council-administrator* form, an administrator is appointed by, and responsible to, the elected council to carry out directives.

The *council–elected executive* form features two branches of government: the executive and the

Table 3 Cumulative Distribution of U.S. Counties

Classification	All counties	Population 2,500 and over	5,000 and over	10,000 and over	25,000 and over	50,000 and over	100,000 and over	250,000 and over	500,000 and over	Over 1,000,000
Total, all counties	3,033	2,921	2,748	2,362	1,494	857	474	200	90	27
Population group										
Over 1,000,000	27	27	27	27	27	27	27	27	27	27
500,000-1,000,000	63	63	63	63	63	63	63	63	63	...[1]
250,000-499,999	110	110	110	110	110	110	110	110	...	...
100,000-249,999	274	274	274	274	274	274	274	...	...	...
50,000-99,999	383	383	383	383	383	383	...	...	...	...
25,000-49,999	637	637	637	637	637	...	...	...	...	...
10,000-24,999	868	868	868	868	...	...	...	...	...	...
5,000-9,999	386	386	386	...	...	...	...	...	...	...
2,500-4,999	173	173	...	...	...	...	...	...	...	...
Under 2,500	112	...	...	...	...	...	...	...	...	...
Geographic region										
Northeast	189	189	188	183	174	129	85	45	19	3
North-Central	1,052	1,005	912	745	444	228	124	45	19	7
South	1,371	1,345	1,300	1,151	683	364	177	65	27	6
West	421	382	348	283	193	136	88	45	25	11
Geographic division										
New England	45	45	45	43	40	24	14	6	2	...
Mid-Atlantic	144	144	143	140	134	105	71	39	17	3
East North-Central	437	436	433	407	298	165	94	33	15	5
West North-Central	615	569	479	338	146	63	30	12	4	2
South Atlantic	544	542	534	481	313	192	100	38	16	2
East South-Central	360	358	356	323	175	73	27	7	2	...
West South-Central	467	445	410	347	195	100	50	20	9	4
Mountain	276	245	215	159	93	54	32	14	7	2
Pacific Coast	145	137	133	124	100	82	56	31	18	9
Metro status										
Central	455	455	455	455	452	437	375	194	88	27
Suburban	341	340	339	331	283	177	68	6	2	...
Independent	2,237	2,126	1,954	1,576	759	243	31	...	...	...
Form of government										
County commission	1,728	1,639	1,501	1,215	665	303	130	46	17	4
Council-manager/administrator	817	805	788	736	545	357	216	87	43	15
Council-elected executive	488	477	459	411	284	197	128	67	30	8

1 (...) indicates data not applicable or not reported.

legislative. The independently elected executive is considered the formal head of the county.

The use of varying types of local government is an institutional response to the needs, requirements, and articulated demands of citizens at the local level.

Within each type of local government, structures are developed to provide adequate services. These structural adaptations are a partial result of the geographic location, population, metropolitan status, and form of government of the jurisdiction involved.

Consolidated Governments

The Bureau of the Census defines a consolidated government as a unit of local government in which the functions of a primary incorporated place and its county or minor civil division have merged.[4] There are several categories of consolidations: city-county consolidations that operate primarily as cities (Table 4), metropolitan governments operating primarily as cities (Table 5), and areas that maintain certain types of county offices but as part of another city or township government (Table 6). In addition, the District of Columbia is counted by the Census Bureau as a city, a separate county area, and a separate state area. To avoid double counting in survey results, ICMA counts the District of Columbia only as a city.

The Census Bureau defines independent cities as those operating outside of a county area and administering functions commonly performed by counties (Table 7). The bureau counts independent cities as counties. For survey research purposes, ICMA counts independent cities as municipal, not county governments.

Uses of Statistical Data

The *Municipal Year Book* uses primary and secondary data sources. ICMA collects and publishes the primary source data. Secondary source data are data collected by another organization. Most of the primary source data are collected through survey research. ICMA develops questionnaires on a variety of subjects dur-

Table 4 Legally Designated Consolidated City-County Governments Operating Primarily as Cities, 2007

State	Consolidated government
Alaska	City and Borough of Anchorage
	City and Borough of Juneau
	City and Borough of Sitka
California	City and County of San Francisco
Colorado	City and County of Broomfield
	City and County of Denver
Hawaii	City and County of Honolulu
Kansas	Kansas City and Wyandotte County
Montana	Anaconda-Deer Lodge
	Butte-Silver Bow

Table 5 Metropolitan Governments, 2007

State	Consolidated city
Tennessee	Hartsville-Trousdale County
	Lynchburg-Moore County
	Nashville-Davidson

Note: The Census Bureau treats these as consolidated cities.

Table 6 Areas That Maintain Certain Types of County Offices but as Part of Another Government, 2007

State	County	Other government
Florida	Duval	City of Jacksonville
Georgia	Chattahoochee	Cusseta-Chattahoochee County unified
	Clarke	Athens-Clarke County unified
	Georgetown-Quitman County	Georgetown-Quitman County unified
	Muscogee	City of Columbus
	Richmond	City of Augusta
	Webster and cities of Preston and Weston	Webster County unified
Hawaii	Kalawao	State of Hawaii
Indiana	Marion	City of Indianapolis
Kentucky	Lexington-Fayette Urban County	Lexington-Fayette
	Louisville-Jefferson County	Louisville-Jefferson
Louisiana	Parish of East Baton Rouge	City of Baton Rouge
	Parish of Lafayette	City of Lafayette
	Parish of Orleans	City of New Orleans
	Terrebonne Parish	Terrebonne Parish consolidated
Massachusetts	County of Nantucket	Town of Nantucket
	County of Suffolk	City of Boston
New York	County of Bronx	New York City
	County of Kings	New York City
	County of New York	New York City
	County of Queens	New York City
	County of Richmond	New York City
Pennsylvania	County of Philadelphia	City of Philadelphia

Table 7   Independent Cities

State	Independent city
Maryland	Baltimore City
Missouri	St. Louis
Nevada	Carson City
Virginia	Alexandria
Virginia	Bedford
Virginia	Bristol
Virginia	Buena Vista
Virginia	Charlottesville
Virginia	Chesapeake
Virginia	Colonial Heights
Virginia	Covington
Virginia	Danville
Virginia	Emporia
Virginia	Fairfax
Virginia	Falls Church
Virginia	Franklin
Virginia	Fredericksburg
Virginia	Galax
Virginia	Hampton
Virginia	Harrisonburg
Virginia	Hopewell
Virginia	Lexington
Virginia	Lynchburg
Virginia	Manassas
Virginia	Manassas Park
Virginia	Martinsville
Virginia	Newport News
Virginia	Norfolk
Virginia	Norton
Virginia	Petersburg
Virginia	Poquoson
Virginia	Portsmouth
Virginia	Radford
Virginia	Richmond
Virginia	Roanoke
Virginia	Salem
Virginia	Staunton
Virginia	Suffolk
Virginia	Virginia Beach
Virginia	Waynesboro
Virginia	Williamsburg
Virginia	Winchester

ing a given year and then pretests and refines them to increase the validity of each survey instrument. Once completed, the surveys are sent to officials in all cities above a given population level (e.g., 2,500 and above, 10,000 and above, etc.). For example, the city managers or chief administrative officers receive the ICMA *Economic Development Survey*, and finance officers receive the *Police and Fire Personnel, Salaries, and Expenditures* survey.

ICMA conducts the *Police and Fire Personnel, Salaries, and Expenditures* survey every year. Other research projects are conducted every five years, and some are one-time efforts to provide information on subjects of current interest.

Limitations of the Data

Regardless of the subject or type of data presented, data should be read cautiously. All policy, political, and social data have strengths and limitations. These factors should be considered in any analysis and application. Statistics are no magic guide to perfect understanding and decision making, but they can shed light on particular subjects and questions in lieu of haphazard and subjective information. They can clarify trends in policy expenditures, processes, and impacts and thus assist in evaluating the equity and efficiency of alternative courses of action. Statistical data are most valuable when one remembers their imperfections, both actual and potential, while drawing conclusions.

For example, readers should examine the response bias for each survey. Surveys may be sent to all municipalities above a certain population threshold, but not all of those surveys are necessarily returned. Jurisdictions that do not respond are rarely mirror images of those that do. ICMA reduces the severity of this problem by maximizing the opportunities to respond through second and (sometimes) third requests. But although this practice mitigates the problem, response bias invariably appears. Consequently, ICMA always includes a "Survey Response" table in each article that analyzes the results of a particular survey. This allows the reader to examine the patterns and degrees of response bias through a variety of demographic and structural variables.

Other possible problems can occur with survey data. Local governments have a variety of record-keeping systems. Therefore, some of the data (particularly those on expenditures) may lack uniformity. In addition, no matter how carefully a questionnaire is refined, problems such as divergent interpretations of directions, definitions, and specific questions invariably arise. However, when inconsistencies or apparently extreme data are reported, every attempt is made to verify these responses through follow-up telephone calls.

Types of Statistics

There are basically two types of statistics: descriptive and inferential.

Descriptive

Most of the data presented in this volume are purely descriptive. Descriptive statistics summarize some characteristics of a group of numbers. A few numbers represent many. If someone wants to find out something about the age of a city's workforce, for example, it would be quite cumbersome to read a list of several hundred numbers (each representing the age of individual employees). It would be much easier to have a few summary descriptive statistics, such as the mean (average) or the range (the highest value minus the lowest value). These two "pieces" of information would not convey all the details of the entire data set, but they can help and are much more useful and understandable than complete numerical lists.

There are essentially two types of descriptive statistics: measures of central tendency and measures of dispersion.

Measures of Central Tendency These types of statistics indicate the most common or typical value of a data set. The most popular examples are the mean and median. The mean is simply the arithmetic average. It is calculated by summing the items in a data set and dividing by the total number of items. For example, given the salaries of $15,000, $20,000, $25,000, $30,000, and $35,000, the mean is $25,000 ($125,000 divided by 5).

The mean is the most widely used and intuitively obvious measure of central tendency. However, it is sensitive to extreme values. A few large or small numbers in a data set can produce a mean that is not representative of the "typical" value. Consider the example of the five salaries above. Suppose the highest value was not $35,000 but $135,000. The mean of the data set would now be $45,000 ($225,000 divided by 5). This figure, however, is not representative of this group of numbers because it is substantially greater than four of the five values and is $90,000 below the high score. A data set such as this is "positively skewed" (i.e., it has one or more extremely high scores). Under these circumstances (or when the data set is "negatively skewed" with extremely low scores), it is more appropriate to use the median as a measure of central tendency.

The median is the middle score of a data set that is arranged in order of increasing magnitude. Theoretically, it represents the point that is equivalent to the 50th percentile. For a data set with an odd number of items, the median has the same number of observations above and below it (e.g., the third value in a data set of 5 or the eighth value in a data set of 15). With an even number of cases, the median is the average of the middle two scores (e.g., the seventh and eighth values in a data set of 14). In the example of the five salaries used above, the median is $25,000 regardless of whether the largest score is $35,000 or $135,000. When the mean exceeds the median, the data set is positively skewed. If the median exceeds the mean, it is negatively skewed.

Measures of Dispersion This form of descriptive statistics indicates how widely scattered or spread out the numbers are in a data set. Some common measures of dispersion are the range and the interquartile range. The range is simply the highest value minus the lowest value. For the numbers 3, 7, 50, 80, and 100, the range is 97 (100 – 3 = 97). For the numbers 3, 7, 50, 80, and 1,000, it is 997 (1,000 – 3 = 997). Quartiles divide a data set into four equal parts similar to the way percentiles divide a data set into 100 equal parts. Consequently, the third quartile is equivalent to the 75th percentile, and the first quartile is equivalent to the 25th percentile. The interquartile range is the value of the third quartile minus the value of the first quartile.

Inferential

Inferential statistics permit the social and policy researcher to make inferences about whether a correlation exists between two (or more) variables in a population based on data from a sample. Specifically, inferential statistics provide the probability that the sample results could have occurred by chance if there were really no relationship between the variables in the population as a whole. If the probability of random occurrence is sufficiently low (below the researcher's preestablished significance level), then the null hypothesis—that there is no association between the variables—is rejected. This lends indirect support to the research hypothesis that a correlation does exist. If they can rule out chance factors (the null hypothesis), researchers conclude that they have found a "statistically significant" relationship between the two variables under examination.

Significance tests are those statistics that permit inferences about whether variables are correlated but provide nothing directly about the strength of such correlations. Measures of association, on the other hand, indicate how strong relationships are between variables. These statistics range from a high of +1.0 (for a perfect positive correlation), to zero (indicating no correlation), to a low of –1.0 (for a perfect negative correlation).

Some common significance tests are the chi square and difference-of-means tests. Some common measures of association are Yule's Q, Sommer's Gamma, Lambda, Cramer's V, Pearson's C, and the correlation coefficient. Anyone seeking further information on these tests and measures should consult any major statistics textbook.[5]

Inferential statistics are used less frequently in this volume than descriptive statistics. However, whenever possible, the data have been presented so that the user can calculate inferential statistics whenever appropriate.

Summary

All social, political, and economic data are collected with imperfect techniques in an imperfect world. Therefore, users of such data should be continuously cognizant of the strengths and weaknesses of the information from which they are attempting to draw conclusions. Readers should note the limitations of the data published in this volume. Particular attention should be paid to the process of data collection and potential problems such as response bias.

Notes

1. The terms *city* and *cities*, as used in this volume, refer to cities, villages, towns, townships, and boroughs.
2. See census.gov/population/www/estimates/aboutmetro .html.
3. The vast majority of the text describing metropolitan areas has been taken from the website cited in footnote 2.
4. See U.S. Census Bureau, *Consolidated Federal Funds Report for Fiscal Year 2009: State and County Areas* (August 2010), Appendix A, census.gov/prod/2010pubs/cffr-09.pdf.
5. For additional information on statistics, see Tari Renner's *Statistics Unraveled: A Practical Guide to Using Data in Decision Making* (Washington, D.C.: ICMA, 1988).

Management Trends and Survey Research

1

Reflections on the First Decade of the 21st Century: Leadership Implications for Local Government

Robert J. O'Neill Jr.
ICMA

Ron Carlee
ICMA and George Washington University

People faced the beginning of the 21st century with trepidation, and by the end of its first decade, they had come to realize many of their fears: terrorism, natural disaster, financial uncertainty, political polarization, and technological challenges. While local governments will face a host of challenges in the coming decade, it is undeniable that they met many of the challenges of the past decade with perseverance and commitment. They have successfully dealt with emergencies large and small every day, and have provided basic services at levels of competence that are mostly taken for granted. They are balancing their budgets and building communities that are economically and environmentally sustainable. Millions of people live healthy and productive lives with an extremely high standard of living. And despite the challenges ahead—natural, human, and technological threats; uneven economic recovery; and persistent social inequity—local leaders continue to accept the challenges and work toward building ever better communities that further improve the lives of all people.

This article reflects on the past decade, on the lessons we have learned, and on implications for local government leadership in 2011 and beyond. It addresses the need for sustainability, which encompasses the environment, the economy, and social equity, and for the effective management of two compelling forces that affect sustainability: disaster

SELECTED FINDINGS

Competence and ethics remain the foundation on which professional local government management rests; however, today's local government leader must also be able to engage citizens in forging a common vision of the community they want to build.

Pensions and health care costs will create increasing pressures on constrained local budgets.

Environmental efforts will be largely focused on promoting energy-efficient building practices and pursuing alternative sources of energy, fuel, and financing.

With so many social issues tearing at the fabric of our society—immigration reform, gay rights, religious diversity, to name a few—there will be an ever-growing need for professional managers with the leadership skills to bring rationality to public discourse, promote civility, and prevail over those who seek to polarize and inflame the public.

response and rapidly changing technologies. The premise is that the achievement of these societal objectives requires leadership, especially from professional local government managers. These managers cannot do the job by themselves, but as leaders, they must serve as catalysts and facilitators to bring all sectors of the community together. Thus, we begin with the issue of leadership.

Leadership

Not only is 2011 the beginning of a new decade, but it also moves ICMA closer to its hundred-year anniversary in 2014 and thus presents an opportunity to reassess what it means to be a city, town, or county manager. In 1911 the United States was coping with the industrial age and with rapidly growing urban areas where the interdependencies of cities and the complexities of society could no longer tolerate the luxuries of corruption and incompetence in local government. Professional managerial skills were critically needed to build new metropolises: water plants and distribution systems, sanitary and storm sewer systems, roads and bridges, streetcars, schools and libraries, recreation centers and parks, law enforcement systems, fire and emergency services, public health services, and building codes.

The first appointment to a position akin to city manager was made in Staunton, Virginia, in 1908. From those early days on, the profession was very much about "management"—about bringing professionalism to the "business" of local government. It was the job of professional managers to bring objective, analytical decision making to the tasks at hand. These managers created personnel, budget, and purchasing systems to serve the public's interests, not their own political allegiance and certainly not their own interests. Competence, honesty, and objectivity were core, and these were the skills emphasized by ICMA, which was founded in 1914 as the City Managers' Association to support those early managers who were bringing reform and accountability to local government.

Ethical integrity remains at the center of professional leadership today as it did at the dawn of the profession. A stark reminder of why ethics matter came just this past year from Bell, California. A suburb of Los Angeles, Bell is a city of 2.6 square miles; its population of less than 40,000 is 90% Latino and has a median household income of $30,000 to $40,000. What has set Bell apart, however, was a massive corruption scheme uncovered in 2010, at the center of which was a manager who has since been censured and expelled from the profession and is currently under criminal indictment. According to an investigation by, the California state auditor and investigations by the *Los Angeles Times*, the manager worked in collusion with elected and other appointed officials

to raid the city treasury for personal gain, mostly through a hidden compensation agreement.[1] There was a lack of communication with and transparency to the public, as well as a lack of public engagement demanding such. Attorneys, auditors, and a host of staff, as well as voters and taxpayers, failed in their oversight and stewardship responsibilities, empowering those driven by greed to think that they could get away with just about anything. Bell is a case study on how the total institution of government can fail.

The important lesson from Bell is that ethical conduct and integrity cannot be taken for granted. Dishonest people will always do bad things, so institutionally there is a need to build stronger safeguards, greater transparency, and a culture of stewardship. While the egregious acts in Bell were ultimately exposed by the press, reporters of the *Los Angeles Times* actually stumbled onto the story while researching something entirely different. Professional journalism has sharply declined over the past decade, severely reducing the ability of the press to serve as a check on the inappropriate use of power at the local level. Thus, it is incumbent upon professional managers to make institutional changes to ensure preservation of the public trust. In 2010, ICMA adopted new guidelines for making such changes as they relate to transparency in the adoption and content of compensation agreements for managers. Just as they were at the beginning of the 20th century, competence and ethics remain the foundation on which professional managers can credibly engage the public and build communities of intent.

But competence, ethics, and professional management skills will not be sufficient in the next decade and for the balance of the century. The challenges facing local governments of the 21st century will require leadership that transcends those qualities. The goal is to build communities that are not only safe and healthy but also places to which residents feel connected and in which they want to live as a matter of choice—that is, communities of intent. These are commonly referred to "sustainable communities."

Sustainable communities are built around three principles: the environment, the economy, and social equity. Creating such communities requires leadership skills to help people collectively engage in forging a common vision of the community they want. While it is the elected officials who may actually lead the public in that effort, it is the role of the professional manager to help the elected officials understand the need for engagement. The professional manager provides the elected officials with the tools and approaches for engaging the public and the sound analysis to inform the decisions. He or she is then responsible for implementing the community vision, evaluating its progress, and creating mechanisms for review and evaluation—all of which involve continued engagement with elected officials and the public.

Sustainability

Sustainability took center stage in the past decade, mostly with regard to the environment but also, closing out 2010, with a focus on economic decline and increasing economic disparity. These will remain important issues in the coming years, which will also see continuing debates on immigration, gay rights, and religious tolerance. Developments in each of these pillars of sustainability—the economy, the environment, and social equity—are discussed below in the context of leadership challenges for local government professionals. A fourth area for managers is the sustainability of their own local government organizations. Leadership is required both within local government to create organizations that can meet community needs and with residents to help develop shared expectations and shared ownership in the interests of the greater good.

The Economy

The economy will always be a concern of local governments, and this was certainly true over the past decade. After starting the new millennium with a recession, the United States enjoyed an economic boom, especially in housing and commercial development. With local governments in most states financed largely with property taxes, the boom enabled many of those governments to increase employee salaries and benefits and expand services, especially for public safety. The boom collapsed in 2007, the aftermath of which remains at the dawn of 2011. Even though the business sector and stock markets have improved, local governments continue to be financially squeezed. In many communities, predictions are for continuing declines in revenues and more budget cuts, possibly well into 2012. Prospects for state governments are similarly bleak.[2]

As with most challenges, there is a silver lining in the economic clouds. Whereas inertia and comfort with the status quo often mask inefficiencies and can impede community growth, economic crises present opportunities for professional managers to assert leadership and challenge assumptions in ways that would have been unthinkable in better times. During this current recession, city, town, and county managers have employed a range of strategies to not merely weather the crisis but introduce permanent changes that will enhance their communities' efficiency and sustainability.

In the new decade, two major drivers will continue to challenge old ways:

- *Pensions.* As the new decade begins, taxpayer concern about public employee pensions appears to be growing. The defined benefit pension—guaranteed retirement income for life—has all but disappeared in the private sector, where it has been replaced by defined contribution plans (401-K and Keogh plans). The magnitude of the public sector pension liability is coming into sharper focus with the dramatic drop in interest earnings and the increasing demand from the retirement of baby boomers.[3]

- *Employee and retiree health care.* This second area of escalating costs has spawned a new acronym: OPEB, or other post-employment benefits. New accounting standards have directed state and local governments to account for the future costs of retiree health care in the same manner as they do pension liabilities. For many communities, the resulting liability numbers have been staggering. And the passage of national health care legislation in 2010 has not improved the situation. How the legislation will affect local government as an employer is unclear, as are its long-term financial implications. As 2010 ended, the landmark legislation was under attack in the courts, and some members of the new Congress have pledged to repeal the act or deny funding for its implementation. Regardless the outcome at the national level, however, local leaders will continue to struggle with the rising cost of employee health care, searching for the appropriate level of cost sharing with employees and for effective incentives to create a healthy workforce.[4]

It has long been argued that superior benefits are necessary for the recruitment and retention of public employees given that their salaries tended to lag behind salaries in the private sector. This conventional wisdom will be challenged in the coming decade. Private sector pay is currently flat, unemployment remains relatively high, and private sector benefits, especially pensions, have eroded. In this environment, will the taxpaying public support substantially higher benefits for public employees than private sector workers are receiving? There are indicators that public opinion is beginning to shift regarding pay and benefits, including those for public safety employees.[5]

The challenge for professional managers is to ensure that public employees are paid fairly and that public jobs do not become employment of last resort. This requires a much stronger analysis of the overall employment market in a community and of the changing expectations of the younger workforce. Sub-par pay in exchange for a deluxe 30-year pension plan and free health care is yesterday's paradigm. Local government leaders must envision and implement human resource systems for a new generation—systems imbued with work that has meaning (i.e., the value of public service); opportunities to grow and take ownership for one's work; total compensation (pay and benefits) that is fair in the market; and flexibility, especially around telework and alternative scheduling.

The Environment

There is no denying that much of the environmental debate of the last decade was shaped by the documentary film *An Inconvenient Truth*. Absent a clear national environmental strategy, local governments have recognized that the impacts of failed policies will be felt in the communities where people live and that they must act on their own. Consequently, local governments—in the United States and internationally—have become test beds for environmental innovation, with many taking action long before *An Inconvenient Truth*. The effects of droughts, floods, hurricanes, snowstorms, and energy costs are not hypothetical policy discussions at the local level. The leadership challenge is to take a community beyond the capacity to respond to immediate events, and not only create plans and systems that can sustain it in the face of uncertainty but also make that community resilient when bad things do occur.

While there is no single approach that is right for every community, local government leaders must adapt leading practices to address environmental issues in ways that resonate with their residents. The framing of the issues varies: mitigating climate change, reducing the carbon footprint, creating green space, conserving or enhancing water quality, ensuring efficient land use, enhancing mass transportation, increasing energy efficiency, and reducing oil dependency. Some communities address all these environmental issues comprehensively; other communities find it more effective to take a targeted approach. In general, most local governments are working on energy efficiency, and many are actively pursuing innovative alternatives to energy sources, fuels, and the financing of such improvements.

Energy-Efficient Building Practices LEED building standards, developed by the U.S. Green Building Council (GBC), added another term to our lexicon and shaped how local governments began to design and construct public buildings. Local governments are also applying these standards to private development. The standards themselves continue to evolve as do the technologies to implement them, such as LED lighting.

Alternative Energy Solar energy and wind energy reached new levels of acceptance over the past decade. Local governments are working in these areas to determine which of the technologies warrant public investment. Additionally, local governments are grappling with how to deal with zoning and land use issues that are created when home owners and businesses implement these technologies.

Alternative Fuel *Peak oil* is a term that was increasingly used over the last decade and will be discussed with increasing frequency. It applies to the point at which oil production in the world is at its maximum level, after which production declines to its inevitable conclusion. There is no consensus on when the peak will be reached or on how long supplies will last thereafter. The fluctuations in oil demand and oil pricing make the concept of peak oil even more difficult to comprehend. Nonetheless, there is an increasing recognition that the price of oil can and will spike and that oil supplies may well be disrupted. Consequently, local governments are increasingly focused on energy management for practical and financial reasons. Local government leaders need to determine the extent to which their communities should invest in and develop long-term plans for the possibility of a world without oil.

Many local governments have invested in hybrid, alternative-fuel, and plug-in vehicles to lower their fuel costs and reduce their vulnerability to increasing oil prices and the possibility of limited oil availability. The use of ethanol, however, appears to be in decline. In 2011, General Motors will introduce its first mass-produced plug-in car in selected markets. While the commercial success of plug-ins is as yet unknown, local governments are evaluating the extent to which they should provide or require the private sector to provide plug-in facilities to support all-electric vehicles.

Alternative Financing PACE (Property Assessed Clean Energy) programs and ELTAPs (Energy Loan Tax Assessment Programs) were similar efforts that local governments initiated to make loans available to residential home owners for energy-efficiency improvements. Within these programs, a loan would be made in the form of a tax assessment (similar to assessments used to build sidewalks and sewer systems), which would be tied to the property, not the home owner; this would make it possible to amortize the cost of energy improvements over a longer period of time and at lower out-of-pocket costs. The programs, however, were challenged by the mortgage industry in 2010 because, in case of default, liens by local governments have priority over mortgages. Currently, the programs remain on hold, but regardless of the outcome, local governments will continue to search for ways to reduce not only their government's dependency on oil but also the community's dependency overall.

In the coming decade, local governments will be evaluating the STAR Community Index, a national, consensus-based framework for gauging the sustainability and livability of U.S. communities. The index is in development through a partnership among the GBC, ICLEI–Local Governments for Sustainability, and the Center for American Progress.[6] The goal of STAR is to provide a planning and measurement system by which local governments can assess their sustainability efforts in terms of the environment, the economy, and social equity.

Social Equity

The vision statement for ICMA talks about building sustainable communities that "improve lives worldwide," and the ICMA Code of Ethics requires managers to "recognize that the chief function of local government at all times is to serve the best interests of all people." At the same time, the code requires managers to "uphold and implement local government policies adopted by elected officials." When policies and laws are discriminatory, however, managers face a dilemma. Segregation by race and sex were once officially supported in laws and policy. Over the past decade, the areas creating the hottest social equity debates in law and policy have been immigration and gay rights. Emerging areas of concern revolve around religious discrimination, specifically pertaining to Muslims, and economic disparity. In the coming years, all four areas will affect the social fabric of communities as well as of the local government organization itself. As leaders, it will be incumbent upon professional managers to facilitate communication, bring reason and objectivity to discussions, and combat those who seek to inflame passions and polarize the public.

Immigration People from Central and South America came to the United States in large numbers over the last decade, providing the workforce that filled many of the construction jobs during the development boom and most of the low-wage agricultural positions across the country. For many communities, the large influx of immigrants challenged their values, and while some communities embraced the new populations, others actively worked to drive the newcomers out. As the national economy deteriorated,

immigrants (with and without legal status) became convenient scapegoats despite a lack of evidence that they were indeed taking jobs away from citizens.[7] Exacerbating the situation was the failure of Congress to enact comprehensive immigration reform, leading to a patchwork of controversial state and local actions, the most noted of which occurred in 2010 in Arizona.

Because it is unlikely that Congress will clarify the situation through national reform any time soon, states will continue to address immigration in diverse and piecemeal ways. This requires local leaders to understand immigration and its implications within their own communities. Legal status, for example, is nuanced and complex. Someone who has overstayed a student visa is not the same as someone who has robbed a gas station; the former violation is more like a mistake or misstatement on one's income taxes. Leaders will also have to deal with influences, both internal and external, that promote political agendas. In some instances, managers will be called upon to implement policies and laws that may conflict with their own values or with the stated values of their citizens. As leaders, it will be up to them to set the example in the community, to perform their professional duties in helping elected leaders understand the implications of any actions that are taken, and to keep dialogue and options open.

Gay Rights Advancing steadily over the decade were gay rights, which came known as LGBT—lesbian, gay, bi-sexual, and transgender—rights. Gay marriage now is now a reality in six states; extension of employee fringe benefits to domestic partners has become increasingly common. One of the last acts of Congress in 2010 was to repeal the military's Don't Ask, Don't Tell policy, eliminating the most nationally visible form of overt discrimination against gays and lesbians. While there will probably be efforts to roll back the clock in state legislatures and in voter referenda, the coming decade is likely to see national acceptance of some form of civil union for same-sex couples. Members of the LGBT community will be increasingly open, creating adaptation challenges for organizations and communities. Not everyone will be accepting of these social changes. Once again, it will be up to the leaders to promote tolerance and civility along with equity and justice.

Religious Discrimination The jihadist campaign of al-Qaeda and its attacks against the United States on September 11, 2001 (referred to universally as simply 9/11), created tensions with the Muslim community. While there is no question that al-Qaeda does not represent the Muslim faith, its visibility and the threat it poses can result in stereotypes and discrimination toward Muslims (or people who "appear" to be Muslim) who have no connection to or sympathy for terrorism or al-Qaeda. Plans to build an Islamic cultural center in New York City was, at its core, a local zoning issue; however, it became the obsession of national commentators who claimed that the center would be an affront to those who died at "Ground Zero" (another new term during the decade). Demonstrating how quickly such controversies can spread to places previously immune from them, the pastor of a small church in Gainesville, Florida, became internationally known in 2010 when he announced that he would burn a copy of Koran on 9/11 in protest of the Islamic cultural center. Suddenly, international media descended on a local government far removed from the zoning issues of New York City.

Economic Disparity In the down economy it has fallen to local governments, as always, to deal with the real issues of homelessness and hunger. Local shelters are full, and food pantries face unprecedented demand. Around the world, heartbreaking stories of poverty and human rights violations reveal the extent to which humankind has not yet advanced; genocide, ethnic cleansing, human trafficking, hunger, and preventable diseases continue to challenge civilized societies. The contrast between the haves and have-nots is sharp. Like their residents, some local governments grow increasingly wealthy and elite while others become more deeply impoverished. And some local governments encompass dramatically disparate neighborhoods within their boundaries. What does such economic disparity portend for the future of local governments? The United States has not seen civil unrest on a large scale since the 1960s. If riots return, will local leaders be prepared? More importantly, will they have paid sufficient attention to the underlying issues of social strife to prevent unrest in the first place?

All four of the above issues will be part of the social equity debate of 2011 and beyond, along with continuing efforts to reconcile relations between blacks and whites and to fully integrate people with disabilities into the mainstream of society. In this area more than any other, professional managers are called upon to rise to a higher level of leadership. And when they do, they may be challenged for being inappropriately engaged in politics and in violation of the ICMA Code of Ethics. In fact, the code does not prohibit managers from engaging in policy discussions; it prohibits involvement in elections and "political activities which undermine public confidence in pro-

fessional administrators." Yet nothing undermines public confidence more than a local government or community that is socially unjust and discriminatory. Ignoring simmering social issues will not make them go away. Local government managers must have the courage to demonstrate meaningful leadership by advancing rational discourse where people can talk openly about their concerns and advance mutual understanding and tolerance.

Terrorism and Natural Disasters

The new millennium began with city, county, and town managers on edge in emergency operations centers. The primary fear was of a massive technological failure should the computers on which society depends suddenly fail at the stroke of midnight, shutting down power grids and utilities, banking systems, and transportation. Would the computer-operated doors of prisons and jails suddenly fling open? Would public safety radio systems die? Would cars start? The secondary fear was that terrorists would exploit the opportunity for a high-profile attack, especially in locations where large numbers of people were gathered. The term *Y2K* (Year 2000) became the shorthand for these anxieties. In fact, Y2K proved to be remarkably uneventful; however, the underlying concerns regarding terrorism proved well founded when coordinated attacks were launched in the United States on 9/11. This event more than any other shaped the last decade.

Much of the 9/11 aftermath has been national in scope: the creation of the Department of Homeland Security, including the Transportation Security Administration, and the national government's military campaigns in Iraq and Afghanistan. Less visible have been the impacts on local governments, especially in larger communities:

- Infusions of federal funds have led to enhancements in a wide range of emergency management capabilities, including command centers and telecommunications upgrades.

- National guidelines have led to significant increases in training and national approaches to organizing emergency responses, known as the National Incident Management System (NIMS) and Incident Command System (ICS).

- Homeland security functions have been created in local governments, usually in police departments, that include higher levels of local intelligence gathering and analysis in coordination with federal agencies and integrated into state or regional "fusion centers."

- An increasing number of surveillance cameras watch all that happens in public.
- Enhanced security can be found around city halls, courthouses, and other public buildings.

Statistically, the likelihood of a terrorist attack in a given community, especially in a small to mid-size one, is low; nonetheless, homeland security has to some degree become a focus of virtually all local governments over the past decade.

The real emergency challenges for most local governments, however, remain natural disasters and human accidents. Disasters of both kinds affected local governments along the Gulf Coast in the past decade. First came Hurricanes Katrina and Rita in 2005; then came the massive oil spill at BP's Deepwater Horizon oil rig in 2010. Over the course of the decade, devastating floods and forest fires have destroyed numerous communities. On the very last day of the decade, six people died in tornadoes in the Midwest and South.

Key lessons from the emergency events of the past decade fall to local government leaders to learn and implement in their communities: identifying the threats, mitigating vulnerabilities where possible, developing an all-hazards approach to response, and building the capacity to recover. Leaders are called upon to take a systems approach in preparing for both the anticipated and the unexpected. They are also required to understand that while local government cannot do it alone, they cannot expect state and federal assistance to be immediately available. Successful response and recovery require a total community effort. It is the job of professional managers as leaders to engage with the community and build relationships across all sectors, public and private, to create an integrated system of resilience—that is, communities that can bounce back quickly after disaster strikes.

Technology

The technology evolution of the past decade may eclipse the revolution that occurred with the advent of the personal computer in the late 1970s and early 1980s. The full impacts are still emerging as the public in large numbers shifts from personal computers to mobile devises. Leading the way are smart phones, which offer previously unimaginable capabilities in a small mobile package. Mobile smartphones are replacing landline telephones and reaching price points that are affordable to large segments of the population. Where once users had bought expensive software on discs, now they are buying "apps" online at costs as low as free. Growing rapidly is tablet technology,

which has been around in some form since the 1990s. Apple's iPad, introduced in 2010, was the first tablet to achieve widespread commercial success and portends a host of competitors in the next decade. Applications and file storage will shift from desktops to off-site locations, accessed through the Internet—so-called cloud computing.

The importance of these technological changes, however, lies less in the equipment itself than in what people are doing with it. Books, newspapers, magazines, television, radio, and movies are all available virtually anywhere at any time. People can shop, bank, and play games with people on the other side of the world. And people are communicating more, with more people, and with a rapidity never before known. Social media (another new term this decade) is changing how society functions. According to the *New York Daily News*, a tweet (yet another new term) began the rise to international status of the aforementioned pastor in Gainesville.[8]

Local governments are still learning what the new technologies will mean for them. They are creating Facebook pages and tweeting to their residents. Many have worked over the decade to create transactional portals on their websites for citizens to pay utility bills, register for recreation classes, and schedule building inspections. Very soon, however, citizens will expect an app for anything they want to do with the local government. They will expect whatever information they want to be readily available online.

Local governments will also be challenged to ensure that access to new technologies is available to all residents, including those in the most rural communities, and that no one gets left behind. A growing body of research during the past decade, much of which was supported by the Bill and Melinda Gates Foundation, demonstrates the critical role that public libraries are playing in providing the public with access to these new technologies.

Local government leaders will have to work hard to avoid lagging too far behind the information curve since being ahead of the curve may be impossible. Information and misinformation will travel quickly throughout a community and include not just text, but also photographs and videos. Parents may be aware of a school incident before the superintendent is. At great risk of being blindsided, managers and elected officials are continually challenged to distribute objective and accurate information as quickly as possible. They may also face liabilities if they fail to inform people of potential threats, as evidenced in the discussions over the way that Virginia Tech managed notifications during the mass shooting in 2007.

Managers will also find that confidential information will land on the web. The international uproar over the WikiLeaks website at the end of the decade foretells a future in which no one can trust that information will be kept confidential and we all can assume that when information is leaked, it is leaked to the entire world.

On the positive side, the new technologies are enabling local governments to engage more directly with their residents than ever before, to inform them of threats in as timely a manner as possible, and to make direct, unfiltered connections at very low cost. New technologies also open areas for innovation, such as the idea of using web-based gaming to link people in the joint problem solving of challenging social issues. An example is "World without Oil," a web-based game designed to help communities adapt to the loss of this resource. Gaming expert Jane McGonigal proclaims that "reality is broken, game designers can fix it."[9] Maybe so.

Conclusion and Summary

Emergency management, economic sustainability, the environment, human rights, and technology were defining areas of the first decade of the 21st century, and they will continue to command the attention of professional local government managers as we move into the second decade. Across these areas local governments can assert vision and self-determination, yet there will always be elements that are beyond their control and beyond prediction.

Given the enormous challenges of the past decade, it has been interesting to observe how local governments have responded, particularly those that appear to have met those challenges successfully. The leaders of the better-performing local governments seem to have certain characteristics and pursue certain approaches that distinguish them from the others.

1. *Focus on the positive.* While they recognize the complexity and the difficulty of the issues facing their communities and organizations, these leaders focus instead on the possibilities that the new normal presents, creating options that can lead to positive outcomes.

2. *Have a vision.* These leaders are able to articulate a vision of the future and, most importantly, describe concrete actions that are likely to advance that vision, and then build the credibility and momentum necessary to ensure that those actions are implemented.

3. *Cross boundaries.* These leaders facilitate and connect the public, private, and nonprofit sectors, and work across disciplines to achieve the outcomes that matter most to those they serve.

4. *Ask questions.* These leaders understand that leadership in a rapidly changing, complex world is about asking the right questions, not about having all the right answers. They engage the community and the organization by asking probing questions, listening to diverse voices, and not being satisfied with the status quo and conventional wisdom.

5. *Take risks.* Despite the risk-averse environment and resource constraints of their local governments, these leaders are constantly on the lookout for innovative solutions and best practices, eager to learn what works elsewhere and what might be adapted to their own organizations.

6. *Connect the dots.* These leaders seem able to connect what appear to be unrelated ideas in order to create innovative approaches to old problems. Similarly, they seem able to pick up on subtle indicators that allow faster reactions when difficult issues arise.

7. *Push performance.* These leaders are relentless in the pursuit of continuous improvement, applying an unusual rigor to the examination of existing performance and the opportunities for improvement.

8. *Create synergy.* These leaders have what Daniel Pink has described as "symphonic" skills—the ability to create synergy from diverse parts.[10] The quintessential skill of the 21st century will be creating a whole that is greater than the sum of the parts.

While no single individual has all these attributes, many of the leaders in transformed organizations possess a good number of them. These leaders build teams with complementary skills so that the overall organization has breadth and depth in a culture of shared leadership.

In the decade ahead, building communities of intent—ensuring the engagement of and ownership by the people who live and work there—will require professional managers who can accept the mantle of leadership, serve as catalysts, facilitate community discussions, and link people across sectors. These are demands that can only be met with courage, foresight, equanimity, a high level of technical competence, and ethical standards that are above reproach.

Communities do not remain the same; they either get better or they grow worse; they move forward or slide backwards. It is during times of challenge that successful communities create their own opportunities and make a better life for all.

Notes

1. John Chaing, *City of Bell Audit Report, State and Federal Expenditures, July 1, 2008, through August 31, 2010* (Sacramento: California State Controller's Office, 2010), sco.ca.gov/Press-Releases/2010/11-10bell-audit-report .pdf (accessed January 12, 2011); Christopher Goffard, "How Bell Hit Bottom," *Los Angeles Times,* December 28, 2010, articles.latimes.com/2010/dec/28/local/la-me-bell-origins-20101228 (accessed January 12, 2011).

2. Elizabeth McNichol, Phil Oliff, and Nicholas Johnson, *States Continue to Feel Recession's Impact* (Washington, D.C.: Center on Budget and Policy Priorities, December 16, 2010), cbpp.org/files/9-8-08sfp.pdf (accessed January 12, 2011).

3. For more on this subject, see Alicia H. Munnell, Jean-Pierre Aubry, and Laura Quinby, *Issue Brief: The Funding of State and Local Pensions: 2009–2013* (Washington, D.C.: Center for State and Local Government Excellence, April 2010), available at slge .org/.

4. For more on this subject, see Jerrell D. Coggburn, *Issue Brief: How Local Governments Are Addressing Retiree Health Care Funding* (Washington, D.C.: Center for State and Local Government Excellence, August 2010), available at slge.org/.

5. See, for example, Jonathan Walters, "Firefighters Feel the Squeeze of Shrinking Budgets," *Governing* (January 2011), governing.com/topics/public-workforce/firefighters-feel-squeeze-shrinking-budgets.html (accessed January 12, 2011).

6. ICLEI–Local Governments for Sustainability, "Star Community Index: A National Framework for Sustainable Communities," at icleiusa.org/star (accessed January 12, 2011).

7. See Michael Greenstone and Adam Looney, *Ten Economic Facts about Immigration* (Washington, D.C.: The Hamilton Project, Brookings Institution, September 2010), brookings. edu/reports/2010/09_immigration_greenstone_looney .aspx (accessed January 12, 2011).

8. Aliyah Shahid, "Pastor Terry Jones: How He Went from Nobody to International Villain," *New York Daily News,* September 11, 2010, nydailynews.com/news/national/2010/09/11/2010-09-11_pastor_terry_jones_how_he_went_from_nobody_to_international_villain .html (accessed January 12, 2011).

9. See "You Found Me," website of Jane McGonigal at janemcgonigal.com/.

20. Daniel H. Pink, *A Whole New Mind: Why Right-Brainers Will Rule the Future* (New York: Berkeley Publishing Group, 2005).

2

Second-Order Devolution?
What City Managers Have to Say

Richard C. Kearney
North Carolina State University

Jodi E. Swicegood
North Carolina State University

Ann O'M. Bowman
Texas A&M University

Since the Federalist Papers were written nearly two and a quarter centuries ago, political scientists, legal scholars, historians, and others have debated the nature of federalism in the United States. Metaphors attempting to depict the evolving relationships among the national, state, and local governments abound. These intergovernmental relationships have been likened to a picket fence, various cakes, a food chain, or water taps and described as cooperative, conflicted, creative, and "new," among many other things. The abundance of such characterizations reflects at least one accepted truth: American federalism is in a constant state of flux.

However one perceives federalism and intergovernmental relations, the reality is that legally, local governments are "creatures of the state," subject to state statutory and constitutional grants of authority and discretion. The powers of counties, municipalities, towns, townships, and other general-purpose local governments go unmentioned in the U.S. Constitution; these powers are to be granted expressly by the states through laws, charters, or broad home rule provisions. And the states have granted them to various degrees, resulting in extensive interstate variance in local discretionary powers.

During most of the twentieth century the national government served, perforce, as the prime mover of federalism. Beginning in the late 1970s, however, the states resurged as responsive, responsible, and progressive actors in American federalism. Enabled by

SELECTED FINDINGS

Most city managers (64%) deemed bills enacted by the state legislature during the past decade to be frequently "intrusive or preemptive of city government powers or authority"; and over 50% reported that states have frequently encroached into their terrain through such actions as mandates, cost shifting, and raids on local government revenues.

Since 2000, the greatest shift in responsibility toward local authority has been in the area of finance: 31% of city managers reported substantial devolution, mostly as a result of states granting local governments greater authority to raise taxes and fees. However, this increased devolution has not extended to local financial administration, as respondents consistently reported decreased power and authority in financial administration (66%).

various "new federalism" initiatives and buoyed by reformed political and administrative institutions, the states became the leading policy innovators, displacing a highly contentious and occasionally impoverished national government.

The new federalism policies of Ronald Reagan and the subsequent "Republican Revolution" of 1994 popularized the notion of devolution of powers and responsibilities to the states. This "devolution revolution" did indeed delegate certain new programmatic responsibilities to the states, and it intimated the possibility that states would, in turn, enhance local governments' discretionary powers and responsibilities. Evidence of this "second-order devolution" may perhaps be found in the Temporary Assistance to Needy Families program that has been largely administered by local governments, and in the increased revenue-raising powers that some states have granted to their local governments. The purported advantages of greater devolution are well known and include service delivery efficiencies, greater accountability and transparency, and higher levels of responsiveness to citizens. But skeptics remain, insisting that from where local governments eat in the fiscal food chain, little has changed on the local menu.

Has devolution been experienced at the local level? This article reports the results of a survey asking city managers about their experiences and perceptions in that regard. In many ways, city managers are well positioned to comment on the impact of devolution at the local level as they are fully aware of how their states have treated municipalities in recent years. Managers' jobs are defined and their actions bounded, in part, by the scope and degree of decision-making authority they hold under state law. Thus, managers' views on second-order devolution should provide valid evidence of the presence or absence of any larger trend in state-local relations.

Methodology

With the cooperation and assistance of ICMA, we drew a random sample of 600 city managers from municipalities with populations of 25,000 and above. Packets—including an explanatory letter, the survey, and a stamped/addressed return envelope—were mailed to respondents during the week of January 11, 2010. After the initial mailing, we were notified of address problems in nine instances; in six other cases, we learned that the manager was no longer employed with the city, thus reducing the total number of possible respondents to 585. Two weeks after the initial mailing, we sent out a reminder and a "thank you" postcard. A total of 234 completed surveys were returned, producing a satisfactory response rate of 40%.

Of the 600 surveys initially mailed, 19% were sent to municipalities in the Northeast region of the country, 25% to the North-Central, 27% to the South, and 30% to the West (Table 2–1). The percentage of responding municipalities from each region was similar to this breakdown. The Northeast was the least represented region with a 12% response rate, while

Table 2-1   Survey Responses by Region

Region	Cities surveyed		Respondents	
	No.	%	No.	%
Total	600	100	234	100
Northeast	113	19	29	12
North-Central	148	25	63	27
South	160	27	75	32
West	179	30	67	29

Note: Percentages may exceed 100% because of rounding.

the South had the highest response rate at 32%. The North-Central and the West regions were represented by 27% and 29% of respondents, respectively. Analysis of respondents' demographic features indicated that the pool reflected the total sample and provided no indication of over- or underrepresentation, or biases, of managers from particular states.

Survey Results

The survey asked managers to reflect on the nature and direction of state-local relations since 2000. Its 12 questions were intended to elicit managers' perceptions of state actions affecting their own cities as well as other municipalities within the state. With a single exception, the questions were closed-ended; the final, open-ended question prompted respondents to report on the overall quality of state-local relations in their municipalities.

Degree of Second-Order Devolution Since 2000

The first portion of the survey presented Likert-type scales prompting managers' views on the frequency of actions taken by the legislature (e.g., statutes, budgets, mandates), state courts (e.g., decisions), and voters (e.g., popular initiatives and referendums) that would connote the presence or absence of second-order devolution. Other questions asked managers to assess the frequency with which state governments "raided" local revenue sources; seized state-shared taxes, fees, and revenues; or shifted new costs to city governments.

Figure 2–1 summarizes the responses concerning selected intrusive actions. When managers were asked to assess how often bills were enacted by the legislature that they deemed "intrusive or preemptive of city government powers or authority," the majority (64%) responded "frequently," with the next largest percentage (31%) reporting "occasionally." Not surprisingly, then, legislative activities are generally per-

Figure 2-1　Frequency of Intrusive State Actions

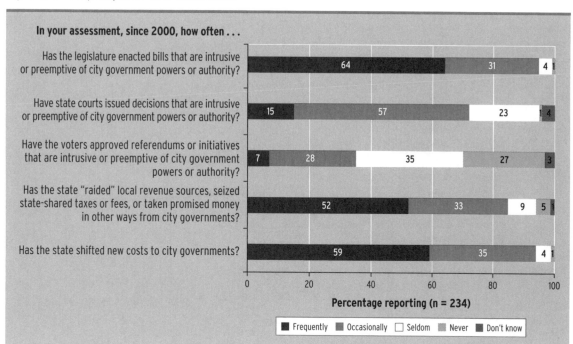

In your assessment, since 2000, how often . . .

Has the legislature enacted bills that are intrusive or preemptive of city government powers or authority?
64　31　4　1

Have state courts issued decisions that are intrusive or preemptive of city government powers or authority?
15　57　23　1　4

Have the voters approved referendums or initiatives that are intrusive or preemptive of city government powers or authority?
7　28　35　27　3

Has the state "raided" local revenue sources, seized state-shared taxes or fees, or taken promised money in other ways from city governments?
52　33　9　5　1

Has the state shifted new costs to city governments?
59　35　4　1

Percentage reporting (n = 234)

■ Frequently　■ Occasionally　□ Seldom　■ Never　■ Don't know

ceived as being intrusive. A second question asked managers how often state courts had issued decisions they perceived as intrusive of city government power or authority. A 57% majority responded "occasionally" and 23% reported "seldom." Managers perceived the frequency of voter-initiated referendums or initiatives that infringed on local government power to be much less of an issue; most (62%) responded "seldom" or "never." Of course, voter initiatives are not authorized in all states.

When requested to assess how often their states placed an extra financial burden on local governments by raiding local revenue sources, seizing state-shared taxes or fees, or confiscating money previously promised to local governments, just over half (52%) of managers reported "frequently" and 33% responded "occasionally." A majority of city managers (59%) indicated that the state had frequently shifted new costs to their local governments. One respondent from New England accused the state of "repeated raids on local revenues, and shifts of responsibility to local government without (new) revenues."

Taken together, responses to the first five survey questions reveal that during the past ten years, most city managers experienced or were aware of intrusive state actions into local affairs. Through mandates and other legislative actions, including the shifting of costs to and raiding of local government revenues, states have encroached into the accepted terrain of

municipalities. In the words of a respondent from the Pacific Northwest, the state has "a top-down mentality." Another western respondent remarked upon the state's "abdication of responsibility" to local governments.

Next, the survey assessed the change in local governments' discretion, power, and authority since 2000 in 12 common municipal policy areas. Figure 2–2 represents managers' perceptions of the direction of change in the service areas of education, public welfare, hospitals, health, highways, police, corrections, natural resources, parks and recreation, financial administration (e.g., budget authority, reporting requirements), land use and planning, and economic development. The most frequent responses were that discretion, power, and authority had "decreased" or "stayed about the same"; there is little indication of increased local discretion during the past decade. The two functional areas in which managers consistently reported decreased power and authority were financial administration (66%) and land use and planning (64%). For two policy areas, parks and recreation (66%) and police (54%), a majority of respondents reported that local discretion had remained about the same.

Table 2–2 shows the mean of responses to the services question above. Possible scores range from − 1 (decreased discretion) to + 1 (increased discretion). Again, city managers perceive that the policy area that

Figure 2-2 Change in Degree of City Government's Discretion, Power, and Authority for 12 Policy Areas

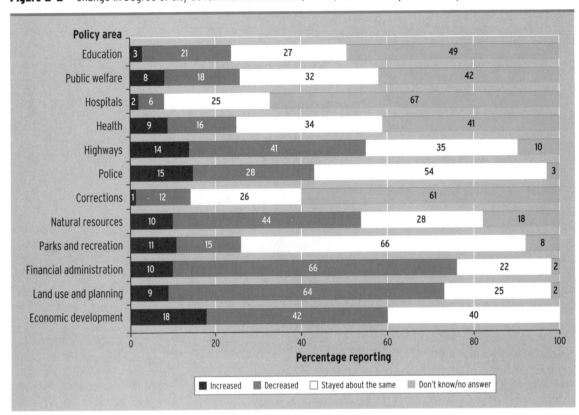

Table 2-2 City Government's Discretion, Power, and Authority

Area	Mean	Standard deviation
Education	−0.36	0.46
Public welfare	−0.17	0.51
Hospitals	−0.14	0.28
Health	−0.12	0.49
Highways	−0.30	0.69
Police	−0.13	0.65
Corrections	−0.27	0.35
Natural resources	−0.42	0.65
Parks and recreation	−0.04	0.50
Financial administration	−0.58	0.67
Land use and planning	−0.55	0.68
Economic development	−0.24	0.73

has experienced the greatest decrease in local authority is financial administration at −0.58, followed by land use and planning with a mean score of −0.55, and natural resources at −0.42. In the case of financial administration, the fiscal crisis that prevailed during the latter part of the past decade may have provoked legislatures and, to a lesser extent, state courts

to restrict and redirect local governments' budgetary authority. Land use planning and natural resources tend to be cross-jurisdictional collective benefits functions that logically call for greater centralized planning and administration as population grows. The policy areas that have been witness to the least loss of discretion, power, and authority are parks and recreation (−0.04), health (−0.12), police (−0.13), and hospitals (−0.14). Higher mean scores in health and hospitals could be explained by the fact that hospitals fall outside the purview of many municipalities. Law enforcement continues to be primarily a local government responsibility.

Table 2–3 shows the degree of devolution, or the shifting of responsibilities from state government to city government, in five broad functional areas: personnel, finance, service provision, administrative authority, and home rule. The data illustrate that since 2000, the greatest shift in responsibility in favor of local authority has been in the area of finance (e.g., the authority to raise revenues, issue debt, etc.), with 31% of city managers reporting substantial devolution. This may be a result of states granting local governments increased authority to raise taxes and fees; however, it is interesting to note that increased

Table 2-3 State Devolution of Responsibility to Local Governments

Functional area	Substantial devolution, %	Modest devolution, %	Minimal devolution, %	No devolution, %	Don't know/not applicable, %
Personnel	5	21	30	36	8
Finance	31	25	22	19	3
Service provision	18	38	29	12	3
Administrative authority	9	26	32	29	4
Home rule	14	18	19	37	12

financial devolution has not been accompanied by enhanced power and authority in local financial administration. Areas in which majorities of city managers reported combined totals of minimal or no devolution are home rule (56%), administrative authority (61%), and personnel (66%).

It is important to consider second-order devolution in the context of local government capacity (the ability to assume new responsibilities) and capability (the ability to perform satisfactorily in devolved areas of responsibility). Ideally, municipalities would acquire substantial levels of administrative authority and personnel before assuming responsibility over other areas of government, such as new services. The devolution of services may be perceived as promoting local autonomy, but in actuality it may result in a struggle to raise revenues to support additional service delivery responsibilities that are mandated but not adequately funded. And as suggested above, the devolution of financial responsibility may have a negative impact on a local government: more times than not, increased financial responsibility, such as that from state legislation permitting local governments to add a penny to the sales tax, provides a convenient excuse for the state to shift new costs to the locality as well. In sum, increased local financial responsibility and control over service provision may paradoxically be indicative of disruptive state policies, particularly when the local government does not have the administrative, human resource, and financial wherewithal to carry out devolved responsibilities with success.

Do city governments have the capacity to manage second-order devolution? When asked "on balance" about public administration capacity, a near majority (47%) of managers logically replied that the answer depends on the policy area (see Appendix Table I). Of the rest, 19% responded that city governments have sufficient public administrative capacity for second-order devolution while 28% indicated that municipalities do not and 6% did not know. Obviously results are likely to vary depending on the respondent municipality and its specific level of financial and

administrative capacity, but the general answer to the question appears to be, "it depends."

How are municipal governments dealing with their enlarged role as providers and financers of state-devolved services? One possibility is to outsource or contract out to entities in other sectors of the economy. A survey question sought to assess what role, if any, for-profit and not-for-profit organizations play in local service delivery—"third-order devolution," if you will. As shown in Appendix Table I, a substantial proportion of city managers reported that their cities involved such organizations frequently or occasionally in service delivery, with regional variance ranging from 78% in the South to 85% in the West. It would appear that for many of the surveyed cities, other sectors of the economy are being tapped to help provide services.

Impact of State Mandates on Local Governments

We also sought to elicit managers' perceptions about the impact of state mandates on local governments. We again presented the 12 policy areas and asked respondents to indicate the levels of significance and impact of mandates on each area. Scores could vary from -2, signifying a significant and negative impact, to $+2$, representing a significant and positive impact. It is apparent from Table 2–4 that in none of the policy areas do city managers perceive the impact of state mandates as positive; all the mean scores are negative. The policy areas in which state mandates are perceived most negatively are financial administration (-1.25) and education (-1.21). Policies for which state mandates are viewed least negatively, although by no means positively, are parks and recreation (-0.29), health (-0.50), hospitals (-0.60), and economic development (-0.62).

One likely reason for the service-associated differences in the impacts of state mandates is variation in local governments' responsibility for specific policies. For example, we acknowledge that many cities do not directly administer hospitals or correction

Table 2-4 Impact of State Mandates

Area	Mean	Standard deviation
Education	-1.21	0.89
Public welfare	-0.69	0.71
Hospitals	-0.60	0.49
Health	-0.50	0.66
Highways	-0.78	0.89
Police	-0.65	0.79
Corrections	-0.67	0.58
Natural resources	-0.84	0.88
Parks and recreation	-0.29	0.65
Financial administration	-1.25	0.81
Land use and planning	-1.05	0.82
Economic development	-0.62	0.99

Note: Scores range from significant and negative impact (-2), modest and negative impact (-1), negligible impact (0), modest and positive impact (+1), to a significant and positive impact (+2).

facilities, and that education may be governed and administered as a special-purpose district. Similarly, responsibility for public welfare and for parks and recreation may be relegated to the county government for smaller municipalities. But several of the service-specific perceptual distinctions are striking. The high significance and negativity calculated for education may be associated with educational reforms imposed first on the states by the federal government under No Child Left Behind (NCLB), and then later by the states on their local governments to ensure that the state would be in compliance with NCLB mandates. State centralization of land use and planning may be perceived negatively in jurisdictions where states have rendered locally unpopular land use decisions.

Perhaps most striking is the highly significant and negative score for financial administration. As noted above in our discussion of Figure 2–2 and Table 2–3, while managers reported that a relatively high degree of financial responsibility has devolved to local governments, that responsibility has not been deemed felicitous. As one city manager put it, "State agencies rarely provide value to local governments, but always steal resources, increase costs...and obstruct local authority." The implication is that financial devolution has two faces: one shows that local governments are receiving enhanced authority, power, and discretion over finances; the other shows that states are increasingly withdrawing state-shared taxes and fees, "borrowing" from state-funded local government accounts, and imposing new financial requirements on local governments. The inequitable exchange is akin to a second-order version of the classic "shift and shaft" federalism usually attributed to the federal government.

Additional support for the "two faces of financial devolution" hypothesis is found in Table 2–5. Respondents were given four critical features of government—structural, functional, personnel, and fiscal—and asked to assess which they felt had "experienced the most significant state intrusion or preemption of power and authority." In each of the four regions, 71%–81% of respondents identified the fiscal area (e.g., taxing, spending, borrowing) as the one that had experienced the greatest state intrusion or preemption. The question that might be posed is whether the financial devolution that has been reported has actually resulted in fiscal deprivation. While a higher percentage of respondents in the South reported state intrusiveness in fiscal areas, respondents in the West registered the highest percentages in the other three areas; most notably, four out of five respondents in the West indicated that their municipalities had experienced state intrusion into personnel (rules and procedures) (83%) and functions (service provision) (81%).

Table 2–6 summarizes the mean state scores on five preemptive and intrusive state activities for which we received five or more survey responses, thereby allowing for a comparison of the responses among the 14 listed states. The state-specific sentiments expressed by managers are largely comparable to those of the total set of respondents summarized above, indicating the frequency of counterdevolutionary measures taken by state governments. The institution viewed as the most intrusive is the state legislature, and the action viewed as most intrusive is state raids on local revenue sources. Clearly, these are not mutually exclusive. Mirroring the comprehensive response set, activities felt to be less intrusive of local autonomy in the listed states are state court decisions and voter referendums and initiatives. States that provide for popular referendums and initiatives are indicated with asterisks. The mean scores (not shown) for initiative-referendum states is 2.62 (indicating relative intrusiveness of this form of direct democracy) versus 3.28 for states without the initiative-referendum option.

The Nature and Direction of State-Local Relations

Nearly all individual comments in response to our open-ended question, which invited respondents to comment in general about the quality of state-local relations in their state, remarked negatively upon a perceived high degree of coercive, intrusive, and preemptive state policies toward local governments. Some managers reported that state governments hide behind a veil of cooperation and partnership while, in reality, they have become masters of deception, devising techniques to shift not only costs to local governments but

Table 2-5 The Most Significant State Intrusion of Power and Authority

Involvement	Northeast Count	%	North-Central Count	%	South Count	%	West Count	%
Structural								
Experienced intrusion	1	3	2	3	3	4	4	6
Has not experienced intrusion	28	97	61	97	72	96	62	94
Functional								
Experienced intrusion	8	28	17	27	23	31	54	81
Has not experienced intrusion	21	72	46	73	52	69	13	19
Personnel								
Experienced intrusion	12	41	19	30	17	23	55	83
Has not experienced intrusion	17	59	44	70	58	77	11	17
Fiscal								
Experienced intrusion	21	72	44	71	61	81	53	79
Has not experienced intrusion	8	28	18	29	14	19	14	21

Note: The results from respondents who answered "don't know" are not reported here.

Table 2-6 State Intrusion: Sources and Actions, by State

State	State legislative intrusion Mean	SD	State court intrusion Mean	SD	Intrusive referendums or voter initiatives Mean	SD	State raids on local revenue sources Mean	SD	State shifting new costs to cities Mean	SD
California	1.35	0.62	1.90	0.62	2.17[1]	0.80	1.10	0.30	1.25	0.49
Florida	1.00	0.00	2.19	0.66	2.31[1]	0.87	1.60	0.73	1.30	0.48
Illinois	1.29	0.46	1.81	0.68	3.30[1]	0.78	2.05	1.02	1.10	0.30
Kansas	2.00	0.71	2.67	1.52	3.40	0.55	1.40	0.55	2.20	1.10
Michigan	1.71	0.49	2.14	1.07	2.71[1]	0.76	1.14	0.38	1.43	0.53
Minnesota	1.38	0.52	2.12	0.35	3.25	0.71	1.38	0.52	1.50	0.53
Missouri	1.60	0.55	2.00	0.00	2.60[1]	0.89	2.40	1.14	2.00	1.00
New Jersey	1.38	0.52	1.75	0.71	3.71	1.39	1.75	1.16	1.50	0.76
Pennsylvania	2.00	0.82	2.29	0.49	3.17	1.50	2.86	1.07	1.71	0.76
South Carolina	1.17	0.41	2.67	0.52	3.00	0.89	1.67	0.52	1.50	0.55
Texas	1.20	0.41	2.22	0.89	2.76	0.88	1.56	0.82	1.28	0.54
Utah	1.22	0.44	2.11	0.60	3.11[1]	0.60	2.33	0.87	1.67	0.50
Washington	1.50	0.55	1.83	0.41	2.17[1]	0.98	2.60	1.47	1.67	0.52
Wisconsin	1.17	0.41	2.17	0.41	3.67	0.82	1.33	0.52	1.83	0.75

Notes: Scores reflect the rate of occurrence and range from 1 (frequent) to 4 (none). Individual state scores are averages of five or more respondents.
  SD = standard deviation.

1 State provides for popular referendums and initiatives.

also responsibilities for policies over which local governments have only limited authority. Several managers roundly excoriated the encumbrances of unfunded mandates and increased responsibility without a corresponding expansion in resource allocation.

Conclusion

The city managers who responded to this survey expressed a general perception that states have been acting intrusively during the past decade. Rather than devolving power, authority, and responsibility to their general-purpose local governments, they have centralized state power and stepped into the affairs of local government. Managers overall reported that their cities lost discretionary authority during the survey period in most or all of the 12 major policy areas presented. Actions by state legislatures—particularly recurring raids and confiscations of local revenues, and refusals to pass along monies legally obligated to localities—came in for special opprobrium. Even as some states trimmed local financial assets, they foisted costly new mandates on their cities.

There was evidence of a paradox in financial affairs. Managers reported that their cities gained financial power and authority while simultaneously acknowledging that they were granted less authority in financial administration. Perhaps this indicates a disconnect between revenue-raising authority and budgetary authority, as local governments are gaining new powers of levying taxes and fees but are suffering from state administrative impositions and mandates. The overall impact is perceived to be negative.

More broadly, the survey results reveal an absence of trust by city managers in state legislatures and a sense that the state is treating them as their water boys or handmaidens. As a manager from a state in the Southwest observed, "The . . . legislature collectively, and legislators individually, see cities as a "subdivision" of the state. They act as a super city council, always reducing our authority and questioning our methods and motives. Thank goodness they only meet for 45 days. No man, woman, or child is safe those 45 days."

The sad situation depicted by managers is one of dysfunctional federalism. Its causes are several, including a certain perceived arrogance on the part of state officials, long histories of shifting and shafting local governments, and, most immediately, the enormous financial crisis pressing down on all but a handful of states. Second-order devolution is an appealing notion, but under the present circumstances, that is all it is: a notion.

Notes

1. Timothy D. Mead, "Federalism and State Law: Legal Factors Constraining and Facilitating Local Initiatives," in *Handbook of Local Government Administration*, ed. John J. Gargan (New York: Marvel Dekker, 1997): 31–45.

2. See Dale Krane, Platon N. Rigos, and Melvin B. Hills Jr., *Home Rule in America: A Fifty-State Handbook* (Washington, D.C.: Congressional Quarterly Press, 2001).

3. Ann O'M. Bowman and Richard C. Kearney, *The Resurgence of the States* (Englewood Cliffs, N.J.: Prentice Hall, 1986).

4. Dale Krane, "Devolution as an Intergovernmental Reform Strategy," in *Strategies for Managing Intergovernmental Policies and Networks*, ed. Robert W. Gage and Myrna P. Mandell (New York: Praeger, 1990).

5. Judith F. Gainsborough, "To Devolve or Not to Devolve? Welfare Reform in the States," *The Policy Studies Journal* 31 (November 2003): 603–623.

6. John Kincaid, "The Devolution Tortoise and the Centralization Hare," *New England Economic Review* (May–June 1998): 13–40; Krane, Rigos, and Hills, *Home Rule in America*.

7. John Kincaid, "De Facto Devolution and Urban Defunding: The Priority of Persons over Places," *Journal of Urban Affairs* 21, no. 2 (1999): 135–167; Kincaid, "Devolution Tortoise and the Centralization Hare."

8. See James H. Svara, "Dichotomy and Duality: Reconceptualizing the Relationship between Policy and Administration in Council-Manager Cities," *Public Administration Review* 45 (January/February 1985): 221–232; Carmine P. F. Scavo, Richard C. Kearney, and Richard J. Kilroy Jr., "Challenges to Federalism: Homeland Security and Disaster Response," *Publius: The Journal of Federalism* 38, no. 1 (2008): 81–110.

9. The coding for the survey was performed by ICMA. Each region is defined in accordance with the U.S. Census Bureau's designation as follows: Northeast (New England and Mid-Atlantic), North-Central (East North-Central and West North-Central), South (South Atlantic, East South-Central, and West South-Central) and West (Mountain and Pacific Coast).

10. There was quite a large number of California cities in the sample, but no more than would be expected considering the prevalence of council-manager governments in that state.

Appendixes

Appendix I: Summary of Survey Responses

	Region									
	Northeast		North-Central		South		West		Total	
	No.	%	No.	%	No.	%	No.	%	No.	%
In your assessment, since 2000, how often has the legislature enacted bills that are intrusive or preemptive of city government powers or authority? (n = 234)										
Frequently	18	62	32	51	54	72	46	69	150	64
Occasionally	8	28	28	44	19	25	18	27	73	31
Seldom	2	7	3	5	2	3	3	4	10	4
Never	1	3	0	0	0	0	0	0	1	0
Don't know	0	0	0	0	0	0	0	0	0	0
In your assessment, since 2000, how often have state courts issued decisions that are intrusive or preemptive of city government powers or authority? (n = 234)										
Frequently	6	17	10	16	7	9	12	18	35	15
Occasionally	16	55	38	60	35	47	44	66	133	57
Seldom	6	21	12	19	26	35	9	13	53	23
Never	0	0	1	2	1	1	1	1	3	1
Don't know	1	4	2	3	6	8	1	2	10	4
In your assessment, since 2000, how often have the voters approved referendums or initiatives that are intrusive or preemptive of city government powers or authority? (n = 234)										
Frequently	0	0	1	2	4	5	11	16	16	7
Occasionally	6	21	13	21	21	28	25	37	65	28
Seldom	9	31	22	35	26	35	24	36	81	35
Never	11	38	26	41	21	28	6	9	64	27
Don't know	3	10	1	2	3	4	1	2	8	3
In your assessment, since 2000, how often has the state "raided" local revenue sources, seized state-shared taxes or fees, or taken promised money in other ways from city governments? (n = 234)										
Frequently	13	45	30	48	36	48	42	63	121	52
Occasionally	9	31	23	37	32	43	14	21	78	33
Seldom	3	10	6	10	4	5	7	10	20	9
Never	4	14	3	5	2	3	3	4	12	5
Don't know	0	0	1	2	1	1	1	2	3	1

(continued on page 22)

Appendix I: Summary of Survey Responses *(continued from page 21)*

	Region									
	Northeast		North-Central		South		West		Total	
	No.	%	No.	%	No.	%	No.	%	No.	%
In your assessment, since 2000, how often has the state shifted **new costs** to city governments? (n = 234)										
Frequently	17	59	36	57	46	61	40	60	139	59
Occasionally	9	31	22	35	26	35	26	39	83	35
Seldom	3	10	4	6	2	3	1	1	10	4
Never	0	0	1	2	1	1	0	0	2	1
Don't know	0	0	0	0	0	0	0	0	0	0
On balance, do city governments have sufficient **public administration capacity** today for more devolution of power and authority from the state government? (n = 234)										
Yes	7	24	14	22	12	16	12	18	45	19
No	4	14	21	33	18	24	23	34	66	28
Depends on policy area	15	52	26	39	40	53	28	42	109	47
Don't know	3	10	2	3	5	7	4	6	14	6
Since 2000, in which of the following areas has your city experienced the **most significant state intrusion or preemption of power and authority?**[1] (n = 301)										
Structural	1	3	2	3	3	4	4	6	10	3
Functional	8	28	17	27	23	31	13	19	61	20
Personnel	12	41	19	30	17	23	11	16	59	19
Fiscal	21	72	44	70	61	81	53	79	179	58
Don't know	0	0	0	0	1	1	0	0	1	0
In your assessment, since 2000, how often has your city involved for-profit and not-for-profit organizations in service delivery? (n = 234)										
Frequently	7	24	13	21	25	33	30	45	75	32
Occasionally	16	55	37	59	34	45	27	40	114	49
Seldom	4	14	11	17	12	16	10	15	37	16
Never	2	7	1	2	2	3	0	0	5	2
Don't know	0	0	1	2	2	3	0	0	3	1

1   Respondents were allowed to pick more than one area. Only those that elected that their city had experienced preemption are included here.

Appendix II: Change in Degree of City Government's Discretion, Power, and Authority since 2000 in 12 Policy Areas

Policy area	Increased		Decreased		Stayed the same		Don't know/NA	
	No.	%	No.	%	No.	%	No.	%
Education	7	3	50	21	64	27	113	48
Public welfare	19	8	43	18	76	32	96	41
Hospitals	4	2	15	6	59	25	156	67
Health	21	9	37	16	79	34	97	41
Highways	33	14	96	41	83	35	22	9
Police	36	15	65	28	126	54	7	3
Corrections	3	1	28	12	62	26	141	60
Natural resources	23	10	104	44	66	28	41	18
Parks and recreation	25	11	34	15	155	66	20	9
Financial administration	23	10	155	66	51	22	5	2
Land use and planning*	22	9	150	64	58	25	3	1
Economic development	41	18	97	41	93	40	3	1

*One response was coded incorrectly, so the total sample size here is 233, not 234.

Appendix III: Impact of State Mandates on Cities since 2000 in 12 Policy Areas

Policy area	Significant and negative		Modest and negative		Negligible		Modest and positive		Significant and positive		Don't know/NA	
	No.	%	No.	%	No.	%	No.	%	No.	%	No.	%
Education	53	23	45	19	13	6	3	1	3	1	117	50
Public welfare	23	10	47	20	42	18	9	4	0	0	113	48
Hospitals	10	4	24	100	39	17	0	0	0	0	161	69
Health	17	7	42	18	59	25	11	5	0	0	105	45
Highways	50	21	83	35	63	27	15	6	1	0	22	9
Police	33	14	91	39	88	38	12	5	0	0	10	4
Corrections	15	6	33	14	44	19	1	0	0	0	141	60
Natural resources	51	22	75	32	54	23	12	5	1	0	41	18
Parks and recreation	12	5	51	22	135	58	12	5	1	0	23	10
Financial administration	99	42	90	38	32	14	4	2	1	0	8	3
Land use and planning	70	30	110	47	37	16	11	5	0	0	6	3
Economic development	48	21	73	31	74	32	22	9	5	2	12	5

Notes: State mandates include legislative enactments, public referendums, regulatory actions, administrative actions, and court decisions. Respondents (n = 234) were allowed to choose more than one area.

Appendix IV: Degree of Devolution of Responsibility from State Government to City Government since 2000 in Five Functional Areas

	Substantial devolution		Modest devolution		Minimal devolution		No devolution		Don't know/NA	
	No.	%	No.	%	No.	%	No.	%	No.	%
Personnel	11	5	49	21	71	30	85	36	18	8
Finance	73	31	59	25	52	22	44	19	6	3
Service provision	42	18	89	38	68	29	29	12	6	3
Administrative authority	20	9	61	26	76	32	67	29	10	4
Home rule	32	14	41	18	45	19	87	37	29	12

Note: Respondents (n=234) were allowed to choose more than one area.

3

Alternative Notions of Community: Understanding Local Government Responses to Immigrants

Nadia Rubaii-Barrett
Binghamton University, State University of New York

In 2010, the most prominent news story regarding immigration centered on the state of Arizona's enactment of SB 1070. Signed into law on April 23, 2010, the "Support Our Law Enforcement and Safe Neighborhoods" Act is widely characterized as one of the broadest and most stringent laws against illegal immigration in recent decades. The law contains provisions that would make it a state misdemeanor to be in Arizona without carrying required documents; allow police to arrest individuals suspected of being undocumented immigrants and detain them without a warrant; ban the solicitation or performance of work by day laborers; and impose penalties on those who shelter, hire, or transport undocumented immigrants. The explicit intent of the law is to achieve "attrition through enforcement."[1]

SB 1070 has not been fully implemented because some of its provisions have been struck down and still others face legal challenges. Nonetheless, reactions to the law from the general public, other governmental entities, professional associations, and private corporations reveal that it has further polarized people around an already contentious issue. One substantive point of contention is whether Arizona has overstepped its authority to legislate on a matter of national jurisdiction.

Immigration policy is widely understood to be the responsibility of the national government, and

SELECTED FINDINGS

Local government policies regarding immigrants fall into four broad categories: anti-immigrant, neutral or laissez-faire, community cohesion, or pro-immigrant. Survey responses indicated that policies that are at either extreme of the continuum are much less prevalent than those that are more moderate, such as providing local government materials in languages other than English (55%) and referring immigrants to religious and nonprofit organizations for services (40%).

Collectively, three dimensions—how immigrants are perceived, what citizens and policy makers think about assimilation, and whether local policies are more likely to defer to or challenge policies at higher levels—can indicate whether local leaders view their role as either defending an existing notion of community or helping the community expand its sense of self in response to change and diversity.

yet across the United States, local and state governments are expressing frustration with the federal government's inaction and ineffectiveness. Proponents of Arizona's sweeping legislation acknowledge that the law was in large part a response to a perceived failure of the federal government to pass and implement immigration reforms that would stop the influx of undocumented immigrants and remove those already in the country. Opponents of the Arizona statute also express frustration with federal inaction, although they focus more on the need for comprehensive immigration policies in areas other than border control and enforcement. Pro-immigrant advocates for comprehensive immigration reform stress the need for federal policies that would allow businesses to lawfully hire needed immigrant workers, vigorously enforce labor laws to protect the rights of immigrants and citizens alike, speed processing times and reduce backlogs for visas, and create a path to legal citizenship for undocumented individuals already living and working in the country.

Despite the national government's legal and practical responsibility to establish and enforce immigration policies, the reality is that growing numbers of immigrants live in local communities across all regions of the country, challenging the service delivery and financial resource capacities of towns, villages, cities, and counties of all sizes. The local ordinances, programs, and practices that have been instituted in response could affect the experiences of immigrants more directly and immediately than any policy changes at the national level. These responses, which are wide-ranging and not easily understood solely on the basis of demographic trends or political ideology, also reflect broader notions of how to define community and of whether local government responsibilities for creating and maintaining community are primarily for the benefit of long-term residents or extend equally to new and diverse populations.

The attention given to the Arizona law may have shifted public and media attention away from local immigration policies as some localities interested in enacting similar policies have adopted a wait-and-see approach while the lawsuits are resolved. But in many other localities across the country, officials continue to adopt policies, implement programs, and otherwise respond to the challenges of an increasingly diverse immigrant population within their communities. Thus, a careful review of local government policies and practices is warranted, as is an effort to understand the factors influencing the selection of a particular local policy response.

The Context for Local Immigration Policies

Although it is widely characterized as "a nation of immigrants," the United States has a long and contentious history with new arrivals.[2] Each new wave of immigrants has usually been viewed with suspicion or outright hostility and often been made the scape-

goat for whatever economic or social ills are contemporaneous with their arrival. Immigrant integration and assimilation is a matter of enduring debate in the United States, with some individuals viewing "a country composed of diverse ethnic populations" as providing "promise of new vigor and growth" while others perceive "the presence of these strange people" as constituting "threats to the very core of [America's] heritage."[3] As time passes, each group ultimately transitions from newcomer status to part of the core population. Prior waves of immigrants are then viewed in a nostalgic and idyllic light relative to the groups that follow.

Several characteristics of recent immigration trends—most notably, overall rates of immigration, growing language and cultural diversity, and more disperse settlement patterns—have prompted increased policy activity by local governments. Compounding the impact of these demographic trends is continued gridlock and inaction in Washington, D.C., on the issue of comprehensive immigration reform.

Rates of Immigration

Overall rates of immigration are a function of factors both in the country of origin and in the United States. So-called push factors include the civil wars, natural disasters, political unrest, religious persecution, and economic hardships in an immigrant's home country. In contrast, pull factors include job opportunities, political and religious freedoms, and relative peace within the United States. As Figure 3–1 illustrates, the United States has experienced a steady and noticeable increase in the percentage of foreign-born residents since the 1970s, reaching a record number and a near-record proportion of the total population: as of 2009, an unprecedented number of foreign-born individuals—more than 36 million, both legal and undocumented—resided in the United States, representing more than 12% of the nation's population.[4] The economic recession in 2009 and 2010 served to slow the influx of new immigrants somewhat; the most dramatic decrease was in the number of undocumented immigrants, which was estimated to drop from 12 million in March 2007 to 11.1 million in March 2009, with the biggest changes occurring in the states of Arizona, California, Florida, New Jersey, and New York.[5] Despite these reductions, however, there was little impact on aggregate numbers.

Diversity of Language and Culture

Not only are immigration rates approaching or exceeding record levels, but new immigrants are also increasingly likely to come from developing countries in Latin America, Asia, and Africa rather than from developed countries in Europe. English-language proficiency

Figure 3-1 Foreign-Born Population of the United States: 1850-2010

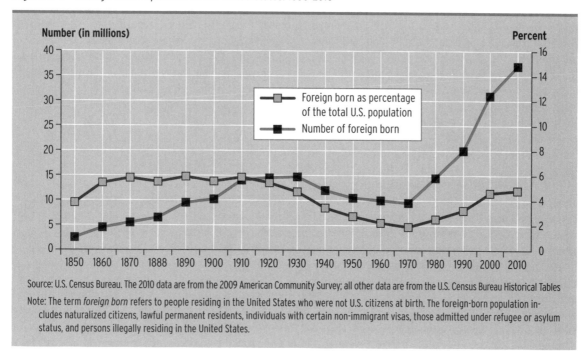

Source: U.S. Census Bureau. The 2010 data are from the 2009 American Community Survey; all other data are from the U.S. Census Bureau Historical Tables

Note: The term *foreign born* refers to people residing in the United States who were not U.S. citizens at birth. The foreign-born population includes naturalized citizens, lawful permanent residents, individuals with certain non-immigrant visas, those admitted under refugee or asylum status, and persons illegally residing in the United States.

among new immigrants is low, and the range of languages spoken is vast.[6] While Spanish predominates overall, many communities have sizeable populations of new immigrants who speak Chinese, Tagalog, Vietnamese, Korean, Arabic, French, French Creole, Russian, Italian, German, Polish, and a multitude of African languages and dialects. Few communities outside of major metropolitan areas have resident populations with abilities in these languages. Additionally, as immigration scholar Alejandro Portes has observed, "the surge of immigration into the United States during the past 30 years has brought a proliferation of foreign languages, and with it fears that the English language might lose its predominance and cultural unity may be undermined."[7] Along with speaking languages other than English, the new immigrants bring with them cultural traditions and norms that may differ dramatically from those of the communities where they settle.

Settlement Patterns

Beyond the sheer numbers and the language and cultural diversity, perhaps the single greatest factor driving local government immigration policies are the settlement patterns, which differ sharply from the patterns of prior waves of immigrants. Traditionally, immigrants have settled in or near so-called gateway cities, such as Boston, Chicago, New York, and San Francisco. These gateways have a long tradition of receiving and integrating immigrants, and they have

the social infrastructure to do so effectively. While traditional gateways continue to receive large numbers of immigrants, an increasing number of suburbs as well as rural towns and villages have also seen an influx of immigrants.[8] Rather than merely following their predecessors to the gateway cities, new immigrants are settling in communities on the basis of abundant job opportunities and affordable housing. Maps of the United States showing the foreign-born populations, both on an aggregate level and by country of origin, are available on the website of the Migration Policy Institute (migrationpolicy.org/datahub); these maps illustrate that every region of the country and almost every state includes some pockets of immigrant populations.

The National Response

Of course, no discussion of subnational responses to immigration is complete without a discussion of the shortcomings of national policies. To the media and the general public, the most obvious problems are associated with the failure to prevent undocumented persons from entering the United States. Undocumented immigrants—or "illegal aliens," as they are often called—may have entered illegally or may have entered legally and then overstayed their visas. The overwhelming majority of them are hard-working, law-abiding individuals; some would like to pursue U.S. citizenship while many others would prefer to be living and working in their native countries if it were economically feasible to do so. A small proportion of undocumented immigrants are involved in criminal activities, such as drug smuggling, human trafficking, and violent gang activities, and it is this image that has captured the attention of many anti-immigrant groups as they promote more stringent border controls, penalties for those who would house or employ undocumented individuals, and aggressive use of detention and deportation.

Illegal immigration needs to be understood within the context of the problems with the system designed to screen applicants for legal access to the country. While border control and immigration enforcement by Immigration and Customs Enforcement (ICE) has been a priority in U.S. immigration policy since September 11, 2001, other elements of that policy have received less attention. Applications for legal permanent residence (green cards) and naturalization are backlogged. So, too, are applications for visas: entering the United States legally, whether to pursue work or to reunite with family members, may happen quickly or may take anywhere from 6 years to 15 years, depending on the type of visa sought.

Although ICMA and its counterpart associations that make up the "Big 7" (i.e., Council of State Governments, National Association of Counties, National Conference of State Legislatures, National Governor's Association, National League of Cities, and U.S. Conference of Mayors) recognize the need for and advocate to have comprehensive immigration reform at the national level, Washington seems unable to act. National immigration policies reflect a series of often conflicting policy objectives, such as maintaining border control, reunifying families, filling needed work skills, creating jobs, protecting residents, practicing fiscal responsibility, ensuring homeland security, and providing humanitarian relief. In light of such wide-ranging goals, it is no wonder that efforts at comprehensive immigration reform have repeatedly failed to secure necessary congressional approvals, regardless of which political party controls the chambers. And given federal inaction, it is not surprising that local and state policies have filled the void.

Research on Local Immigration Policies

In 2008, ICMA conducted a survey of local government leaders to learn about their experiences, attitudes, and local policies regarding immigrants. The results of that survey have been supplemented by additional research on the more recent practices of local governments and the reactions of local governments to Arizona's 2010 law. The intent is to provide an overview of the various policy and program options that local governments are using, and the frequency with which those options are being pursued. Additionally, this article helps to frame the understanding of local immigration policies within a broader framework.

The ICMA survey asked respondents to indicate to what extent they have experienced an influx of immigrants, what kinds of challenges immigrants have created for the community, and how the community has responded. Completed surveys were received from 517 jurisdictions ranging in population from 120 residents to 1.3 million; respondents were from 47 states in all regions of the country, with no single region predominating. Nearly half (45%) of the respondents indicated that immigrant populations within their communities grew over the preceding decade; close

Figure 3-2   Continuum of Local Responses to Immigrants

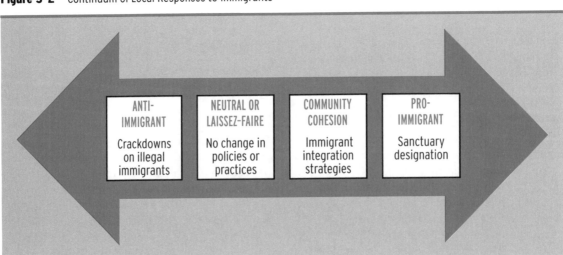

to one-third (32%) reported that recent immigrants are from a variety of countries and regions of the world; more than one-quarter described immigrants as a large proportion of the population; and almost all respondents (98%) reported that they were unable to accurately determine the relative proportion of legal and undocumented immigrants in their communities (not shown).[9] More than half (57%) identified language diversity and the lack of English proficiency among immigrants as a major barrier to immigrant integration in their communities (not shown).

Local government responses to immigrant populations can be broadly characterized as falling into one of four categories: anti-immigrant, neutral or laissez-faire, community cohesion, or pro-immigrant. Figure 3–2 depicts these categories along a continuum, and Figure 3–3 provides a detailed list of local policy or program responses in each category.[10] Survey

Figure 3-3   Local Policy and Program Responses Associated with Categories

Anti-immigrant

- Strict ordinances (penalties for hiring, housing or transporting undocumented persons)
- 287g agreements with Immigration and Customs Enforcement
- Limited ordinances (e.g., restrict work opportunities for individuals without documentation)
- Local law enforcement personnel required to check documents
- Local law enforcement personnel required to report to federal authorities
- Adopt English-only ordinances
- Allow foreign flags to be flown only if accompanied by U.S. flag
- Targeted police enforcement at day labor centers
- Use of housing, trespassing, or antisolicitation ordinances at day labor centers

Neutral/ laissez faire

- Referral of immigrants to religious or nonprofit organizations
- Educating all residents about codes enforcement
- Encouraging cultural competence among employees
- Broad-based community policing efforts
- Adopt resolutions calling for comprehensive national immigration reform
- No designated local policies or practices regarding immigrants

Community cohesion

- Provide English language instruction
- Encourage civic participation
- Community policing with language and cultural competence

- Mandating cultural competence training for local employees
- Providing local government materials (print and electronic) in multiple languages
- Community events to promote diversity
- Facilitated community dialogues
- Mission statement emphasizing the value of cultural diversity
- Providing translation services at local proceedings

Pro-immigrant

- Local agencies and officials required to protect confidentiality of individuals
- Promote naturalization and citizenship
- Establishment of local day labor hiring centers
- Create a local welcome centers for immigrants
- Accept Matriculas Consulares as a valid form of identification
- Provide community ID cards to all residents for access to local services
- Adopt resolution calling for reform to create a legal path to citizenship
- Adopt resolution supporting humane immigration reform
- Fund organizations that provide services to immigrants
- Hire an immigrant liaison
- Create a local office of immigrant services
- Create immigrant affairs committees, councils, and advisory boards
- Adopt "Don't Ask, Don't Tell" policies regarding immigration status
- Adopt a sanctuary designation

Figure 3-4 Local Policies and Practices in Responses to Immigrants

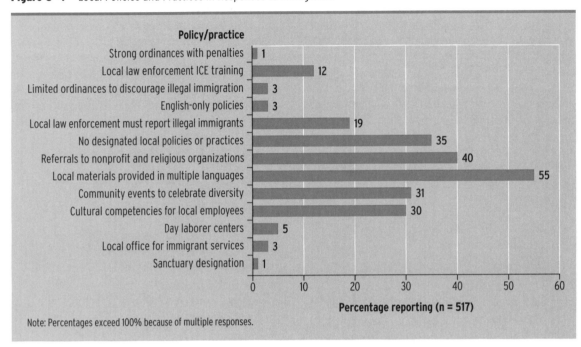

Note: Percentages exceed 100% because of multiple responses.

respondents were provided with an abbreviated list of policy options representing the four categories; from their responses, which are shown in Figure 3-4, it is clear that policies at either end of the continuum—that is, those that are clearly anti-immigrant or pro-immigrant—are much less prevalent than are those that are more moderate. Such moderate policies include providing local government materials in languages other than English (55%), referring immigrants to religious and nonprofit organizations for services (40%), holding community events to promote immigrant contributions and/or celebrate cultural diversity (31%), and encouraging or requiring local government employees to obtain cultural competencies (30%) (Figure 3-4).

The survey responses correspond to broader patterns of local policy across the country. Among the nearly 40,000 general-purpose local governments in the United States, fewer than 90 cities and 60 counties have enacted strong anti-immigrant ordinances directed at employment, housing, police enforcement, or English-only language restrictions.[11] According to ICE reports, 60 local law enforcement agencies in 21 states have signed memorandums of understanding (MOUs) under the 287(g) program;[12] these MOUs delegate federal civil and criminal immigration authority to select trained and certified state and local law enforcement officials, effectively empowering them to act as immigration authorities. At the other end of the spectrum, fewer than 30 local governments

have adopted sanctuary ordinances of one form or another,[13] and roughly 60 local governments have created—or have partnered with nonprofit organizations to create—day labor centers.[14] While the communities enacting policies at these two ends of the spectrum receive the most attention, particularly those undergoing court challenges to their stringent anti-immigration policies, the vast majority of local governments are responding with less contentious policies and programs.

Not reflected in the survey data are how local governments have responded since Arizona enacted its landmark anti-immigration statute in April 2010. Close to 20 cities and counties—ranging in size from Gallup, New Mexico (population 20,000), to Cook County, Illinois (population 5.3 million), and spanning all regions of the country—acted swiftly to impose boycotts on travel to and purchases from Arizona by local employees and agencies.[15] Other localities enacted nonbinding statements of opposition to the Arizona law. A small number of cities and counties expressed strong support for the law, however, and some indicated a desire to enact similar measures should the state law withstand judicial challenges.

Factors Influencing Local Immigrant Policies

So what explains such divergent local policies? Several recent studies have used multiple linear regression and logistic regression to try to pinpoint the variables with the greatest capacity to predict local government responses—specifically, whether anti-immigrant or pro-immigrant policies are adopted. These analyses are inherently limited by the relatively small number of jurisdictions that adopt policies at either extreme. Even with the limitations, however, the results are worth noting.

One study of 108 communities that considered anti-immigration ordinances between 2000 and 2006 concluded that such policies at the local level are most likely to be enacted when "communities are undergoing sudden demographic changes at the same time that salient national rhetoric politicizes immigration," and it explained this phenomenon in terms of perceived racial threats to longtime residents.[16] But while such findings provide an intuitively appealing explanation, the study that generated them was limited by its focus solely on communities that had formal proposals for anti-immigrant policies. Other communities that were not included in the analysis had experienced similar sudden demographic changes during times of polarized national debate but reacted differently, either by considering pro-immigrant policies and/or adopting pro-immigrant policies, or by not considering any immigrant-specific policies at all.

A more comprehensive analysis of local ordinances reached different conclusions. In this case, the sample included 25,108 communities, of which 72 considered pro-immigrant ordinances, 92 considered anti-immigrant ordinances, and 24,944 did not consider any immigrant ordinances.[17] The analysis found that more important than the recent influx of immigrants was the partisan balance in the county. Specifically, while the growth in the Hispanic population had only a weak effect on the passage of anti-immigrant ordinances, counties with Republican majorities were more likely to both propose and enact restrictive immigration policies. Interestingly, communities with a higher percentage of recently arrived immigrants were found to be more likely to propose and adopt pro-immigrant ordinances.

As an alternative to regression analysis, variation in local immigration policies can be considered from a more qualitative perspective in terms of the underlying values and priorities reflected in the policy discourse and decisions. Specifically, local policies can be characterized in terms of the attitudes they reflect about the role that immigrants play in the community; competing theories of assimilation; and the relative authority of national, state, and local governments to govern immigrant experiences at the community level.[18] Specifically, one can assess whether immi-

grants are considered to be a threat to the community, a burden on public resources, a population in need of protection, or useful and contributing members of the community. Records of debates can also provide evidence of what citizens and policy makers think about assimilation. Do they consider it to be impractical or undesirable, likely to occur only if forced upon immigrants through "tough love" policies, or something that will occur naturally with the passage of time? Or do they consider mutual adaptation to be a more appropriate concept than immigrant assimilation. Similarly, local discourse reveals the extent to which local decisions are guided by either deference to or a willingness to challenge state and federal policies. Collectively, these three dimensions—how immigrants are perceived, what citizens and policy makers think about assimilation, and whether local policies are more likely to defer to or challenge policies at higher levels—provide a sense of how local leaders view their role in either defending an existing notion of community or helping the community expand its sense of self in response to change and diversity.

Summary

Rates of overall immigration, increasing diversity of language and national origin, and more disperse settlement patterns, coupled with repeated failed attempts at national immigration reform, have created a context in which a growing number of local governments have enacted policies directed at the immigrant populations in their communities. The policies are many and quite varied. Arrayed along a continuum, it is clear that relatively few localities have adopted measures at the extremes, but many have taken steps that nonetheless have an impact on both new and long-term residents.

In many ways the range of policies identified in the studies referenced above reflect the tradeoffs associated with any debate that positions individual rights in competition with collective security, or that challenges local leaders to articulate and advance a particular model of community. Anti-immigrant policies stem from a concern about protecting the safety of long-standing residents; they focus on illegal or undocumented immigrants; and they are willing to accept as collateral damage any negative consequences for legal immigrants. In contrast, pro-immigrant policies tend to focus on the value of individual human rights, diversity, and mutual adaptation; they stress the rights of individuals regardless of legal status; and they are willing to accept that some of those rights extend to undocumented persons as well. Just as Thomas "Tip" O'Neill, longtime Speaker of the U.S. House of Representatives, observed that "all politics is local," one writer has noted that "all immigration politics is local."[19]

Future research on local government responses to immigration should be directed toward the policies that fall in the middle of the continuum. While not as glamorous as the policies at the extremes, the multitude of policies that can be characterized as either neutral/laissez-faire or community cohesion are much more prevalent and thus deserving of greater attention. Having a better understanding of these policies and programs is important, not only because these are the policies and programs that will be of use to a larger number of local government administrators but also because they ultimately affect a larger proportion of both the immigrant population and the citizens of the United States.

Notes

1. Arizona Senate Bill 1070, Section 1 "Intent" (2010).

2. Michael LeMay and Elliott R. Barkan, eds., *U.S. Immigration and Naturalization Laws and Issues: A Documentary History* (Westport, Conn.: Greenwood Press, 1999).

3. Stanley Lieberson, *Ethnic Patterns in American Cities* (New York: The Free Press of Glencoe, 1963), 1.

4. U.S. Census Bureau, *American Community Survey—* 2009, census.gov.

5. Jeffrey S. Passel and D'Vera Cohn, *U.S. Unauthorized Immigration Flows Are Down Sharply since Mid-Decade* (Washington, D.C.: Pew Hispanic Center Report, September 1, 2010), pewhispanic.org/files/reports/126 .pdf (accessed December 21, 2010).

6. Michael Fix and Jeffrey S. Passel, *Immigration and Immigrants: Setting the Record Straight* (Washington, D.C.: Urban Institute, 1994).

7. Alejandro Portes, "English-Only Triumphs, but the Costs Are High," in *Critical Social Issues in American Education: Democracy and Meaning in a Globalizing World*, 3rd ed., ed. H. Svi Shapiro and David E. Purpel (Mahwah, N.J.: Lawrence Erlbaum Assoc., 2005), 209.

8. Audrey Singer, *The Rise of New Immigrant Gateways* (Washington, D.C.: Brookings Institution, 2004).

9. Data from the 2008 survey are available on the ICMA website under "Aggregate Survey Results: ICMA Snapshot of Immigration, 2008," at icma.org/en/results/ surveying/survey_research/survey_results.

10. A similar continuum was presented by Abraham David Benavides at the 2010 ICMA Annual Conference. Referring back to a presentation he gave at the Midwest Political Science Association's 67th Annual National Conference in April 2009 (see note 11), he labeled the extremes of the continuum as enforcement cities and sanctuary cities, and the middle ground as neutral cities.

11. Abraham Benavides, "Sanctuary Cities, Neutral Cities, Enforcement Cities, and Immigration: The Conundrum for Local Municipalities" (presentation delivered at the Midwest Political Science Association's 67th Annual National Conference, Chicago, Ill., April 2, 2009).

12. U.S. Department of Homeland Security, Immigration and Customs Enforcement, "Fact Sheet: Delegation of Immigration Authority Section 287(g) Immigration and Nationality Act," ice.gov.

13. Benavides, "Sanctuary Cities, Neutral Cities."

14. Abel Valenzuela Jr. et al, *On the Corner: Day Labor in the United States* (Los Angeles: Center for the Study of Urban Poverty, UCLA, 2006), sscnet.ucla.edu/issr/csup/ uploaded_files/Natl_DayLabor-On_the_Corner1.pdf (accessed December 21, 2010).

15. "Who Is Boycotting Arizona?" *Arizona Central*, August 27, 2010, azcentral.com/business/articles/2010/05/13/ 20100513immigration-boycotts-list.html (accessed December 21, 2010).

16. Daniel J. Hopkins, "Politicized Places: Explaining Where and When Immigrants Provoke Local Opposition," *American Political Science Review* 104, no. 1 (2010): 40, journals.cambridge.org/action/displayFulltext?type = 1& fid = 7449420&jid = PSR&volumeId = 104&issueId = 01&a id = 7449412 (accessed December 21, 2010).

17. S. Karthick Ramakrishnan and Tom (Tak) Wong, "Partisanship, Not Spanish: Explaining Municipal Ordinances Affecting Undocumented Immigrants," in *Taking Local Control: Immigration Policy Activism in U.S. Cities and States*, ed. Monica W. Varsanyi (Stanford, Calif.: Stanford University Press, 2010). It should be noted here that the data in the original Table 4.1 of this source are incorrect; however, corrected data are available on the author's website at karthick.com/ publications.html (accessed December 28, 2010).

18. Nadia Rubaii-Barrett, "The Micro-Politics of Immigration: Local Government Policies of Inclusion and Exclusion," in *The Politics of Inclusion and Exclusion: Identity Politics in Twenty-First Century America*, ed. David Ericson (New York: Routledge, 2010).

19. Michael S. Danielson, "All Immigration Politics is Local: The Day Labor Ordinance in Vista, California," in *Taking Local Control*, 239–254 (see note 17).

4

Economic Development Strategies for Recessionary Times: Survey Results from 2009

Mildred E. Warner
Cornell University

Lingwen Zheng
Cornell University

Through its economic development surveys, ICMA has been tracking the use of economic development strategies among local municipalities every five years. Business attraction strategies—namely, firm-specific incentives and subsidies—have been the most common strategies reported. However, over the decade of 1994–2004, local governments took a more comprehensive approach, complementing these strategies with strategies to promote business retention and expansion as well as small-business and community development.[1] To these they added increased attention to the importance of accountability measures and the use of written business attraction plans.[2] Local governments have become savvier in their economic development practice.

ICMA's *Economic Development Survey 2009* occurred at a time of great economic uncertainty. Financial markets began crashing in 2008, and by the next year, the "Great Recession" was already leading to business closures and rising unemployment across the United States. As the survey findings reveal, local governments responded by increasing their use of business incentives in an effort to attract business. However, they also maintained support for more comprehensive approaches—business retention and expansion, small-business development, community development, and investments in quality of life.

SELECTED FINDINGS

In response to the recession, local governments' use of business incentives rose from 72% of respondents in 2004 to 95% in 2009.

The majority of respondents (73%) give top priority to programs supporting quality of life (education, recreation, arts and culture), high-quality physical infrastructure (59%), and affordable housing (48%).

Sixty percent of respondents reported using clawback agreements, which require firms to pay back incentives if they do not deliver the promised employment benefits.

At the same time, accountability measures, which had been on the rise, fell slightly.

The challenge in these difficult times is to balance efforts to attract new business with investments in existing local businesses, infrastructure, and quality of life, all the while maintaining accountability. With citizens scrutinizing public expenditures, local governments that apply performance measures to their economic development activities will find greater citizen support.

The *ICMA Economic Development Survey 2009* was made possible in part with funding from the W. K. Kellogg Foundation. The Peppercorn Foundation provided support for analysis. The survey was conducted in collaboration with the National League of Cities.

Survey Methodology and Response Rate

The *ICMA Economic Development Survey 2009* was sent to chief administrative officers of all municipalities/counties with a population of 10,000 or more in October 2009. Of the 3,283 cities and 556 counties surveyed, 734 cities and 110 counties responded for a response rate of 22% (Table 4-1). Respondents were relatively evenly distributed across all population groups except for the largest and smallest municipali-

Table 4-1 Survey Respondents, 2009

Classification	No. of municipalities/counties[1] surveyed (A)	Respondents No.	Respondents % of (A)
Total	3,839	844	22
City[1]	3,283	734	22
County[1]	556	110	20
Population group			
Over 1,000,000	34	6	18
500,000-1,000,000	73	14	19
250,000-499,999	116	32	28
100,000-249,999	370	89	24
50,000-99,999	629	157	25
25,000-49,999	784	185	24
10,000-24,999	1,833	361	20
Geographic region			
Northeast	971	112	12
North-Central	1,062	273	26
South	1,081	265	25
West	725	194	27
Geographic division			
New England	361	46	13
Mid-Atlantic	610	66	11
East North-Central	781	187	24
West North-Central	282	86	31
South Atlantic	565	171	30
East South-Central	195	23	12
West South-Central	320	71	22
Mountain	194	58	30
Pacific Coast	531	136	26
Metro status			
Central	849	203	24
Suburban	2,225	500	23
Independent	765	141	18

1 For a definition of terms, please see "Inside the *Year Book*," xi.

ties, which had lower response rates (20% or less). The response rates among central and suburban municipalities were similar (24% and 23%, respectively), but the independent (rural) municipalities had a lower response rate (18%). Across geographic regions, the West North-Central, Mountain, South Atlantic, and Pacific Coast had the highest response rates (over 25%), while the Mid-Atlantic, New England, and East South-Central had the lowest (11%–13%).

The Economic Base and Tax Revenue

Each year it is conducted, the survey asks local officials what best describes the condition of the local government's economic base over the previous five years and what they anticipate it to look like in the next five years. The results from the 2009 survey are telling. Whereas 43% of respondents described rapid or moderate economic growth over the previous five years, only 23% foresaw rapid or moderate growth in the coming five years (Figure 4-1). The majority, 53%, saw a future of slow growth. Interestingly, however, whereas 14% reported a declining economic base over the preceding five years, only 9% predicted a future of slow, moderate, or rapid decline despite the prevailing recession. Local government leaders are optimistic: they must be, as their tax bases depend upon economic growth.

When asked to identify their local government's primary economic base and the primary focus of its economic development activities, respondents listed retail/services first on both counts (44% and 42%, respectively) (Figure 4-2). Manufacturing, which is still recognized as a leading source of well-paying jobs and a major component of the property tax base, is next, identified as the primary economic base for 29% of respondents but as the primary focus of economic development activity for 34%. Telecommunications is also seen as an important economic development driver: although only 10% listed it as their primary economic base, 27% identified it as the primary focus of their economic development activities.

Given that over half the sample is suburban, it is not surprising to find that 26% of respondents described their primary economic base as residential. However, only 7% reported the residential sector to be a primary focus for their economic development efforts. This may be a reflection of the mortgage foreclosure crisis. In a similar vein, although 18% of respondents identified institutions (military, government, universities) as their primary base, only 9% named this sector as a primary focus of their economic activities. Although these institutions provide stable employment, their nonprofit and tax-exempt nature limits their benefit to the local prop-

Figure 4-1 Past and Projected Condition of Local Economic Development Base, 2009

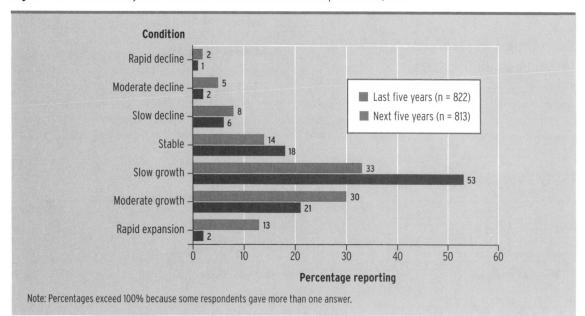

Figure 4-2 Primary Economic Development Base and Focus of Economic Development Efforts, 2009

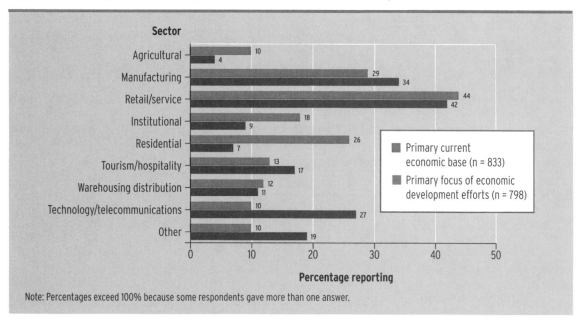

erty tax base. Indeed, on average, respondents reported that 17% of their land is tax-exempt (not shown).

Economic development strategy is closely tied to concerns over the local tax base. On average, local governments fund 88% of the economic development budget (not shown), and the goal is to increase the number of local jobs and the tax base. Income and sales taxes are important, but they are procyclical, rising and falling with the business cycle; just over half of the respondents

(52%) collect a local sales tax, and only 11% levy a local income tax (not shown). It is the property tax that provides the local government's primary source of revenue (reported by 91%, not shown), and it is normally a stable revenue source. However, the recession that began in late 2007 was caused by a housing bubble, and readjustments in housing prices will cause declines in assessed value, which will lead to declines in the property tax base unless there is economic growth.[3] This is why the fiscal crisis for local governments is deepening even as Wall Street is bouncing back.

Economic Development Strategies for Recessionary Times

Responding to both an economic recession and a public sector fiscal crisis requires balanced economic development strategies. Local governments employ a comprehensive array of such strategies to achieve this—strategies focused on business attraction, business retention and expansion, and small-business and community development.

Business Attraction

Business attraction strategies are usually firm specific and primarily characterized by financial incentives and subsidies. During the decade of 1994 to 2004, there was a gradual shift away from business incentives;[4] however, the 2009 survey data indicate a

Table 4-2 Economic Development Strategies: Business Incentives and Attraction

	2004		2009	
Strategy	No. using strategy	%	No. using strategy	%
Business incentives				
Total reporting	(N = 562)		(N = 792)	
Total offering business incentives	407	72	753	95
Incentives offered (total reporting)	(n = 396)		(n = 760)[1]	
Tax abatements	226	57	359	47
Tax credits	94	24	164	22
Tax increment financing	231	58	414	55
Locally designated enterprise zones	96	24	199	26
Federal-state-designated enterprise zones	131	33	202	27
Special assessment districts	94	24	202	27
Free land or land write-downs	122	31	215	28
Infrastructure improvements	265	67	434	57
Subsidized buildings	36	9	68	9
Low-cost loans	133	34	205	27
Grants	151	38	270	36
Zoning/permit assistance	271	68	521	69
One-stop permit issuance	164	41	311	41
Utility rate reduction	50	13	62	8
Regulatory flexibility	49	12	109	14
Relocation assistance	69	17	108	14
Employee screening	59	15	85	11
Training support	116	29	192	25
Other	49	12	60	8
Business attraction				
Total reporting	(N = 576)		(N = 805)	
Total seeking to attract new business	566	98	792	98
Strategies used (total reporting)	(n = 537)		(n = 662)	
Participation in industry-specific trade shows/conferences	284	53	418	63
Promotional and advertising activities (e.g., direct mail, CD-ROM, video, other media advertising)	336	63	426	64
Local government representative calls on prospective companies	306	57	449	68
Other	75	14	147	22

Source: Data from the 2004 survey are available on the ICMA website under "Aggregate Survey Results: Economic Development, 2004," at icma.org/en/results/surveying/survey_research/survey_results.

1 Because the request for respondents to indicate which incentives their local government offers was posed separately rather than limited to those respondents who had reported in a prior question that their local government offers incentives, the base for this question includes seven respondents who had responded negatively to the prior question.

significant rebound in their use. In 2004, 72% of local governments used business incentives,[5] but in 2009, 95% reported using them (Table 4–2). The survey data suggest that, confronted with the most severe economic recession since the Great Depression, local governments have reverted back to business incentives in an effort to attract firms for both the tax base and jobs.

However, tax abatements are not the primary business incentive strategy: use of tax abatements dropped from 57% of the sample in 2004 to 47% in 2009. Instead, the primary focus is on zoning and permit assistance (69%) to facilitate the development process. Infrastructure improvements remain the second most important business incentive strategy (57%), but their usage dropped 10 percentage points from 2004—possibly owing to fiscal stress. The American Recovery and Reinvestment Act (the stimulus bill) was not passed until February 2009, so investments in infrastructure as a result of this bill may not have occurred in time to be reflected in this survey. The less expensive business attraction strategies, such as calls on companies, promotional and advertising activities, and participation in trade shows, all rose slightly in the 2009 survey.

Business Retention

Since the late 1980s local governments have recognized that local economic development and job creation largely depend on the success of local businesses.[6] Business retention programs focus on retaining businesses that are already in the community.[7] Partnering appears to be the most common strategy: local governments are most likely to partner with the chamber of commerce and other nongovernmental organizations in these efforts (84%) as well as with other local governments (56%) (Table 4–3). Surveying local businesses is the second most common strategy (62%), followed by business roundtables (42%). Recognition of the need to promote business clusters and industrial districts has risen to 33% of respondents in 2009 as compared to 26% in 2004. Planning has increased as well. In 2009, 27% of respondents reported having a written plan as compared to 24% in 2004. Use of revolving loan funds is down slightly (from 31% to 24%), but this may be a result of the general shortage of capital available during the financial crisis (see discussion of barriers below).

Small-Business and Community Economic Development

Small businesses, a source of innovation in our economy, are very independent. However, they are also fragile, and three out of five fail within the first five years,[8] which makes it difficult for local governments to reach out to this group. In general, support for small businesses is lower than the level of attention given to business retention: only 16% of local governments have written small-business development plans (Table 4–4)

Table 4-3 Economic Development Strategies: Business Retention

Strategy	2004		2009	
	No. using strategy	%	No. using strategy	%
Total reporting	(N = 549)		(N = 778)	
Have business retention plan	129	24	209	27
Strategies used (total reporting)	(n = 523)		(n = 709)	
Surveys of local business	313	60	435	62
Business roundtable	247	47	299	42
Revolving loan fund program	161	31	170	24
Ombudsman program	114	22	195	28
Local business publicity program (community-wide)	175	34	216	31
Replacing imports with locally supplied goods	15	3	42	6
Export development assistance	62	12	71	10
Partnering with chamber, others	421	81	594	84
Partnering with other local governments	272	52	394	56
Business clusters/industrial districts	138	26	235	33
Other	50	10	62	9

Source: Data from the 2004 survey are available on the ICMA website under "Aggregate Survey Results: Economic Development, 2004," at icma.org/en/results/surveying/survey_research/survey_results.

Table 4-4 Economic Development Strategies: Small Business

Strategy	2004		2009	
	No. using strategy	%	No. using strategy	%
Total reporting	(N = 531)		(N = 782)	
Have small-business development plan	90	17	121	16
Strategies used (total reporting)	(n = 346)		(n = 505)	
Revolving loan fund	167	48	203	40
Small-business development center	190	55	214	42
Business incubator	100	29	132	26
Microenterprise program	63	18	67	13
Matching improvement grants–physical upgrades to business	98	28	179	35
Vendor/supplier matching	29	8	52	10
Marketing assistance	117	34	187	37
Management training	72	21	85	17
Executive on loan/mentor	35	10	57	11
Other incentives	77	22	101	20

Source: Data from the 2004 survey are available on the ICMA website under "Aggregate Survey Results: Economic Development, 2004," at icma.org/en/results/surveying/survey_research/survey_results.

compared with 27% that have business retention plans. But small-business development is important—especially in low-income neighborhoods, in rural communities, and among immigrants. Small firms are also important to maintain viable Main Streets. Thus, actual support for small-business programs is higher than the percentage of local governments with small-business development plans would suggest.

The most common activity among local governments in support of small businesses is funding a small-business development center (42%), followed closely by offering revolving loan funds (40%) (Table 4-4). But both of these are down from percentages reported in 2004. Marketing assistance, reported by 37% of respondents, and business incubators, found among 26% of respondents, may also help small firms survive. And local governments can provide matching improvement grants for physical upgrades that enhance the appeal of downtown streets to consumers and residents. This form of public-private partnership, which can help beautify downtown streets and increase small business viability, increased from 28% in 2004 to 35% of respondents in 2009.

Along those same lines, local governments are giving attention to a broader array of community development activities to enhance economic welfare. Richard Florida's *The Rise of the Creative Class* (2002) has drawn attention to the role that amenities play in attracting and retaining a high-quality workforce.[9] Communities now compete to be the "best place to live." But more recent research shows that it

is investment in the fundamentals—schools, physical infrastructure, and social services—that makes communities more economically vibrant over the long term and supports their well-being.[10]

The majority of respondents (73%) in 2009 reported that their local governments give top priority to programs supporting quality of life (defined as social services: good education, recreation, and culture and arts programs) (Figure 4–3). Next in importance are high-quality physical infrastructure (59%) and affordable housing (48%). Many communities' zoning rules limit the production of affordable multifamily housing, but the 2009 survey shows that, from an economic development perspective, affordable housing is a critical component of local economic development strategy. Local government support is also strong for efficient transportation systems, including transit (43%), and for environmental sustainability (38%).

More traditional community development approaches, such as job training, community development corporations and loan funds, are still important but are no longer the key focal points for public investment. Child care is a target of community development investment among only 10% of local governments, but 14% (not shown) use economic development tools (grants, loans, business assistance) to support child care. Given the lack of affordable, quality child care in most communities, child care providers, who are themselves small businesses, would benefit from economic development attention.[11]

Figure 4-3   Local Government Support of Community Development Activities, 2009

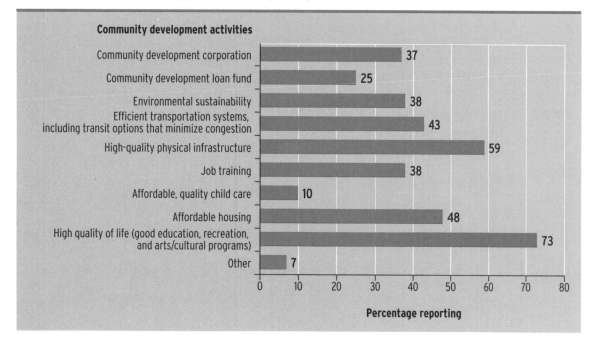

Barriers, Participation, and Competition

Cost and availability of land continue to be identified as the top barriers facing economic development (Table 4–5). However, with the ongoing economic crisis, the 2009 survey finds that lack of capital has replaced the lack of building availability as the third most common barrier, reported by 50% of respondents compared to only 36% in 2004. The economic crisis has actually eased some of the other barriers: for example, the constraint on building availability, cited by 45% of respondents in 2004, dropped to 37% in 2009. Similarly, only 15% of respondents reported the high cost of housing as a barrier—down from 20% in 2004. As the foreclosure crisis deepens, however, affordable rental housing may become more of a concern for cities. Meanwhile, respondents who perceived the high cost of labor as an economic development barrier also decreased slightly from 11% in 2004 to 8% in 2009. Traffic congestion fell by about eight percentage points from 2004, but this could be a result of both the recession and the increased community development attention to transportation issues noted above.

Although quality of life was given high priority under community development investments, only 6% of local governments reported poor quality of life as a barrier to economic development. This may be because higher attention has been given to quality-of-life issues over the last few years. Quality of life has

many components, and one special focus in the 2009 survey was access to affordable, quality child care. Only 6% of responding governments saw inadequate child care supply as an economic development barrier, and yet studies around the country have shown that most communities lack an adequate supply. Indeed, in surveys of economic developers in New York and Wisconsin, this lack was cited as a barrier by the majority of respondents.[12] This suggests that a broader array of participants may be needed in the economic development process to ensure that the full range of economic development concerns is addressed.

ICMA's economic development survey tracks which local constituencies participate in the economic development process. In 2009, almost 90% of local governments surveyed reported that their city governments participate in this process (not shown); more than 65% indicated the involvement of chambers of commerce; and over half reported that county governments are involved in developing their local strategies (53%). Other commonly identified participants include economic development corporations (44%), private business/industry (40%), regional organizations (38%), citizen advisory board/commission (36%), public-private partnership (36%), and state government (34%).

Interlocal competition has been a concern in economic development policy as local governments may bid against their neighbors to attract firms, which leads to a "race to the bottom." Efforts to promote more regional collaboration to avoid destructive local competition were noted over the 1994–2004 decade.[13] As shown in Table 4-6, the 2009 survey reflects a slight increase in interlocal competition among close neighbors (nearby local governments and those within the same state), and a slight decrease in competition with governments in surrounding states, other states, and foreign countries. Given the ongoing economic crisis, the fact that proximate competition slightly increased while competition from distant sources became less important shows that local governments are competing with other local governments to promote economic development.

Table 4-5   Economic Development Barriers, 2004 and 2009

	2004		2009	
Strategy	No. reporting (A)	% of (A)	No. reporting (B)	% of (B)
Total reporting	564	100	796	100
Availability of land	324	57	417	52
Cost of land	298	53	425	53
Lack of building availability (due to space or costs)	253	45	297	37
Inadequate infrastructure (e.g., no fiber-optic cable, water and wastewater)	156	28	226	28
Lack of skilled labor	97	17	140	18
High cost of labor	62	11	67	8
Lack of affordable, quality child care	–	–	47	6
Limited number of major employers	180	32	271	34
Lack of capital/funding	201	36	399	50
Taxes	101	18	161	20
Distance from major markets	87	15	129	16
Lengthy permit process	72	13	99	12
Environmental regulations	124	22	181	23
Citizen opposition	123	22	183	23
Lack of political support	57	10	86	11
Declining market due to loss of population	28	5	72	9
High cost of housing	115	20	119	15
Poor quality of life (inadequate education, recreation, and arts/cultural programs)	29	5	50	6
Traffic congestion	132	23	119	15
Other	106	19	94	12

Source: Data from the 2004 survey are available on the ICMA website under "Aggregate Survey Results: Economic Development, 2004," at icma.org/en/results/surveying/survey_research/survey_results.

Table 4-6   Economic Development Competition, 2004 and 2009

	2004		2009	
Type of competition	No. reporting (A)	% of (A)	No. reporting (B)	% of (B)
Total reporting	540	100	781	100
Competition in attracting investment				
Nearby local governments	414	77	606	78
Other local governments within the state	364	67	535	69
Local governments in surrounding states	300	56	396	51
Other states	298	55	416	53
Foreign countries	152	28	176	23
Other	14	3	7	1

Source: Data from the 2004 survey are available on the ICMA website under "Aggregate Survey Results: Economic Development, 2004," at icma.org/en/results/surveying/survey_research/survey_results.

The Importance of Accountability

Local governments recognize the importance of accountability in economic development policy. The vast majority, 85%, have instituted performance agreements as a condition for providing business incentives (Table 4–7), and over 70% conduct cost/benefit analyses prior to offering business incentives. From 2004 to 2009 we see a small rise in the percentage of governments that do not use performance agreements (11% to 15%) or cost/benefit analyses (25% to 28%). These may be governments that are using incentives for the first time. Experienced governments have learned that the use of incentives without performance measures in place limits effectiveness and can lead to more citizen opposition. Given the

potential for abuse in business incentives, it is important that these governments employ accountability measures. Setting clear expectations up front is important, but so too is measuring the effectiveness of the business incentives after investment. In 2009, 92% of respondents reported that they measure the number of jobs created, and 62% reported measuring the amount of money invested in construction materials and labor. The 2009 survey also included a new question regarding clawback agreements, in which firms are required to pay back all or part of the local government subsidy if they do not deliver the promised employment benefits, and 60% of respondents reported using such agreements. This shows that local governments are concerned that the community receives a return on public investment.

Table 4–7 Accountability Measures, 2004 and 2009

Accountability measures	2004, %	2009, %
Performance agreement as a condition for providing business incentives	(n = 390)	(n = 717)
Always	61	56
Sometimes	28	29
Never	11	15
Cost/benefit analysis prior to offering business incentives	(n = 387)	(n = 713)
No	25	28
Yes	75	72
Measure of the effectiveness of business incentives	(n = 390)	(n = 721)
No	16	29
Yes	84	71
If yes	(n = 326)[1]	(n = 501)[1]
Amount of jobs created by the new business	90	92
Amount of money invested in construction materials and labor	63	62
New dollars invested in land	48	43
Company revenue/sales	32	32
Cost/benefit analysis	45	52
Number of new business relocating or expanding in jurisdiction	47	41
Other	11	9
Use performance measures to assess the effectiveness of its economic development efforts	(n = 533)	(n = 701)
No	67	52
Yes	33	48
If yes	(n = 173)[1]	(n = 327)[1]
Input measures	31	28
Output measures	69	53
Efficiency measures	47	41
Clawback agreement	–	60
Other	20	9

Source: Data from the 2004 survey are available on the ICMA website under "Aggregate Survey Results: Economic Development, 2004," at icma.org/en/results/surveying/survey_research/survey_results.

1 Percentages exceed 100% because respondents were able to check off multiple answers.

Conclusion

The *ICMA Economic Development Survey 2009* was conducted at a difficult time for most local governments. The financial crisis and meltdown on Wall Street was felt in communities all across America. The well-being of both local economies and local government budgets is intricately tied to the economy. Frozen real estate markets, rising foreclosure rates, and rising unemployment translate into reduced revenue for local governments at a time when citizen demand for services is increasing. Local officials want to use economic development policies to boost the local economy, but tax incentives do not build the tax base in the short term and may not lead to sustained employment gains in the long term.[14] Governments that pursue a balanced strategy that addresses the needs of local firms (retention), small businesses, and local residents (quality of life) may have the best chance of weathering the economic storm. High-quality public services ensure a high quality of life and a favorable climate for economic growth. A comprehensive economic development strategy appears to be the best approach for improving a community's economic well-being.

Notes

1. Lingwen Zheng and Mildred E. Warner, "Local Economic Development, 1994–2004: Broadening Strategies, Increasing Accountability," in *The Municipal Year Book 2010* (Washington, D.C.: ICMA, 2010), 3–9.

2. Lingwen Zheng and Mildred E. Warner, "Business Incentive Use among US Local Governments: A Story of Accountability and Policy Learning," *Economic Development Quarterly* 24, no. 4 (2010): 325–336.

3. Christopher Hoene and Michael Pagano, *City Fiscal Conditions in 2010* (Washington, D.C.: National League of Cities, 2010), nlc.org/ASSETS/AE26793318A645C795C9CD11DAB3B39B/RB_CityFiscalConditions2010.pdf.

4. Zheng and Warner, "Local Economic Development, 1994–2004," 5.

5. Thomas S. Lyons and Steven G. Koven, "Economic Development and Public Policy at the Local Government Level," in *The Municipal Year Book 2006* (Washington, D.C.: ICMA, 2006), 14–15. Complete data from the 2004 survey are available on the ICMA website under "Aggregate Survey Results: Economic Development, 2004," at icma.org/en/results/surveying/survey_research/survey_results.

6. David L. Birch, *Job Creation in America: How Our Smallest Companies Put the Most People to Work* (New York: The Free Press, 1987).

7. Raymond C. Lenzi, "Business Retention and Expansion Programs: A Panoramic View," *Economic Development Review* 9 (1991): 7–12, springerlink.com/content/k6212266130rknp7/ (accessed November 30, 2010).

8. Bruce D. Phillips and Bruce A. Kirchhoff, "Formation, Growth and Survival; Small Firm Dynamics in the U.S. Economy," *Small Business Economics* 1, no. 1 (1989): 65–74.

9. Richard L. Florida, *The Rise of the Creative Class: And How It's Transforming Work, Leisure, Community and Everyday Life* (New York: Basic Books, 2002).

10. Laura Reese, "Creative Class or Procreative Class: Achieving Sustainable Cities" (paper presented at International Making Cities Livable Conference, Charleston, South Carolina, October 17–21, 2010).

11. Mildred E. Warner, "Putting Child Care in the Regional Economy: Empirical and Conceptual Challenges and Economic Development Prospects," *Community Development: Journal of the Community Development Society* 37, no. 2 (2006): 7–22, economicdevelopmentandchildcare.org/documents/special_journal_issues/jcds/warner.pdf (accessed November 30, 2010).

12. Mildred E. Warner, "Child Care and Economic Development: Markets, Households and Public Policy," *International Journal of Economic Development* 9, no. 3 (2007): 111–121, economicdevelopmentandchildcare.org/documents/special_journal_issues/ijed/warner.pdf (accessed November 31, 2010).

13. Zheng and Warner, "Business Incentive Use among US Local Governments."

14. Greg LeRoy, *The Great American Jobs Scam: Corporate Tax Dodging and the Myth of Job Creation* (San Francisco: Berrett-Koehler, 2005).

5

The Early Stage of Local Government Action to Promote Sustainability

James H. Svara
School of Public Affairs, Arizona State University

Sustainability has emerged as a major public policy issue facing countries throughout the world. As ICMA asserted in a 2007 report, sustainability is "'the issue of our age.'"[1] It is a comprehensive concept that captures many of the major problems facing society today, problems that have arisen from practices that will eventually deplete resources, lower quality of life, and fragment societies if they are not modified. The concept also indicates that the path toward addressing these problems requires attention to long-term interests. The most commonly used "official" definition of sustainability comes from the 1987 United Nations' landmark report *Our Common Future*, where the term is defined broadly as "meet[ing] the needs of the present without compromising the ability of future generations to meet their own needs."[2] Classic definitions of sustainability have focused on the three "e's": environment, economy, and social equity. This view of sustainability is based on the goal of promoting economic change within communities that enhances environmental quality and benefits all segments of society.

Sustainability requires a broad range of actions in which all levels of government, all sectors of the economy, and all citizens must participate. City and county governments are uniquely positioned to make

SELECTED FINDINGS

Survey responses reflect two opposing tendencies: most local governments are becoming active in sustainability, but most are also involved at a relatively low level, and few of the possible sustainability actions are in wide use.

Western local governments have the highest average adoption ratings in 10 of the 12 activity areas—most notably, in measures related to water, vehicles and lighting, transportation alternatives, and transportation improvements. Almost half of the local governments in the top 10% of sustainability activity, however, are outside the West.

At least 50% of local governments of all population sizes provide residential recycling pickup, recycle internally, and have bike and walking trails, and all but the smallest local governments also recycle household hazardous waste and electronic equipment; improve the efficiency of government buildings; purchase fuel-efficient vehicles; support a farmers' market; and require sidewalks in new developments.

I would like to thank Tanya Watt, doctoral student in public administration at Arizona State University, for her data analysis and literature review, and Abigail Wischnia, undergraduate research assistant in the College of Public Programs, for her assistance in preparing the data set for this chapter.

a significant contribution to this effort for several reasons: they are directly involved in providing or regulating many of the human activities that affect resource use, such as transportation, building construction, and land use; they are actively involved in efforts to promote economic development; and they provide services that help to determine whether persons from all economic levels and all racial and ethnic groups are protected and included. ICMA's *Local Government Sustainability Policies and Programs, 2010* survey was a major effort undertaken to examine what local elected officials and administrators have done so far to address the sustainability challenge, and how they work with citizens as partners to advance shared goals and change behaviors to advance sustainability.[3]

Actions to Promote to Sustainability

The sustainability movement began with an effort to reconcile economic growth and environmental protection.[4] From this initial emphasis on sustainable development, the range of issues has broadened considerably. Many of the challenges addressed by this movement—for example, air and water quality, resource conservation, reduced energy consumption, balanced economic development, individual and family well-being, and smart growth—have been the target of numerous policies and programs for decades. Today, however, the movement differs in two ways from earlier efforts. First, the wide range of sustainability issues is approached from a unified perspective in hopes of finding integrated solutions. Second, sustainability now entails a comprehensive strategy that adds a large number of new program initiatives to long-standing policies.

The ICMA survey reported on in this article examines the priorities that local governments have established for a number of sustainability issues, the measures they have taken to plan and organize the sustainability effort, and the wide range of actions they have taken to promote sustainability. Specific indicators—policies, programs, and activities that local governments can take to advance sustainability—were drawn from a number of sources,[5] and a comprehensive set of 160 indicators was developed by the Alliance for Innovation and field tested by local governments in the Sustainability Cities Network of the Global Institute on Sustainability at Arizona State University. From that set, 109 indicators were included in the ICMA survey, chosen intentionally to cover commonly used techniques as well as rarely used practices. As a consequence, the number of actions taken by the responding governments is likely to vary widely.

The challenge in this summary of the survey results is to highlight general patterns while also providing insights about the use of component strategies and specific practices. The approach taken is to rely on an overall measure of a local government's activity level—a total sustainability action rating—based on the level of activity in 12 major areas. The specific activities reported are then divided into five tiers, from the most commonly used to the least commonly used. This approach points to an overall interpretation of the survey results in terms of the diffusion of innovation.

Survey Methodology and Measurement of Sustainability Actions

The *Local Government Sustainability Policies and Programs, 2010* survey was mailed in the summer of 2010 to all city-type governments with a population of 2,500 and above and to all counties with an appointed administrator/manager or elected executive. Local governments that did not respond to the first survey received a follow-up reminder. Overall, 25% of local governments responded (see Table 5–1).[6]

The 109 specific sustainability activities that were included in the survey were divided into the 12 major areas. For each, the average percentage of governments using specific activities within that area was calculated (see the appendix table at the end of this article).

The major areas are presented in Table 5–2 along with two measures of use. For example, 9 out of 10 responding governments are doing some recycling, but only a third of all recycling activities listed in the survey are being used across all local governments. The major area used least is alternative electrical energy generation, reported in any form by less than one-quarter of respondents. On average, only 7% of alternative energy options are being used. The overall adoption rating, which is based on the average level of adoption across the 12 activity areas, is 18%.[7]

To simplify the presentation of results, the overall adoption rating is the indicator used most commonly in this presentation to capture both the amount of activity and the spread of activity across the major areas.[8] As indicated in Figure 5–1 (see page 46), most governments are found toward the low end on the 100-point rating scale, and substantially more than half (60%) (not shown) have a rate of adoption that is below the average for all the responding governments. On the other hand, some governments are undertaking a large number and wide range of sustainability activities.

Generally, cities and counties engage in sustainability actions at approximately the same rate, and as

Table 5-1   Survey Response

Classification	No. of municipalities[1] surveyed (A)	Respondents No.	% of (A)
Total	8,569	2,176	25
Population group			
Over 1,000,000	34	13	38
500,000-1,000,000	73	21	29
250,000-499,999	116	32	28
100,000-249,999	370	120	32
50,000-99,999	629	196	31
25,000-49,999	1,060	272	26
10,000-24,999	2,156	556	26
5,000-9,999	2,011	480	24
2,500-4,999	2,095	483	23
Under 2,500	25	3	12
Geographic region			
Northeast	2,082	382	18
North-Central	2,491	716	29
South	2,696	625	23
West	1,300	453	35
Geographic division			
New England	750	160	21
Mid-Atlantic	1,332	222	17
East North-Central	1,624	432	27
West North-Central	869	284	33
South Atlantic	1,304	366	28
East South-Central	548	90	16
West South-Central	844	170	20
Mountain	503	169	34
Pacific Coast	795	283	36
Metro status			
Central	859	268	31
Suburban	4,501	1,151	26
Independent	3,209	757	24
Form of government			
Mayor-council	3,162	606	19
Council-manager	3,548	1,164	33
Commission	143	29	20
Town meeting	341	60	18
Representative town meeting	63	15	24
Council-administrator (manager)	821	228	28
County executive	491	74	15

1   For a definition of terms, please see "Inside the *Year Book*," xi.

Table 5-2   Level of Use of Major Sustainability Activity Areas

Major activity area	Average percentage of activities used, %	Local governments using one or more activities, %
Overall adoption rating across all activity areas	18	60
Greenhouse gas reduction and air quality	12	52
Water quality	28	62
Recycling	33	90
Energy use in transportation and exterior lighting	22	72
Reducing building energy use	19	81
Alternative energy generation	7	23
Workplace alternatives to reduce commuting	8	36
Transportation improvements	22	82
Building and land use regulations	12	58
Land conservation and development rights	15	44
Social inclusion	21	58
Local production and green purchasing	18	68

Note: Percentages of local governments using one or more activities are based on total respondents (n = 2,176).

Table 5-3   Overal Adoption Ratings in Major Activity Areas, City vs. County

Major activity area	City, % (n = 1,874)	County, % (n = 302)	Total, % (n = 2,176)
Total average	18	18	18
Greenhouse gas	12	9	12
Water	30	18	28
Recycling	34	32	33
Vehicles and lighting	23	19	22
Energy buildings	19	23	19
Alternative energy	6	10	7
Transporation alternatives	7	12	8
Transportation improvements	23	20	23
Building and land use	12	11	12
Land conservation	14	22	15
Social inclusion	20	27	21
Local purchase	18	15	18

shown in Table 5–3, their overall adoption ratings are virtually identical. There are three areas, however, in which their levels of activity differ. Cities are more involved than counties in the service of providing water, and they have a higher rating for sustainability actions related to water quality and conservation.

Figure 5-1   Local Governments Arranged by Level of Sustainability Action

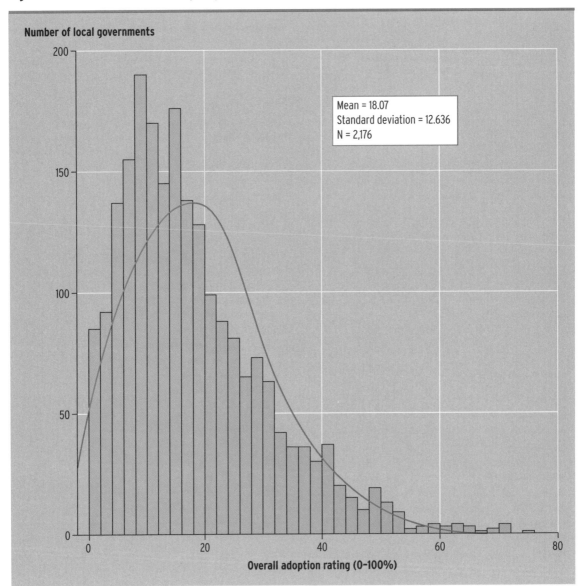

Counties provide more social services and have a higher social inclusion rating than cities. In addition, counties are more likely to be involved in land conservation and the use of development rights to promote sustainability goals, presumably because of their larger geographic size and amount of land devoted to forests and farming.

The overall responses in this survey demonstrate two opposing tendencies: most local governments are becoming active in sustainability; however, most governments are also involved at a relatively low level, and most of the possible sustainability actions are not being widely used.[9] These themes will be developed throughout this article.

Sustainability and Policy Priorities

Communities differ in the level of priority they give to a number of policy issues. (The survey asked "To what extent are the following [issues] a priority in your jurisdiction?" Presumably, the responses indicate the views of officials who are interpreting the preferences of citizens.) As indicated in Figure 5–2, most local governments—almost 7 in 10—assign a very high priority to their economy, and most of the rest make it a high priority. Well over three-fifths also consider energy conservation and the environment to be high or very high priorities (70% and 62%, respectively). However, less than half consider housing for

Figure 5-2   Local Government Priority Levels for Policy Actions

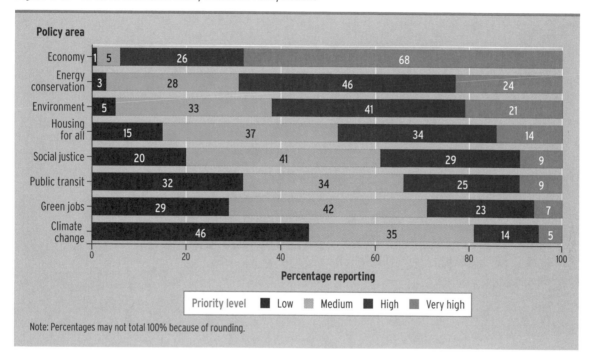

Note: Percentages may not total 100% because of rounding.

all, social justice, public transit, or green jobs to be a high priority, and climate change is a high or very high priority for only one local government in five. Clearly, the early sustainability foci on stabilizing the economy and the environment, along with the newer emphasis on saving energy, are important concerns in most local governments. Social equity, the new interest in green jobs, and the contested issue of combating climate change are assigned less importance.

By and large, both the nature and the level of policy priorities are related to the extent of actions taken to advance sustainability. Placing a higher priority on the economy has only modest effect on sustainability action, as indicated in Figure 5-3 (see page 48). For all the other policy areas, an increasing priority leads to substantially higher overall adoption ratings. In particular, prioritizing green jobs and climate change are linked to substantially higher levels of activity. Although these are the least common high-priority areas, they have the strongest association with action.

When officials and citizens share a broad-ranging commitment to all aspects of sustainability, the conditions are favorable for extensive action. When the level of commitment in the community is lower, the government may back off trying to promote sustainability action, as Figure 5-3 indicates. An alternative approach, however, is suggested by City Manager Michael Willis, who moved from a high-commitment city in Australia to a low-commitment city in England:

I figured that before we could take the sustainability message out into the community, we needed to be able to assert our moral authority as an organization to offer such leadership in the first place, which could best be achieved by making ourselves more sustainable. That way, we could offer a positive example and not just empty proselytizing. We decided to work from the inside out, rather than the outside in....[10]

Limited community support may cause an initial focus on internal government operations (e.g., energy use in government buildings and purchasing practices) rather than on policy issues or community action, but it does not need to derail the government's commitment to sustainability. In time, citizens may start following the example of the government.

Organizing Sustainability Action

For a local government to take effective action to promote sustainability, it is advantageous to pursue a broad strategy aimed at meeting stated goals rather than simply taking a number of disconnected specific actions with little attention to results.

Goals, Targets, and Citizens' Committees

Beyond improved coordination, a commitment in the form of a resolution by the governing board stating policy goals and the adoption of a plan with specific

Figure 5-3   Overall Adoption Ratings by Level of Policy Priority

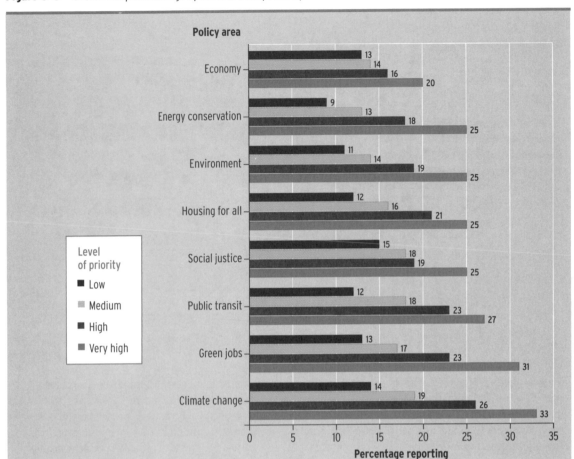

targets will likely contribute to expanded action. Overall, 29% of the responding governments have set goals, and 19% have set targets (Table 5–4). When looking at the two actions together, however, two-thirds of local governments have not taken either of these steps, and another 15% have a resolution without a specific plan (i.e., goals but no targets). Only 14% have done both, and another 5% have targets but not general goals.

Another organizing action that local governments can take is to appoint a citizens' committee or commission to provide ideas and encourage public involvement, as more than one-quarter of the responding governments have done.

When these various steps toward organizing the sustainability effort are considered together, each one increases activity level, and the multiple steps have a positive combined effect. Having either goals or targets increases the activity rating above the average for all local governments, whereas having a citizens' committee in the absence of goals and/or targets does

Table 5-4   Use of Organizing Actions and Overall Adoption Ratings: Policy Goals, Plan with Targets, and Citizens' Committee

Number of organizing actions	Overall activity rating	Local governments	
		No. reporting	%
Average for all local governments	18	2,176	100
None of the three	13	1,214	56
Citizens' committee only	18	234	11
Goals only	22	186	9
Goals and citizens' committee	24	139	6
Targets only	22	65	3
Targets and citizens' committee	26	38	2
Goals and targets	29	129	6
Goals, targets, and citizens' committee	34	171	8

not. Having all three organizing actions is associated with a substantially higher overall adoption rating (34%). Unfortunately, only one in 12 local governments (8%) uses all three methods.

National Campaigns

There are two major efforts to encourage local governments to make a commitment to take action in support of sustainability: the Mayors Climate Protection Agreement and ICLEI's Cities for Climate Protection campaign.

In 2005, the U.S. Conference of Mayors endorsed the Mayors Climate Protection Agreement.[11] To reduce global warming pollution levels, the agreement urges action on the national and local government levels. Among the city governments responding to ICMA's sustainability survey, 281 (13%) have adopted the agreement.[12]

ICLEI—Local Governments for Sustainability (formerly, the International Council for Local Environmental Initiatives) is an association of over 1,200 local governments internationally whose members are committed to sustainable development.[13] ICLEI members become part of the Cities for Climate Protection (CCP) campaign by passing a resolution to undertake specific actions to reduce greenhouse gas (GHG) emissions from their local government operations and throughout their communities.[14] Over 600 local governments in the United States are ICLEI members. Among governments responding to the ICMA survey, 10% are members (not shown).

Local government affiliation with either of these efforts is linked to a substantially higher average adoption rating for sustainability-related activities (not shown):

- Mayors Climate Protection Agreement: 281 signees, 30% rating; 1,895 nonsignees, 16% rating
- ICLEI-Local Governments for Sustainability: 211 members, 34% rating; 1,935 nonmembers, 16% rating.

As noted, the Mayors Climate Protection Agreement started in 2005, so this effort has been ongoing for a relatively short time. As for ICLEI membership, there is evidence that it has increased substantially in California over the past five years. Whereas only 25 governments in California had signed on between 1992 and 2005, the number was over 150 by the beginning of 2010.[15]

Form of Government

Form of government makes a difference in the approaches taken and the level of sustainability activity. As indicated in Figure 5–4, governments organized with the council-manager or county administrator form—forms with a governing board and appointed administrator—are more likely to have established specific targets and benchmarks than mayor-council and county executive governments. Council-manager governments are also more likely to have joined ICLEI and signed the Mayors Climate Protection Agreement. Even though that agreement has been associated with mayor-council cities and the initiatives of strong

Figure 5-4 Sustainability Commitments, by Form of Government

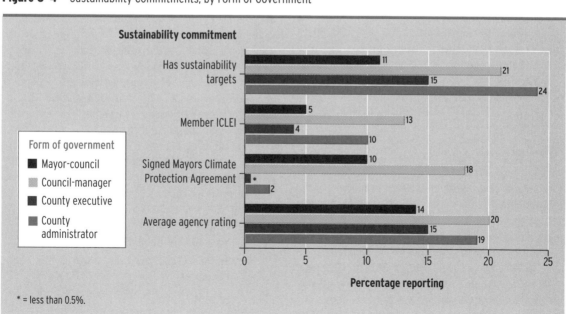

Sustainability commitment

Has sustainability targets: 11, 21, 15, 24

Member ICLEI: 5, 13, 4, 10

Signed Mayors Climate Protection Agreement: 10, 18, *, 2

Average agency rating: 14, 20, 15, 19

Form of government
- Mayor-council
- Council-manager
- County executive
- County administrator

Percentage reporting

* = less than 0.5%.

mayors, more council-manager cities have agreed to its terms and adopted sustainability actions than have mayor-council cities overall.

In addition, council-manager governments have higher overall adoption ratings (cities, 20%; counties, 19%) than mayor-council cities (14%) and elected-executive counties (15%) (Figure 5–4).[16] The governing boards in council-manager governments can set goals and approve strategies that may be hard to achieve when there is a separation of powers between an elected executive and a council. Professional administrators have declared a strong commitment to sustainability action,[17] and the cities and counties in which they work are more active in setting targets, joining sustainability efforts, and undertaking activities than mayor-council cities and elected-executive counties.

Other Major Determinants of Sustainability Actions

Two additional factors deserve special attention for their strong association with greater action to promote sustainability: state and region, and population.

State and Region

Local governments in different parts of the country vary in their likelihood of taking sustainability action. To some extent, there is a state effect as well. Local governments in states that have approved more climate change initiatives are more likely to have higher activity levels—in some cases because they are mandated to do so by the state. For example, California, which according to a Pew Center report has the most state initiatives (21), also has the highest activity level among local governments, with an average adoption rating of 33%.[18] Dividing the states into two groups according to the number of initiatives reveals a clear difference in overall adoption ratings related to the number of state initiatives:

- Twenty-three states with 11 or fewer initiatives: rating of 14%

- Twenty-six states with 12 or more initiatives: rating of 20% (not shown).[19]

The five states with the fewest initiatives—five or fewer—tend to have low overall adoption ratings, but they vary from Alabama (9%), Mississippi (10%), and South Dakota (11%) (ranks of 46, 45, and tied for 41, respectively, among the state overall adoption ratings), to Tennessee at 13% (tied for 38) and Nebraska at 16% (tied for 26) (not shown). And despite the correspondence of California's top rank on both lists, the other states that lead in initiatives are generally highly ranked but vary in their overall adoption rat-

ings. Among the four states tied for second place below California with 19 state initiatives, the average ratings are 22% for Massachusetts and Washington (tied for rank of 8), 19% for Oregon (tied for 16), and 15% for New York (rank of 29) (not shown). State initiatives can provide a generally positive or negative climate for sustainability programs, but they do not by themselves determine how active local governments will be.

Regions, on the other hand, differentiate activity level to a greater extent. As indicated in Figure 5–5, local governments in the West have the highest average adoption ratings in 10 of the 12 activity areas.[20] The exceptions are recycling and land conservation, which are used most commonly in the Northeast. By a large margin, local governments in the West (followed by those in the South) are most active in measures related to water, vehicles and lighting, transportation alternatives, and transportation improvements; promoting alternative sources of energy, although still uncommon, is also happening more in the West than in other regions. The higher levels of activity in the West can be explained in part by natural resource issues such as water scarcity and by the need to control air pollution and handle growing transportation needs. Western cities also tend to be larger than those in other regions, and they make more extensive use of council-manager governments.[21]

Population

Regardless of region, population size is also a major determinant of sustainability action. On average, the larger the city or county, the more that is being done to promote sustainability. The appendix table provides the average adoption ratings for all the specific activities within the major activity areas. The presentation includes the overall percentage of local governments using each activity and a breakdown for each activity by the five major population groups.[22] The largest size category—cities and counties over 500,000 in population—have an overall adoption rating (39%) that is three times that of the smallest category—governments under 10,000 in population (13%).

Looking at specific activities, only three are conducted by at least 50% of responding governments in all five size categories: residential recycling collection, internal governmental recycling, and the addition of bike and walking trails. When the smallest governments (those under 10,000 in population) are set aside, at least 50% of the remaining cities

- Recycle household hazardous waste and electronic equipment

- Conduct energy audits and improve the efficiency of office lighting in government buildings

- Purchase fuel-efficient vehicles

- Support a farmers' market
- Require sidewalks in new developments.

A majority of the jurisdictions in the top three size categories (over 50,000) take on seven additional activities:

- Implement more building energy measures:
  — Install energy management systems
  — Improve heating and air conditioning systems

- Increase traffic signal efficiency
- Expand dedicated bike lanes
- Provide financial support for affordable housing
- Plan for tree preservation and planting
- Purchase hybrid vehicles.

It is important to note that only one additional activity is provided by a majority of cities over 100,000 in population: offering educational programs on the

Figure 5-5   Average Adoption Ratings in Major Activity Areas, by Geographic Region

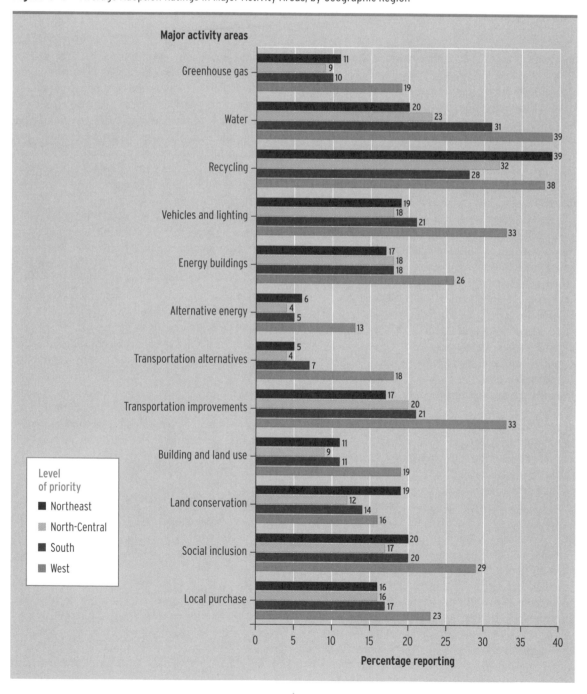

Table 5-5 Overall Adoption Ratings of Top 10% of Communities, by Population and Region

| Population | Region, % | | | | Total | |
	Northeast (n = 19)	North-Central (n = 29)	South (n = 52)	West (n = 118)	No. reporting (A)	% of (A)
Total reporting	9	13	24	54	218	100
500,000 and over	1	–	6	3	21	10
100,000-499,999	1	3	8	15	59	27
50,000-99,999	1	3	5	12	45	21
10,000-49,999	5	5	4	17	68	31
Under 10,000	1	2	1	8	25	12

Note: Percentages may exceed 100% because of rounding.

environment and energy conservation. Thus, only 18 activities are in widespread use among a range of local governments, and even for these, the range for most activities is progressively confined to larger places. In the cities and counties over 500,000 in population, on the other hand, at least half are making use of 23 additional activities (discussed further in the next section).

A number of factors may explain the substantial differentiation based on population. Some activities, such as changes related to transportation, are influenced by larger population and geographic size. Many activities require resources to install or retrofit facilities, or to provide incentives to home owners and businesses. Standards for private buildings can be more easily instituted in larger jurisdictions that have a bigger impact on the regional construction market. There is also likely to be greater pressure for change from mass media and more organized groups in larger places. Among the activities being used by at least 50% of local governments in different size categories, the only one that smaller communities may have an easier time putting in place is a farmers' market; indeed, these markets are more common in smaller (but not the smallest) jurisdictions than in the largest ones. Otherwise, the characteristics associated with a smaller population tend to reduce the likelihood of sustainability activity.

The higher usage in larger places and certain regions is not a negative factor, nor is it necessarily a fixed condition. For many kinds of new approaches, a relatively small proportion of local governments act as pioneers and early adopters. These innovators provide a demonstration effect that other governments will follow. Furthermore, even at the present time, smaller communities and those outside the West are not automatically consigned to lower levels of activity. Of the top 10% of the participants in the survey—218 governments with an average rating of 36% or higher—only one in 10 is over

500,000 in population, and most of these large governments are not in the West (Table 5–5). Over 40% of the top 10% of local governments have a population under 50,000, and almost half are outside the West.

It is plausible to expect that greater population growth would be a factor associated with more attention to and higher action on sustainability. There is little connection, however, between the percentage growth rate and sustainability action overall, and the linkages to specific activity areas are weak. There are modestly more actions taken related to water, transportation improvements, and buildings and land use in faster-growing local governments, but there is virtually no relationship between growth rate and actions on land conservation.[23] The supposition that fast growth would increase (or, some might presume, decrease) the concern about preserving land is not supported by findings from this survey.

In conclusion, active involvement in sustainability increases with population size and is most commonly found in the West, but the activity level in each community is not predetermined. The decisions of leaders and citizens can take any jurisdiction into the leading ranks of sustainability communities even if the conditions in those communities are not highly favorable or can leave them lagging behind.

Variations in Activity Areas

It is important here to briefly examine the approaches to sustainability in more detail. Referring once again to the appendix table, the focus is now on variation in how extensively the 109 specific activities are being used. The survey presented respondents with, in effect, a challenging multiple choice exam that was designed to provide options that might be considered in very committed communities. There was no expectation that any government would be using all the activities listed. It follows that not all the activities would be used extensively even in governments with a high level of commitment to sustainability.

The extent that specific activities are adopted can be divided into five tiers of declining usage. The first tier contains the activities that are adopted most often. The review in the preceding section of the practices used in at least half of local governments in two or more size categories provides a list of the 18 activities used most often. When some of the indicators are combined, recycling, improving energy usage in buildings and traffic signals, expanding opportunities for bicycling, supporting farmers' markets, planting trees, and, in larger places, supporting affordable housing and educational programs are the activities most likely to be included in a local government's portfolio of sustainability actions.

The second tier of activities consists of those used by one-quarter to one-half of all local governments. They include the following, presented singly or in clusters of related actions, with actions taken by half or more of the largest government shown in italics:

- Expanding recycling, including locating recycling containers close to refuse containers in public places, *picking up from commercial properties,* and collecting organic material for composting
- Increasing support for bicycling, such as expanding dedicated lanes and *adding bike parking facilities*
- Widening sidewalks
- Using zoning codes to encourage more mixed-use development
- Using public land for community gardens
- Taking action related to water quality, including protecting aquifers, using water price structure and *other incentives to encourage conservation,* and setting limits on impervious surfaces on private property
- *Improving efficiency in streetlights and/or other exterior lighting* (beyond traffic signals)
- *Permitting telework for staff members*
- *Providing housing options for the elderly*
- *Providing access to information technology for persons without connection to the Internet*
- *Providing after-school programs for children.*

The third tier contains activities that are used by less than a quarter of local governments overall but by at least half of the largest local governments. These include

- Increasing energy efficiency of pumps in the water or sewer systems
- Using brownfields, vacant property, or other programs to revitalize abandoned or underused land and using a land conservation program

- Permitting higher-density development near public transit nodes
- Expanding or planning light-rail or subway systems
- Providing incentives to local government staff to carpool or use mass transit to get to work
- Using greywater and/or reclaimed-water use systems
- Providing supportive housing to people with disabilities or to homeless persons within the community
- Changing government operations, such as installing solar panels on government facilities, requiring all new government construction projects to be LEED or Energy Star certified, purchasing vehicles that operate on compressed natural gas, and purchasing only Energy Star equipment.

Looking across all these activities that are used by at least 50% of local governments in one or more major population categories (most often the largest), or by a quarter or more of all local governments, 49 activities out of the 109 potential actions can be viewed as being extensively used by at least some governments or fairly broadly used by all local governments. Either of these distributions could be the basis for expansion as use trickles down or spreads out for these practices that have established a beachhead. Note, however, that this not a debate about whether the glass is half empty or half full; rather, it is an observation that at least one group of governments, based on size, has a glass that is half full or that the collective glass is at least one-quarter full.

In contrast, most of the activities covered in the survey are not being used much overall or extensively by any population group of local governments. This fourth tier consists of 24 activities that are somewhat more widely used in large cities (by 25%–49%) but are rarely used overall (by less than 25% of all local governments). These include

- Measuring baseline GHG emissions in the community and the government, and setting targets or goals for reducing emissions in government operations
- Implementing governmental actions to generate electricity through municipal operations, reducing dust and particulate matter, making green and low-waste purchases, and requiring all retrofit government projects to be LEED or Energy Star certified
- Supporting building and land use initiatives, such as weatherization of residences and zoning changes to permit alternative energy installations

- Permitting land use changes such as higher-density infill development and ancillary dwelling units
- Purchasing or transferring development rights to preserve open space or historic property
- Reporting on community quality-of-life indicators, funding for pre-school education, and energy reduction and transportation programs targeted specifically to assist low-income residents
- Expanding bus routes, offering incentives for local government employees to bike to work, and providing charging stations for electric vehicles
- Requiring dark sky–compliant outdoor light fixtures.[24]

Finally, the fifth tier contains another 36 activities that are used by 10% or less of all local governments and by less than a quarter of the largest local governments. These include

- Setting GHG reduction targets for single-family residences, multifamily residences, or businesses
- Providing energy audits to residences and businesses, and supporting the installation of solar equipment or the purchase of energy-efficient appliances with grants, loans, or tax incentives
- Applying LEED Neighborhood Design standards
- Using a compressed workweek with government offices closed one day, or a setting a specific target for the percentage of the government workforce that will telework
- Reducing fees, accelerating reviews, or offering tax incentives for environmentally friendly development
- Offering density incentives for "sustainable" development or incentives for new single-family residential or commercial development that is LEED certified or the equivalent
- Having a program for the purchase or transfer of development rights to create more efficient development
- Using a Pay-As-You-Throw (PAYT) program with charges based on the amount of waste discarded
- Offering incentives or setting restrictions regarding the use of locally grown produce or locally produced material or products, or the use of plastic bags by grocery or retail stores.

These approaches have not yet gotten much of a foothold in local government practice although a few local governments are using them.

Summary

In sum, sustainability may be the issue of our age, but the transition from agenda setting to action is slow, uneven, and incomplete. Most governments assign a high priority to certain policies related to sustainability—in particular, the economy, the environment, and energy reduction—but most do not emphasize green jobs or GHG reduction. Higher priorities in all areas are linked to higher action, and the effect is greatest when the community feels it is highly important to promote green jobs and reduce GHG emissions. Beyond the different levels of priority, most local governments lack goals, targets, or specific plans. Only a quarter of them have citizens' committees and staff dedicated to sustainability, and although local governments are spending money on specific actions, only one in six has a separate budget to promote sustainability. Establishing priorities, making commitments, creating an advisory committee, and organizing activities with dedicated staff and budget are all linked to higher activity levels.

Cities and counties are similar in their overall level of sustainability action. Council-manager governments are more likely to join efforts to promote sustainability and are somewhat more active than elected-executive governments—mayor-council and county executive. Regions differ in their activity levels, with the highest activity in the West. Five of the 10 states with the highest overall adoption ratings are in the West. The lowest activity levels are in the South and North-Central regions, where 9 of the 10 states with the lowest adoption ratings are found. Population size is a major determinant of sustainability action. Still, many governments that are showing high commitment and leadership in sustainability are smaller governments, and they are found in all regions.

Depending on their frequency of adoption, activities undertaken for sustainability can be divided into five tiers. Those used most often or with greater uniformity across local governments of various sizes are related to recycling, air and water quality, tree preservation, and energy savings in buildings. Most of these approaches are long-standing commitments, are required by higher levels of government, or help governments save money.[25] Many of the other approaches are relatively new or untried, or require resources that are difficult to find in local governments. In earlier years, these activities may have suffered from competition with other established commitments; in recent years, they have been held back by the general squeeze on financial and manpower resources during the fiscal crisis. Steps to produce savings are welcome in the current climate, but those that require new resources are difficult to implement unless supported with federal funds.[26]

Still, there are many approaches to organizing the effort, and many of the activities can be achieved with focus, commitment, and ingenuity rather than with money or large amounts of staff time. For example, the two least commonly adopted activity areas are developing alternative energy sources—a resource-intensive change—and promoting transportation alternatives, most of which can be embarked upon through changes in priorities, procedures, and work rules. Activities in other areas can be accomplished through new partnerships with citizens. Indeed, the future of sustainability and citizen engagement are intimately connected not only because citizens can help with programs but also because citizen willingness to change behavior is essential to achieving a substantial impact.[27]

The level and spread of sustainability activity is similar to the diffusion of other kinds of innovation.[28] Typically, the pioneers who operate at the cutting edge and the early adopters represent about one government in six. Most organizations are bunched around the middle, with a third that are above average and a third below in terms of the pace or extent of adoption; mirroring the proportion of early adopters, about one local government in six lags behind or refuses to change. At any point in time, the number of new practices that are adopted represents a bell-shaped curve. The striking feature in the adoption of sustainability practices is that most governments are bunched at the low end in the number of adoptions, and the pioneers and early adopters are way out ahead of the rest (see Figure 5–1). It appears that American local governments are still in the early stage of innovation, with most local governments closer to the lower end of the spectrum rather than in the middle or at the higher end. This is puzzling in that sustainability is not a new idea, but it may be understandable given the relative newness of sustainability as a challenge that local governments are taking on beyond the traditional and mandated activities that they have been doing for some time.

Experience with other areas of innovation suggests that the rate of adoption will increase over time. If this happens with regard to sustainability, the number of activities performed by governments in the middle range will increase dramatically. An encouraging finding from the survey is that some governments are engaging in widespread experimentation. A lot of sharing of experience is needed, but it can be expected to come. To advance sustainability, most governments need to broaden the scope of their activity. They also need to improve the planning and coordination of the activities they undertake. City Manager Rick Cole's words from 2007 have not yet been sufficiently heeded: "The world is changing. We can lead or we can follow. We can't hide. Finding creative and practical local solutions is what we are all about."[29] It will also be important to keep checking on the progress over time. This study provides a baseline for measuring future expansion of activity.

Notes

1. "Sustainability," *ICMA Management Perspective* (October 2007), 1, icma.org/fileimages/full/ ~ legacy ~ / icma_data/bc/attach/%7be92cf435-1512-47f3-a14b-26dea69f6e1d%7d08-078%20mgmt%20prsptv%20 sustainability%20v04.pdf (accessed January 14, 2011).

2. World Commission on Environment and Development, *Our Common Future* (New York: Oxford University Press, 1987), un-documents.net/ocf-02.htm#I (accessed January 14, 2011).

3. The survey was developed with input from ICMA's Center for Sustainability Communities, the Center for Urban Innovation at Arizona State University (ASU), ASU's Global Institute of Sustainability (ASU GIOS), the Alliance for Innovation, and others. Its distribution was conducted through a collaboration of ICMA, ASU GIOS, and the ASU Sustainable Cities Network, a multijurisdictional partnership. The survey was provided in a print format because the local government response rate is both higher and more scientifically representative from a paper survey than from an electronic survey. Almost 12% of the responding governments chose to submit the form electronically.

4. Kent E. Portney, *Taking Sustainable Cities Seriously* (Cambridge: MIT Press, 2003).

5. The sources included SustainLane (sustainlane.com/us-city-rankings/); "Visible Strategies: Framework Adapted from U.S. Mayors" (usmayors.visiblestrategies.com/); Portney, *Taking Sustainable Cities Seriously*, 65; Go Green Virginia Green Community Challenge (gogreenva .org/?/challenge/participate/id/1); and the ICMA Center for Performance Measurement.

6. The response rates by population group, region, and form of government were virtually identical to those in the *State of the Profession Survey, 2009*. There does not appear to be a response bias that pertains specifically to involvement in sustainability activities.

7. The activity areas contain different numbers of specific indicators. For this reason, it is misleading to use the raw count of the number of activities from the total list of 109 as the summary measure of adopting sustainability actions. For example, there are 15 ways to reduce building energy use and 12 ways to promote recycling compared to 5 actions each for water quality and alternative energy generation. Local governments that focus on the areas with more indicators would have a relatively high activity count even if they ignore the other areas. For comparison, the average number of activities adopted is 22.9 and the median is 20.0. The overall adoption rating is 18% and the median is 15%.

8. To provide an extreme example, a government that performed all 15 building energy activities but no other activities would have a rating of 14% if divided by the total activity count of 109. Performing 100% of the indicators in only one major activity area out of 12,

on the other hand, would produce an overall adoption rating of 8% (100/12). In calculations of the overall activity rating, the spread of activities across more areas produces a higher rating than a concentrated effort in fewer areas.

9. Using a method of measurement that appears to be closer to the percentage of governments using one or more activities in Table 5–2, a report from the National Association of Counties (NACo) titled *2010 County Sustainability Strategies* concludes that "the national picture of county sustainability efforts looks very positive" (17), naco.org/newsroom/latest/Documents/2010%20Sustainability%20Strategies%20Publication.pdf (accessed January 14, 2011).

10. Michael Willis, "Advancing Sustainability: What Happens If There Isn't an Appetite for It?" *PM Magazine* 91 (July 2009): 23–24.

11. Available at usmayors.org/climateprotection/documents/mcpAgreement.pdf.

12. In addition, seven cities using commission, town meeting, and representative town meeting forms of government signed the agreement, as did four counties.

13. See ICLEI–Local Governments for Sustainability at iclei.org/.

14. ICLEI–Local Governments for Sustainability was founded in 1990, and the Cities for Climate Protection (CCP) campaign was launched in 1993 as a successor to the organization's initial Urban CO2 Reduction Project. According to the CPP website at iclei.org/index.php?id=810 (accessed January 14, 2011), "The five milestones of the CCP and the methodology behind provide a simple, standardized means of calculating greenhouse gas emissions, of establishing targets to lower emissions, of reducing greenhouse gas emissions and of monitoring, measuring and reporting performance."

15. Adam Millard-Bell, "Do City Climate Plans Reduce Emissions?" (working draft, Stanford University, November, 2010).

16. Respondents in other forms of municipal government had these average adoption ratings, which are not shown: commission, 16% (29 respondents), town meeting, 17% (60 respondents), and representative town meeting, 25% (15 respondents).

17. Randall Reid, "The Moral Imperative of Sustainability," *PM Magazine* 91, no. 4 (May 2009): 27–31.

18. Pew Center on Climate Change, "All State Initiatives," pewclimate.org/docUploads/AllStateInitiatives-01-27-09-a_0.pdf (accessed January 29, 2011). The California Global Warming Solutions Act of 2006 requires all localities with publicly owned utilities to report their emissions.

19. The number of initiatives is from the Pew Report. The overall adoption rating is calculated for the cities in each state responding to the survey. Hawaii is excluded from this comparison because it had only one responding local government.

20. There are regional differences in the number of state initiatives. The average number for the states in each region is 16.8 in the Northeast; 9.8 in the Midwest; 8.6 in the South; and 14.2 in the West.

21. Other studies have determined that the western region has greater adoption of innovations even when controlling for the other factors mentioned.

22. The 10 population categories normally used in ICMA surveys show the same patterns of variation. The 5 categories are used to simplify the presentation.

23. The correlation between growth rate and overall activity rating is only .10—a very weak level of association. The correlation with water is .17, with transportation improvements is .17, and with building and land use controls is .13. All correlations are significant at the .001 level. The correlation with land conservation, on the other hand, is only .05.

24. Dark sky–compliant outdoor light fixtures do not meet the standard criterion for this tier because only 22% of the largest governments require them. The requirement is, however, used in 15% of all local governments, and the fifth tier is limited to practices used by 10% or less of local governments.

25. In the NACo survey results, the most important impact of sustainability activities is cost reduction.

26. An important source of outside assistance in some communities was the Energy Efficiency and Conservation Block Grant Program as part of the American Recovery and Reinvestment Act of 2009.

27. James H. Svara and Janet V. Denhardt, ed., *The Connected Community* (Alliance for Innovation, 2010).

28. Everett Rogers, *The Diffusion of Innovation*, 5th ed. (New York: Free Press, 2003),

29. Rick Cole, "Smart Growth: The Opportunity for Managers to Lead," *PM Magazine* (September 2007): 12.

Appendix   Average Adoption Rate (AAR) for Major Activity Areas, and Corresponding Specific Sustainability Actions, by all Local Governments in Five Population Categories, 2008 Population

Activity area and sustainability action (number of item in survey)	All	500,000 or higher	100,000–499,999	50,000–99,999	10,000–49,999	Under 10,000
Number responding	2,176[1]	36	173	207	853	903
			Percentage reporting			
All indices: Overall adoption rating	18	39	30	26	19	13
Greenhouse gas (GHG) reduction and air quality (AAR)	12	28	21	21	12	8
Baseline GHG emissions of the local government (4a)	14	47	36	32	13	6
Baseline GHG emissions of the community (4b)	9	39	22	23	7	3
GHG reduction targets for local government operations (4c)	11	39	27	21	11	6
GHG reduction targets for businesses (4d)	3	6	5	8	2	1
GHG reduction targets for multifamily residences (4e)	2	3	2	6	1	1
GHG reduction targets for single-family residences (4f)	2	3	3	7	2	1
Locally initiated air pollution measures to reduce dust and particulate matter (4g)	9	33	20	11	9	5
Plan for tree preservation and planting (4h)	45	56	53	56	47	38
Water quality (AAR)	28	47	37	35	30	23
Actions to conserve the quantity of water from aquifers (6a)	34	47	41	41	35	28
Use of grey-water and/or reclaimed-water use systems (6b)	16	64	35	28	16	9
Sets limits on impervious surfaces on private property (6c)	30	28	32	35	36	24
Use water price structure to encourage conservation (6d)	33	39	35	37	33	32
Other incentives for water conservation behaviors by city, residents, and businesses (6e)	28	56	41	43	41	35
Recycling (AAR)	33	41	43	41	35	28
Internal program that recycles paper and plastic and glass in your local government (7a)	72	83	89	87	76	61
Community-wide recycling collection program for paper and plastic and glass for residential properties (7b)	76	78	80	81	79	71
Community-wide recycling collection program for paper and plastic and glass for commercial properties (7c)	45	53	47	49	45	43
Recycling of household hazardous waste (7d)	55	78	80	71	59	42
Recycling of household electronic equipment (e-waste) (7e)	52	69	73	70	54	42
Pay-As-You-Throw (PAYT) program with charges based on the amount of waste discarded (7f)	11	8	14	15	9	10
Community-wide collection of organic material for composting (7g)	33	28	36	35	34	30
Require minimum of 30% post-consumer recycled content for everyday office paper use (7h)	9	25	24	17	8	5
Local government action to reduce the use of plastic bags by grocery or retail stores through *restriction* (24b)	1	3	0	1	1	1
Local government action to reduce the use of plastic bags by grocery or retail stores through *incentive* (24b)	2	0	2	4	2	2
Restriction on purchase of bottled water by the local government (25a)	11	25	22	14	10	7
Locate recycling containers close to refuse containers in public spaces such as streets and parks (25e)	34	44	45	46	37	26

Activity area and sustainability action (number of item in survey)	All	500,000 or higher	100,000-499,999	50,000-99,999	10,000-49,999	Under 10,000
Energy use in transportation and exterior lighting (AAR)	22	57	41	36	23	13
Established a fuel efficiency target for the government fleet of vehicles (8a)	13	39	31	18	13	6
Increased the purchase of fuel-efficient vehicles (8b)	44	94	76	68	50	26
Purchased hybrid electric vehicles (8c)	24	81	65	50	25	7
Purchased vehicles that operate on compressed natural gas (8d)	9	64	31	17	7	2
Installed charging stations for electric vehicles (8e)	5	31	15	12	4	2
Upgraded or retrofitted traffic signals to improve efficiency (8j)	37	72	59	58	42	22
Upgraded or retrofitted streetlights and/or and other exterior lighting to improve efficiency (8k)	31	53	42	46	31	23
Upgraded or retrofitted facilities to higher energy efficiency pumps in the water or sewer systems (8m)	23	58	33	32	24	18
Utilize dark sky compliant outdoor light fixtures (8n)	15	22	20	21	15	13
Reducing building energy use (AAR)	19	40	34	28	19	14
Conducted energy audits of government buildings (8f)	63	97	89	81	68	48
Installed energy management systems to control heating and cooling in buildings (8g)	46	97	76	66	49	32
Established policy to only purchase Energy Star equipment when available (8h)	17	53	30	29	17	11
Upgraded or retrofitted facilities to higher energy-efficiency office lighting (8i)	56	100	86	72	60	41
Upgraded or retrofitted facilities to higher energy-efficiency heating and air conditioning systems (8l)	39	94	71	58	40	26
Local government established any energy reduction programs targeted specifically to assist low-income residents (9)	8	33	23	14	6	5
Local government established any energy reduction programs targeted specifically to assist small businesses (10)	6	13	15	8	5	4
Energy audit-individual residences (11a)[2]	8	17	18	16	6	5
Weatherization-individual residences (11b)[2]	15	42	32	30	11	10
Heating/air conditioning upgrades-individual residences (11c)[2]	8	14	17	13	8	6
Purchase of energy efficient appliances-individual residences (11d)[2]	6	8	14	10	5	5
Energy audit-businesses (11f)[2]	5	11	10	8	4	4
Weatherization-businesses (11g)[2]	4	11	9	6	3	3
Heating/air conditioning upgrades-businesses (11h)[2]	5	11	10	8	3	4
Purchase of energy efficient appliances-businesses (11i)[2]	4	8	9	5	2	4
Alternative energy generation (AAR)	7	29	19	12	6	3
Installed solar panels on a government facility (8o)	13	50	35	22	12	6
Installed a geothermal system (8p)	7	22	14	11	6	4
Generated electricity through municipal operations such as refuse disposal, wastewater treatment, or landfill (8q)	7	47	26	14	6	2
Installation of solar equipment-individual residences (11e)[2]	4	14	9	7	3	2
Installation of solar equipment-businesses (11j)[2]	3	11	8	6	2	2
Transportation alternatives (AAR)	8	35	19	13	7	4
Local government incentives for local government employees to take mass transit to work (12a)	7	69	28	14	5	1
Local government incentives for local government employees to carpool to work (12b)	7	64	23	15	4	1
Local government incentives for local government employees to walk to work (12c)	4	22	13	9	3	2

Activity area and sustainability action (number of item in survey)	All	500,000 or higher	100,000– 499,999	50,000– 99,999	10,000– 49,999	Under 10,000
Local government incentives for local government employees to bike to work (12d)	6	31	18	14	4	2
If your local government offers employees parking, do you charge market rates for employee parking? (13)	5	20	14	3	3	5
Is telework permitted for staff members in your local government? (14)	27	60	45	36	27	19
Do you have a specific target for the percentage of your government workforce that will telework? (15)	1	3	1	1	1	0
Does your local government use a compressed workweek with offices closed one day? (16)	10	17	17	14	11	6
Transportation improvements (AAR)	23	43	35	34	24	15
Expanded dedicated bike lanes on streets (17a)	34	78	61	55	38	19
Added biking and walking trails (17b)	61	86	81	73	65	50
Added bike parking facilities (17c)	28	61	46	46	29	18
Expanded bus routes (17d)	22	44	49	43	23	10
Requiring sidewalks in new development (17e)	54	67	61	65	60	45
Widened sidewalks (17f)	25	28	28	35	27	19
Require charging stations for electric vehicles (17g)	1	6	3	3	0	1
Require bike storage facilities (17h)	8	14	14	23	8	3
Require showers and changing facilities for employees (17i)	4	6	8	10	4	2
Does your community currently have a commuter rail system (subway or streetcar)? (18)	7	59	14	11	7	3
Does your community have a plan to create or expand the use of subway or streetcars? (19)	6	58	22	13	5	1
Has your local government established any transportation programs targeted specifically to assist low-income residents? (20)	21	32	44	36	19	14
Building and land use regulations (AAR)	12	26	20	19	13	7
Require all new government construction projects to be LEED or Energy Star certified (21a)	12	56	26	24	12	6
Require all retrofit government projects to be LEED or Energy Star certified (21b)	7	25	13	14	7	4
Permit higher density development near public transit nodes (21c)	20	61	40	36	22	8
Permit higher density development where infrastructure is already in place (utilities and transportation) (21d)	22	44	35	37	24	14
Incentives other than increased density for new commercial development (including multifamily residential) that are LEED certified or an equivalent (21e)	5	11	12	8	6	2
Incentives other than increased density for new single-family residential be LEED certified or the equivalent (21f)	3	14	9	5	3	1
Apply LEED Neighborhood Design standards (21g)	4	8	5	6	5	2
Provide density incentives for "sustainable" development (such as energy efficiency, recycling of materials, land preservation, storm-water enhancement, etc.) (21h)	10	11	16	13	11	6
Provide tax incentives for "sustainable" development (such as energy efficiency, recycling of materials, land preservation, storm water enhancement, etc.) (21i)	3	8	2	4	3	2
Reduce fees for environmentally friendly development (21j)	3	8	6	8	3	1
Fast track plan reviews and or inspections for environmentally friendly development (21k)	8	19	19	14	9	4
Residential zoning codes to permit solar installations, wind power, or other renewable energy production (21l)	21	36	31	26	22	16

Activity area and sustainability action (number of item in survey)	All	500,000 or higher	100,000– 499,999	50,000– 99,999	10,000– 49,999	Under 10,000
Residential zoning codes to permit higher densities through ancillary dwellings units or apartments (such as basement units, garage units, or in-house suites) (21m)	14	25	21	20	14	10
Zoning codes encourage more mixed-use development (21n)	35	42	46	46	41	26
Land conservation and development rights (AAR)	15	41	27	19	15	10
An active brownfields, vacant property, or other program for revitalizing abandoned or underutilized residential, commercial or industrial lands and buildings (22a)	22	50	42	30	22	16
A land conservation program (22b)	22	58	41	32	23	15
A program for the purchase or transfer of development rights to preserve open space (22c)	16	44	29	19	16	10
A program for the purchase or transfer of development rights to create more efficient development (22d)	6	22	11	6	6	4
A program for the purchase or transfer of development rights to preserve historic property (22e)	8	28	12	6	9	6
Social inclusion (AAR)	21	56	41	35	20	13
Provide financial support/incentives for affordable housing (23a)	33	81	60	56	33	20
Provide supportive housing to people with disabilities (23b)	15	53	35	28	16	7
Provide housing options for the elderly (23c)	27	53	44	43	27	20
Provide housing within your community to homeless persons (23d)	10	64	39	26	7	2
Provide access to information technology for persons without connection to the Internet (23e)	27	53	43	34	26	23
Provide funding for pre-school education (23f)	12	36	27	20	12	7
Provide after-school programs for children (23g)	26	58	44	44	27	17
Report on community quality of life indicators, such as education, cultural, diversity, and social well-being (23h)	15	47	35	29	15	7
Local production and green purchasing (AAR)	18	26	27	25	18	14
Local government action to use locally produced material or products through *restriction* (24a)	2	3	1	1	2	1
Local government action to use locally produced material or products through *incentive* (24a)	9	8	14	13	8	7
Local government action to use locally grown produce through *restriction* (24c)	0	0	0	0	0	0
Local government action to use locally grown produce through *incentive* (24c)	9	8	9	10	9	9
Use of public land for community gardens (25b)	29	42	46	41	30	21
Support a local farmers' market (25c)	52	50	56	65	55	47
Education program in the local community dealing with the environment and energy conservation (25d)	28	56	52	41	30	18
Green product purchasing policy in local government (25f)	13	42	35	26	12	6

1 The rating for "All" is based on 2,176 respondents. The estimated 2008 population is not available for four local governments, so the number of respondents is 2,172 for these five categories combined.

2 Activity can be a direct grant, direct loan, and/or tax incentive.

6

Achieving Greater Accountability in Social Programs

Gail S. Chadwick
Prevention Matters, LLC

Lisa Williams-Taylor
Children's Services Council
of Palm Beach County

Lance Till
Children's Services Council
of Palm Beach County

Alan R. Brown
Prevention Matters, LLC

The goal of prevention programs is to sustain and improve the lives of children, families, and communities.[1] But there is little evidence of their success in addressing serious social problems, from crime to substance abuse to dropout rates. Most of the approaches now in use have never been rigorously evaluated, and some of the most widely used interventions have been shown to be ineffective or harmful. Lacking reliable, research-based information about best practices, many communities invest in untested programs that are based on questionable assumptions, delivered with little quality control, and subject to little or no evaluation.[2] To move toward more rigorous, comprehensive, and scientifically based decision making about preventive services, policy makers need to begin asking new questions:

- What are the most serious problems, and where are they clustered?

- Where are resources being deployed, and for what programs?

- What policies, programs, and practices are most effective, and for what populations?

- What skills and tools do community-based service providers, educators, and other practitioners need to deliver effective programs?

- Is government funding making a positive difference?

Efforts to answer these questions are likely to reveal enormous gaps in knowledge, infrastructure, and practice. To help bridge those gaps, two of the authors, Alan Brown and Gail Chadwick, have developed an account-

SELECTED FINDINGS

Measuring the impact of programs and services allows policy makers and program planners to make informed decisions about future directions, the allocation of resources, and program design, thereby increasing the chance of improved outcomes.

Ideally, evidence-based programs have a significant and sustained effect; lend themselves to successful replication; are cost-effective; and meet the highest standards for research design.

Ultimately, change must come from leaders who seek and accept accountability for better results from government; who are willing to frame and make decisions about the allocation of scarce resources; and who are willing to take the risks to make the hard choices that face them.

ability system that improves outcomes while making the best possible use of public resources. One of the central features of the system is evidence-based programming—that is, decisions about policies, programs, and practices that are based on valid, reproducible research findings. The goal of this article is twofold: first, to acquaint readers with the system; and second, to provide an example of such a system in operation.[3]

The Accountability System

The accountability system presented here is based on a simple principle: namely, that a methodical, orderly, and research-based approach is a prerequisite for sensible decisions about how to use resources (see Figure 6-1). Thus, the system is designed to provide

- A fully rounded picture of needs, including those that decision makers are unaware of or that have not been verified

- Sufficient information to assign priorities among needs

- A means for stakeholders—including policy makers, funders, program managers, practitioners, elected officials, researchers, and community partners—to agree on goals and how to accomplish them.

The system has four basic components that work together to yield a comprehensive prevention system:

- A strategic policy agenda
- A professional development system
- A portfolio of effective programs
- A metrics system.

The components are complementary and interrelated: for the system to work, all four must be in place. Implemented in its entirety, the system offers an effective means of determining how dollars are being spent, whether the activities they support justify the

Figure 6-1 The Accountability System

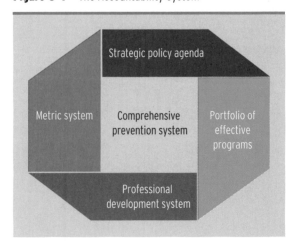

investment, and how the outcomes being "purchased" can be improved.

Strategic Policy Agenda

Solid research data demonstrate that investment in prevention yields human and financial benefits that the alternatives (especially incarceration) do not.[4] But prevention is a long-term solution that requires an integrated approach. The strategic policy agenda, the foundation of the accountability model, provides that integration. Based on systems thinking (see the

---

Highlights of Systems Thinking

Systems thinking is a holistic approach to understanding problems; it focuses on the interdependence of structure, actions, and consequences. The main principles of systems thinking are as follows:

- The parts of a system are interdependent.
- Our "mental models" (worldview, assumptions) influence our actions.
- Systems must be able to learn and adapt.
- Structure drives behavior.
- Our actions have broad consequences that are not necessarily immediate.
- Optimizing one part of a system may lead to poor overall system performance.

Maximizing performance in a system requires

- High-level collaboration
- A shared understanding of system goals
- A willingness to challenge assumptions
- Permeable system boundaries
- The ability to look "upstream" and "downstream"

- Knowledge of customer and client needs
- In most cases, structural redesign.

A systems thinker is someone who

- Sees the whole picture
- Is capable of changing perspectives to identify new leverage points in complex systems
- Looks for interdependence
- Is aware of the ways in which mental models create futures
- Attends to, and gives voice to, the long term
- "Goes wide" (i.e., uses peripheral vision) to see complex cause-and-effect relationships
- Notices where unanticipated consequences emerge
- Is capable of accepting the tension associated with paradox and controversy without trying to resolve it quickly.

accompanying sidebar), it is a proactive response to community problems that has two principal aims: to determine (1) *what* goals the organization is working toward and (2) *how* programs and services can work together to solve problems.

The essential ingredients of a strategic policy agenda are as follows:

- A short list of priorities: which things matter more than other things?

- Integrated use of resources: how can deliberate connections be made among programs that affect children and families?

- A budgetary dimension: how will the policy agenda affect the budget?

- Details about intended results: what are the specific outcomes that are desired?

Through such an integrated approach, local policy makers may determine, for example, that to reduce high school dropout rates among at-risk students (the agenda), they need to bring together the school system, the housing bureau, the police department, and the parks and recreation department (the system).

Professional Development System

Professional development in general, and instruction in systems thinking in particular, are crucial to the success of the accountability model. For staff to become seasoned systems thinkers, the organization—including top management—must be thoroughly committed to creating a climate and developing a skill set that fosters collaboration, innovation, and data-based decision making.

The professional development system should also include a prevention framework and training modules for staff, governing or advisory boards, and providers. The topics addressed within the framework should include, at a minimum, effective prevention, working together, and change and transition. The overall goal of the framework should be to strengthen performance, turn challenges into opportunities, engage and motivate, inspire sustained change, and measurably improve organizational performance.

Portfolio of Effective Programs

Few local governments do a creditable job of inventorying the approaches and outcomes associated with prevention efforts, and replication of successful evidence-based prevention programs—even within the same state—is essentially nonexistent. Although information about such programs is relatively easy to obtain, making use of the information involves more than simply selecting programs from a list.

To begin with, it is important to understand the criteria on which the evidence is based. Ideally, evidence-based programs (EBPs) would (1) have a significant and sustained effect, (2) lend themselves to successful replication, (3) be cost-effective, and (4) meet the highest standards for research design. Randomized clinical trials are the gold standard for determining what works, but such trials are rare in evaluations of programs and policies that address education, crime, or substance abuse.[5]

In recent years, a number of academics, government officials, project managers, and funders (including foundations, government agencies, and corporations) have begun to examine, far more systematically than ever before, which prevention programs succeed and why, and which programs can be replicated or adapted (the Center for the Study and Prevention of Violence [CSPV], at the University of Colorado in Boulder, is an example of such efforts). The early results of this work show promise. Nevertheless, taking constructive action on the basis of a list of effective programs remains a decidedly risky venture unless other factors are taken into consideration; these include the characteristics of the target population, professional development for implementers, and the program's long-term needs. What does seem clear, however, is that evidence-based programming has the potential to offer tremendous cost savings.[6]

Metrics System

Accountability metrics are a means of measuring the indicators of success. Given the enormous expenditures on prevention programs and services, communities should be able to collect and analyze data, and then use the information to track corresponding reductions in the social and economic costs of the problems being addressed. To measure such reductions, it is first necessary to determine what standards will be used to define success. Those standards can then be used to track how program participants have fared over the years and how the results have varied by community.

Measuring the impact of programs and services allows policy makers and program planners to make informed decisions about future directions, the allocation of resources, and program design, thereby increasing the chance of improved outcomes. The following are among the specific aims with which data systems can assist:

- Identifying broad trends (e.g., in the relationship between needs and resources)

- Reducing duplication of effort

- Aligning resource allocations and community needs

- Identifying additional opportunities for evidence-based programming

- Supporting the creation of data-driven needs assessments

- Reducing fragmentation and increasing collaboration

- Tracking progress on targeted issues.

The Importance of Fidelity

The program evaluation field tends to focus on outcomes—that is, on showing what works. As a result, it has largely ignored the intimate relationship between process and product. This gap in the research leaves practitioners with a list of programs that produced favorable outcomes during research trials but with little sense of how to implement those programs. In other words, a great deal more is known about *what* to implement than about *how* to implement.

The importance of the implementation process cannot be overstated. The central concept of implementation science is *fidelity*: process evaluation studies consistently show that programs implemented with fidelity to the original design achieve outcomes that are the same as, or better than, those achieved in the original research. There is also strong evidence that some programs do not work at all unless they are implemented with a high degree of fidelity. As Sharon Mihalic of the CSPV notes, "Most people do not recognize the importance of implementation fidelity and feel that implementation of at least some program components will be better than doing nothing. However, this may be an erroneous belief, since we typically do not know which components of a program may be responsible for the reductions in [problem behavior]."[7] In other words, program implementers cannot omit five of ten sessions and still expect the program to work.

Quite simply, fidelity is a matter of transporting programs to a real-world setting while adhering to the program design used in the original research. As long as an organization can guarantee the integrity of the original program design, it can expect to achieve outcomes similar to those found in research trials. Fidelity is crucial because without it, those outcomes are not assured.[8]

How is fidelity achieved? Five basic factors determine whether a program is being delivered in a way that will produce the expected outcomes:[9]

- *Adherence:* Is the program or service being delivered as it was designed? Specifically, (1) are all core components being delivered to the appropriate population, and (2) have staff been trained appropriately—using the right protocols, techniques, and materials, and in the locations or contexts prescribed?
- *Exposure* (also called *dosage*): Do the number of sessions, the length of each session, and the frequency with which program techniques are used replicate those of the original model?
- *Quality of program delivery:* Does the manner in which a teacher, volunteer, or staff member delivers a program or service (e.g., enthusiasm, preparedness, attitude, and skill in using the prescribed techniques or methods) replicate the

approaches used in the original model?
- *Participant responsiveness:* Do the level and type of participant engagement replicate those of the original design?
- *Program differentiation:* Does the program or service faithfully reproduce the unique features that differentiate it from other programs or services?

Fidelity to a program model is enhanced by several internal and external factors, including the following:[10]

- *Organizational characteristics.* The organization is stable, engages in open and clear internal communications, and is in good fiscal health.
- *Staff characteristics.* Staff have the necessary skills to implement the program, are involved in program selection, are given adequate time to implement the program, and are supported in their efforts to integrate it into daily operations.
- *Strong leadership.* The program has champions among management and key personnel.
- *Adequate training and technical assistance.* Staff are well trained in program delivery and receive ongoing formal or informal training.
- *Community support.* The community has helped to document the need for the program, conflict over turf has been reduced or eliminated, and outside agencies are prepared to cooperate and share data.
- *Adequate planning.* The need for the program has been empirically documented, the program director is committed to the program, and the program receives early support from top leadership.
- *Readiness for implementation.* The program is well developed and includes specific instructions and activities for implementation.

Because various obstacles can undermine implementation, the decision to adopt an EBP does not always guarantee success. Thanks to implementation studies, more is being learned about the capacities and motivation that are necessary to successfully adopt, implement, and sustain evidence-based programs.[11] Nevertheless, widespread replication of effective prevention programs is unlikely to affect the incidence of negative social outcomes until the quality of implementation can be assured.[12]

The Accountability System in Action

The Children's Services Council (CSC) of Palm Beach County, Florida, created in 1986 through a countywide referendum, is an independent special district that levies property tax dollars to fund programs and services for children and families.[13] CSC is founded on the following principles:

- Services and funding will be dedicated to primary prevention and early intervention.[14]
- Programs and services will be innovative and based on high-quality research.
- Programs will be held fiscally and programmatically accountable for measurably improving the well-being of children.

Thus, responsible spending and accountability for outcomes have guided CSC's business decisions since its inception. To the authors' knowledge, Palm Beach County is the only local government that is applying the accountability system outlined in this chapter. Although all elements of the accountability system have been implemented, this discussion focuses on the development of a portfolio of effective programs.

In 2006, in response to emerging interest in evidence-based programming, CSC formed a committee to begin researching programs.[15] The committee's objectives were (1) to research nationally and internationally recognized programs, as well as those that had not been formally rated but that appeared to be promising, given their research backing; and (2) to construct criteria that would allow CSC's locally developed programs to be rated in terms of effectiveness. The second objective was critical because CSC's leaders knew that there were not enough EBPs to meet every need in the county. Since it was not practical to limit funding to only those programs that were evidence based, CSC's program planners needed to develop a mechanism for determining how to move locally developed programs in the direction of being evidence based. (Figure 6–2 lists key questions for evaluating an evidence-based prevention effort.)

Objective 1: Researching Nationally and Internationally Recognized Programs

Using a logic model to help guide the process, the committee explored more than 500 programs.[16] Although the initial goal was to identify possible funding opportunities for CSC, a second goal emerged, which was to identify programs that could be recommended for funding from other agencies or organizations (e.g., the school district, the department of children and families, the criminal justice and juvenile justice systems).

Figure 6-2 Key Questions for Evaluating an Evidence-Based Prevention Effort

Element	Key question
Knowledge of the target population	Are there reasons to believe that the target population will be responsive to the prevention effort?
Clarity and realism of expected results	Are the intended results of the prevention effort clearly defined, and are they realistic in light of the nature of the effort and experiences with it thus far?
Corroborative empirical evidence of potential effectiveness	Does evidence exist from comparable prevention efforts to support claims that the intended results are achievable through efforts of this type and scope?
Conceptual soundness	Does a plausible explanation exist linking the prevention effort to its intended results?
Inclusive participation	Does the prevention effort adequately involve key individuals and organizations in planning and implementation?
System integration	Does the design of the prevention effort adequately account for system interdependency?
Appropriate structuring of the effort	Is the prevention effort scaled in size and complexity to match available resources and possibilities?
Appropriateness of timing, intensity, and duration	Is the prevention effort being implemented at an appropriate time and with sufficient intensity and duration to be effective?
Attention to quality of delivery	Has adequate attention been paid to the execution of each component of the prevention effort to ensure quality services and products?
Commitment to evaluation and effort refinement	Have provisions been made for continual tracking, documentation, evaluation, and feedback to ensure the effectiveness of the effort?

Source: Substance Abuse and Mental Health Services Administration, *Guidelines and Benchmarks for Prevention Programming: Implementation Guide*, 11-13, vvv.dmhas.state.ct.us/sig/pdf/GuidelinesBenchmarks.pdf (accessed January 11, 2011).

The first objective involved five phases:

1. Investigating the organizations that rate programs as evidence based
2. Adopting a definition and criteria for EBPs
3. Developing a list of potential programs
4. Screening the programs
5. Creating a rating system to reevaluate programs and develop a final list.

Phases 1 and 2: Investigating Rating Organizations and Adopting a Definition and Criteria The CSC committee began by examining 26 organizations that rate programs; it then used the definitions and criteria of those organizations to develop definitions and criteria of its own. (The accompanying sidebar lists rating organizations and publications recommended by the committee.) The committee's research revealed considerable variations in terminology (e.g., *evidence based*, *research based*, *best practices*, *evidence informed*) and categorical rankings (e.g., *promising*, *model*, *exemplary*, *effective*).[17]

Ultimately, the committee decided to use the term *evidence-based* and determined that CSC would discuss evidence-based efforts in terms of *programs*, *curricula*, and *practices*. This approach was selected because programs may use various curricula and practices in their delivery of services—some of which may have been researched independently and some which may not. EBPs were defined as a set of coordinated services or activities whose effectiveness had been demonstrated through research. Because of variations in the rating systems used by various organizations, however, the committee further agreed to establish its own criteria for EBPs:

- Evaluation by means of a rigorous research design (experimental, quasi-experimental, or both)
- Demonstrated positive effects
- Demonstrated sustainable outcomes (for at least one year)
- Replicable outcomes.

Phase 3: Developing a List of Potential Programs As the committee collected information on all 500 recognized programs (e.g., target population, research design, outcomes, effectiveness), it eliminated those that did not meet CSC's needs or that failed to meet the criteria that the committee had established for evidence-based programming.[18] By the end of this phase of the process, the 500 programs had been winnowed down to 80.

Phase 4: Screening the Programs To further narrow the number of programs that would be examined in depth, all 80 programs were screened by two to three reviewers. If the findings were inconsistent, the committee met to discuss findings and validate results. The final result was a matrix that included, for each program, information on the following:

- Alignment of outcomes with the goals of CSC
- Research design
- Sustainability
- Replicability (at different sites and with different populations).

Phase 5: Creating a Rating System and Reassessing the Programs To assist with the final phase, which was a more in-depth look at the programs, the committee created a data-gathering instrument that was used to rate programs; ratings were then used as

---

Recommended Sources of Ratings

- Blueprints for Violence Prevention (Center for the Study of Prevention and Violence; colorado.edu/cspv/blueprints/)
- FRIENDS National Resource Center for Community-Based Child Abuse Prevention (friendsnrc.org/cbcap-priority-areas/evidence-base-practice-in-cbcap/evidence-based-program-directory)
- IES What Works Clearinghouse (Institute of Education Sciences, U.S. Department of Education; ies.ed.gov/ncee/wwc/)
- OJJDP Model Programs Guide (Office of Juvenile Justice and Delinquency Prevention; www2.dsgonline.com/mpg/)
- Promising Practices Network on Children, Families, and Communities (promisingpractices.net/default.asp)
- Social Programs That Work (Coalition for Evidence-Based Policy; evidencebasedprograms.org/wordpress/)
- Strengthening America's Families: Effective Family Programs for Prevention of Delinquency (Department of Health Promotion and Education, University of Utah College of Health; strengtheningfamilies.org/)
- "Scientific Standards for Determining Program Excellence," chap. 5 in *Youth Violence: A Report of the Surgeon General* (Office of the Surgeon General; surgeongeneral.gov/library/youthviolence/chapter5/sec2.html).

the basis of recommendations to the CSC leadership. Among the factors assigned ratings were the underlying theory, the core components, the research design, the outcomes, the program infrastructure, and the cost.[19]

Objective 2: Constructing Criteria for Rating Homegrown or Locally Developed Programs

Recognizing that there were not enough EBPs to meet all community needs, the CSC committee created a tool to determine how effective currently funded programs were. The tool, which assesses each program's theoretical background, administrative practices, fidelity, and documented outcomes, has three categories of criteria:

- Foundation and planning (e.g., logic model)
- Operations and implementation (e.g., data quality, fidelity, staff-client relations, staff qualifications, supervision, turnover)
- Evaluation (e.g., research design, intended outcomes, sustainability).

The foundation and operations criteria are designed to identify areas in which the program excels and in which additional support is needed. The evaluation criteria determine to what extent the program can be considered evidence based.

The CSC staff who developed the assessment tool relied on research: for example, the tool examines attrition rates and staff supervision because weaknesses in these areas have been demonstrated to negatively affect implementation.[20] The tool was also evaluated by outside reviewers. After the tool was complete, it was piloted in four different programs to ensure that different raters would obtain consistent findings. The tool is now being used throughout CSC to comprehensively evaluate current programs and to assist with capacity building. Providers use it to undertake self-assessments, which enable them to see how to focus their efforts and make the necessary adjustments.

The goal of the assessment process is to create measurable, verifiable evidence of desirable outcomes. The following steps illustrate how locally developed programs can move in the direction of being evidence based:

1. Only programs that are based on sound theory and a logic model should be implemented.

2. Once programs are implemented, they must maintain fidelity to the original model and engage in high-quality data collection.

3. Assuming that fidelity and data collection are sound, a process evaluation should be undertaken.

4. If the process evaluation demonstrates that process outcomes are being met, more rigorous evaluation designs should be used to identify programmatic outcomes for children and families.

As a result of the accountability system, CSC has put in place many EBPs and is researching additional programs, either for direct implementation or to recommend to other community partners. In addition, CSC has developed a model and a data system to assist all locally developed programs to move in the direction of being evidence based.

Conclusion

When it comes to interventions designed to prevent crime, keep children in school, and reduce substance abuse, much of what has been thought to work had little or no effect.[21] Why do communities continue to fund, and practitioners continue to engage in, programs whose effectiveness has not been demonstrated? Among the many possible reasons, four stand out:

1. Local governments and social service providers are generally untrained in systems thinking, a holistic approach to understanding problems that focuses on the interdependence of structure, actions, and consequences.

2. Practitioners and funders tend to have a limited understanding of research and of the various designs that yield different levels of "knowing."

3. There is a disconnect between science and policy—that is, between what we know and what we choose to do.

4. Only a limited number of programs have been shown, through rigorous testing, to be effective.

The accountability system presented in this article is, at base, a decision support tool. It is designed to improve the well-being of children and families while making the best use of limited public resources. Most importantly, it is securely grounded in lessons learned: the emphasis on EBPs ensures that only those programs that have demonstrable social and financial value will be put in place. Properly implemented, the accountability system offers a robust response to a range of problems that bedevil much governmental activity, enabling policy makers to accurately determine how well taxpayer dollars are being spent, whether the activities being supported justify the investment, and how the job might be done better.

In sum, the accountability system has six goals:

1. Assisting policy makers in establishing priorities

2. Targeting resources to areas of highest need

3. Using resources to purchase the most effective programs available

4. Assisting communities in build the capacity to select and deliver the best programs

5. Promoting a culture of evidence

6. Allowing science to inform and serve policy.

Although the accountability system is a powerful tool, it is not enough in itself to effect the necessary changes. Ultimately, change must come from leaders who seek and accept accountability for better results from government; who are willing to frame and make decisions about the allocation of scarce resources; and who are willing to take the risks to make the hard choices that face them.

Notes

1. This article draws extensively from Lisa Williams-Taylor, *The Journey to Evidence-Based Programming: Changing the Face of Social Services* (Boynton Beach, Fla.: Children's Services Council [CSC] of Palm Beach County, 2010).

2. Scott W. Henggeler et al., *Multisystemic Therapy (MST)* (Denver: Center for the Study and Prevention of Violence [CSPV], University of Colorado at Boulder, 2001), xi.

3. Although the article focuses on the use of the accountability system in a local government setting, the principles of the system are equally applicable to state government.

4. See, for example, Henggeler et al., *Multisystemic Therapy*; Gilbert J. Botvin, Sharon F. Mihalic, and Jennifer K. Grotpeter, *Life Skills Training (LST)* (Denver: CSPV, 2002); David L. Olds et al., *Nurse-Family Partnership (NFP)* (Denver: CSPV, 2001); and Richard Mendel, *Prevention or Pork? A Hard-Headed Look at Youth-Oriented Anti-Crime Programs* (Washington, D.C.: American Youth Policy Forum, 1995).

5. Even more disquieting, the most commonly used nonrandomized study designs often yield incorrect findings—which can lead, in turn, to ineffective or even harmful policy and practice. See Sid Gardner and Alan Brown, "Cost Savings and Achievement Potential of Prevention Programs: Smart Cuts, Dumb Cuts and a Process to Tell the Difference," *PM Magazine* (March 2009): 20–23; Alan Brown, "Determining What Works (and What Doesn't) in the Public Sector," *PM Magazine* (July 2005): 22–25; Lisa Williams-Taylor, "Why Are Evidence-Based Programs So Important?" *PM Magazine* (May 2008): 24–27; and Mendel, *Prevention or Pork?*

6. See, for example, Steve Aos, Marna Miller, and Elizabeth Drake, *Evidence-Based Public Policy Options to Reduce Future Prison Construction, Criminal Justice Costs, and Crime Rates* (Olympia: Washington State Institute for Public Policy, 2006), 15, wsipp.wa.gov/rptfiles/06-10-1201.pdf (accessed January 11, 2011).

7. Sharon Mihalic, *The Importance of Implementation Fidelity* (Denver: CSPV, 2002), 1, incredibleyears.com/Library/items/fidelity-importance.pdf (accessed January 11, 2011).

8. As programs that have been proven effective are implemented in natural settings, under less favorable conditions, it becomes more likely that key components will be modified and that inconsistencies will develop in program delivery. Communities considering adaptations designed to meet their specific needs are advised to contact the program designer to determine whether such an adaptation was tried in the original effectiveness studies and whether it proved effective.

9. Andrew V. Dane and Barry H. Schneider, "Program Integrity in Primary and Early Secondary Prevention: Are Implementation Effects Out of Control?" *Clinical Psychology Review* 18, no. 1 (1998): 23–45.

10. Sharon F. Mihalic and Katherine Irwin, "Blueprints for Violence Prevention: From Research to Real-World Settings—Factors Influencing the Successful Replication of Model Programs," *Youth Violence and Juvenile Justice* 1, no. 4 (2003): 307–329; Sharon Mihalic, Abigail Fagan, and Susanne Argamaso, "Implementing the LifeSkills Training Drug Prevention Program: Factors Related to Implementation Fidelity," *Implementation Science* 3, no. 5 (2008), implementationscience.com/content/3/1/5 (accessed January 11, 2011).

11. Mihalic and Irwin, "Violence Prevention"; Mihalic, Fagan, and Argamaso, "Implementation Fidelity."

12. Mihalic, Fagan and Argamaso, "Implementation Fidelity."

13. This section is an adaptation of "Case Study: The Children's Services Council of Palm Beach County," in Williams-Taylor, *The Journey to Evidence-Based Programming*, 47–67.

14. *Primary prevention* refers to interventions that are undertaken before the onset of symptoms in an effort to avoid future problems.

15. In addition to conducting its own research, the committee consulted with experts from universities and outside organizations, including Arizona State University, the Coalition for Evidence-Based Policy, and the CSPV.

16. Logic models are visual depictions of what needs to be done in order to achieve targeted outcomes or goals.

17. Such inconsistencies create risks for funders and service providers; for example, when a local government selects an "evidence-based" program that has been evaluated by an organization with lax criteria, it risks funding or implementing a program that may not get the best results.

18. Some of the programs that were eliminated were reconsidered for their potential benefit to other systems (e.g., criminal justice, substance abuse, and mental health).

19. For further information about the rating instrument, see Williams-Taylor, *Journey to Evidence-Based Programming*.

20. Among the studies used in the course of developing the assessment tool were Pamela S. Hyde et al., *Turning Knowledge into Practice: A Manual for Behavioral Health Administrators and Practitioners about Understanding and Implementing Evidence-Based Practices* (Boston, Mass.: The Technical Assistance Collaborative, Inc., 2003); and Mihalic, Fagan, and Argamaso, "Implementation Fidelity."

21. For example, see Anthony Petrosino, Carolyn Turpin-Petrosino, and John Buehler, "'Scared Straight' and Other Juvenile Awareness Programs for Preventing Juvenile Delinquency," *Cochrane Database of Systematic Reviews* 2002, Issue 2, and "Youth Illicit Drug Use Prevention: DARE Long-Term Evaluations and Federal Efforts to Identify Effective Programs" (Washington, D.C.: Government Accountability Office, January 15, 2003), at gao.gov/new.items/d03172r.pdf (accessed January 11, 2011).

7

The Hurt Dividend: Residents' Appreciation for Local Government Services in Tough Times

Thomas I Miller
National Research Center, Inc.

Shannon E. Hayden
National Research Center, Inc.

If you enjoyed the last week of 2010, you probably were in Papua New Guinea, where you had only a spotty Web connection and cannibals to contend with. Those local government managers who stayed at home to enjoy the plenty of 2010 ushered in 2011 with headlines like these:

"Bill Would Allow Indiana Cities to Declare Bankruptcy"[1]

"Cuomo's Consolidation Plan a Work in Progress"[2]

"[El Paso, Texas] City Manager Denies Huge Police Shortage"[3]

"Winnebago County [Illinois] May Trim Funding for 10 Service Programs"[4]

"Defaults by Cities Looming as U.S. Mayors Say Deficits Hinder Debt Payment"[5]

Word on the street is that this country's future holidays will be brighter than the last couple, now that the tax compromise has become law, consumer spending is noticeably improved, and the stock market is returning household wealth that investors saw spin down the rabbit hole in late 2008. But if you don't yet see the turnaround, don't blame yourself: most pundits argue that government will remain sickly for months

SELECTED FINDINGS

Despite the severe economic downturn and clear worry about jobs and their own livelihoods, residents reported no decrease in their sentiments about local government services or quality of community life.

At the same time that residents' concerns about the speed of population growth were abating, the ever-present worry about the scarcity of jobs rose steeply. The percentage of respondents assessing job growth as being too slow rose from a low of 66% in 2007 to a high of 83% in 2010. At the same time, however, opinions about the opportunities for affordable housing improved.

Despite publicized cutbacks in local government services, ratings of the overall quality of life in the community have held relatively steady since 2004, averaging at about 65%, with partial results from 2010 showing a possible uptick.

after the private sector has revitalized. What could be worse than the economic tornado that swept away street sweeping, along with public safety personnel, library hours, the foliage in our street medians, and the lights on our streets? What could do more damage to the reputation of our hard work and the goodwill of our residents than to either deny services long expected or charge more for even less service than before?

This could be worse: your fine community could ruin your winning track record by slashing service ratings. Wouldn't attitudes of residents denied snow removal, code inspection, road repair, jobs, and economic development be as depressed as the housing and consumer markets that first impelled the service cuts? It is expected that with the country's fall off the economic cliff, those who received local government services fueled by revenue back when times were good will now record their dissatisfaction with lower service delivery ratings.

Background and Methodology

National Research Center, Inc. (NRC) has been leading innovation in citizen survey methods and reporting since 1990, and we have conducted more than 1,000 surveys to gather residents' perspectives since 1995. In 2001 NRC partnered with ICMA to offer The National Citizen Survey™ (The NCS™) to local governments. After nine years of responses to core questions asked of a representative sample of residents in hundreds of locales from Honolulu, Hawaii, to Montpelier, Vermont, we have grown a hardy repository of opinions of over 180,000 residents, a database that we tend meticulously. Over time, we have tested different wording and methods. From the thousands of responses we have received regarding scores of local government services and many characteristics of community quality, we (and others) have been able to reflect on current trends in resident opinions.

Sometimes we have found ourselves with an opportunity to analyze the impacts of phenomena of historic proportions. (Did residents' perspectives in surveys received just before September 11, 2001, differ from those in surveys received just after it? No. Does a once-in-100-year snowstorm shake residents' confidence in their local government's snow removal service? Yes. Can residents return to feeling safe even after a sniper terrorizes their city? Yes.)

So the fall 2008 financial meltdown and subsequent world economic crisis offered NRC the opportunity for another experiment. NRC researchers examined how residents reacted to the steep economic decline and, after comparing results across several years of data, found—as expected—that downbeat opinions reflected the bad times. It should be noted that the set of jurisdictions surveyed each year is not identical (some jurisdictions respond to the survey every year and most respond every other year) and does not represent a random subset of all U.S. cities and counties. Nevertheless, the volume of data gathered each year (from a couple thousand respondents in the first year to over 15,000 in each subsequent year) and the nature of broadly similar experiences among communities across the country during this time make these findings compelling.

The data for these analyses come from The NCS™, administered in a methodologically rigorous and transparent way in each community. The standard survey protocol involves a mailed survey with multiple contacts to a scientifically selected random sample of households. Surveys for participating jurisdictions are conducted year-round, and unless the questions are inapplicable to specific communities (e.g., questions pertaining to snow removal where snow removal is not an issue), the same questions are asked of all communities.

Findings

When residents were asked to speculate about the likely impact of the economy on their own household's financial well-being in the upcoming months, we found a slow but steady leading indicator of worsening worry that started in 2006, with 32% of respondents anticipating a negative impact, and spiked in 2009, the year following the worst quarter of stock market losses in generations (see Figure 7–1). By August of 2010, when the data for this report were analyzed, pessimism was abating, down from 37% to 33%, but economic doubts about the future remained about as strong as they had been in the time leading up to the start of the recession.

Another expected finding relates to residents' sentiments about population growth. Although for many years the word *growth* had virtually been an expletive that majorities in communities wanted deleted from the lexicon, as the economy worsened in 2008 (but even beginning in 2006), residents became less worried about their communities growing too fast—no doubt because migration had slowed as jobs, the engine of population growth, had slowed. After peaking in 2005, worry about speedy population growth (see Figure 7–2) started to decline just as pessimism about personal economic futures began to grow.

Two years later, the ever-present worry about too few jobs rose steeply. Over the decade, the fraction of respondents assessing job growth as being too slow rose by over 25% (Figure 7–3).

Considering the noticeable and predictable disquiet of residents during this period, NRC researchers and our clients wondered if personal concerns about the economy might have spread to an overall negative view of community and service. This point of view might be considered the "Pervasive Pain" suspicion. It assumes that the economic cloud that shadows our own homes and jobs pervades the entire landscape of local government services, darkening residents' sentiments about service quality and their communities as well. If that is

Figure 7-1 Expectations of the Economy's Negative Impact on Household Income in the Next Six Months

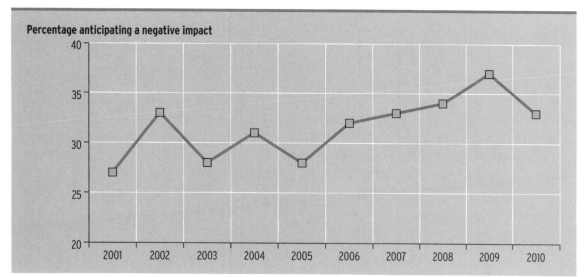

Figure 7-2 Assessment of Population Growth

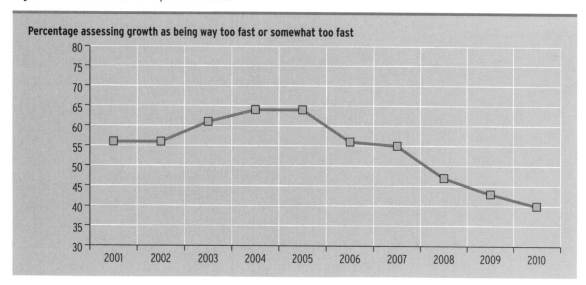

what occurred, one might also expect to see a decline in community ratings (e.g., for quality of life, the city as a place to live or retire or raise children) and service ratings (e.g., for police, fire, trash haul) over this period if the need to trim or eviscerate budgets impaired the quality of community and service delivery. If opinions get worse because services are cut, we might call this the "Poverty Penalty," a cut assessed to quality ratings concomitant with services that are not delivered at formerly high levels because of revenue shortfalls.

As it happened, all this commonsense speculation about service ratings going down when cupboards go bare turned out to be wrong. Across the thousands of

residents and hundreds of jurisdictions in our database, we found that dismal personal economic forecasts over these troubled times have not been predictive of feelings about the community. Nor have residents reported dissatisfaction with service delivery from their local government—at least not yet. While portents of a difficult personal economic future have not fully abated and worries about flagging job growth deepen, residents currently are either holding steady in their opinions of community life and service delivery or giving them even higher ratings than they did in better times past.

One dividend of the economic downturn has been a greater availability of affordable quality housing. While

Figure 7-3 Assessment of Job Growth

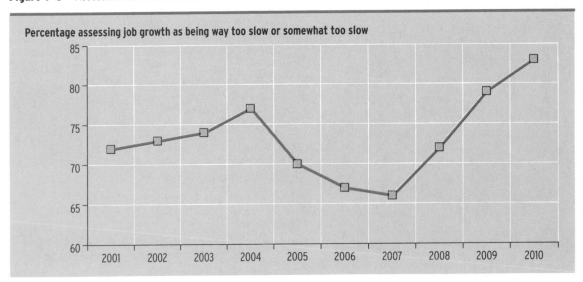

Figure 7-4 Perceptions of the Availability of Affordable Quality Housing

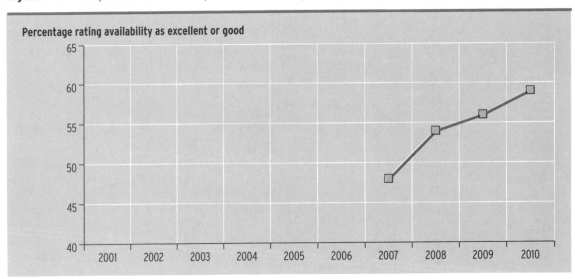

the spate of foreclosures that has accompanied the economic crisis has created a severe hardship for many who have lost their homes, the steep drop in housing prices across the country has meant, for others, homes that are more affordable. From 2007 to 2010, respondents' awareness of the opportunity presented in lower-cost housing rose by more than 10 percentage points (see Figure 7–4). Although the greater availability of affordable quality housing is a sad benefit of a market collapse, the drop in home prices, like respondents' growing pessimism about their personal economic futures or worries about job growth, still represents a direct measure of resident sentiment about the economy.

What about general ratings of community quality or service delivery that are not proxies for economic conditions? Here is where the surprise comes in. Ratings of the overall quality of life have held relatively steady since 2004, with close to two-thirds of respondents giving positive ratings; moreover, partial results from 2010 show a possible uptick (Figure 7–5). The same trend appears in answers to questions about the neighborhood or city as a place to live or retire (not shown). Despite the economic storm, residents still feel positively about where they live. Could these be signs of gratitude for the stability that community offers in tough times?

Figure 7-5   Perceptions of the Overall Quality of Life in the Community

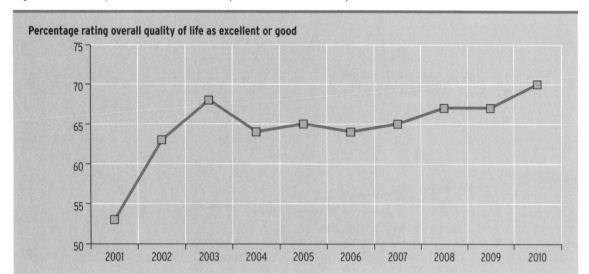

Figure 7-6   Perceptions of Police Services

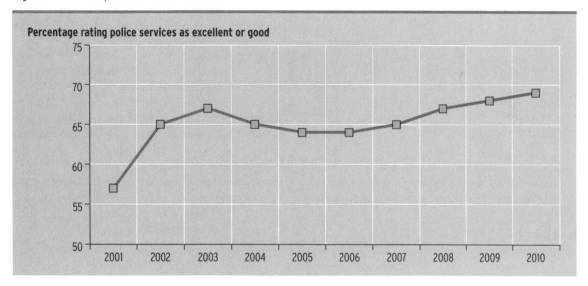

But even if we see stability or improvement in community ratings, what about ratings of local government services? Here, too, we find an unexpected dividend of the bad economy—something we call the "Hurt Dividend," indicative of an appreciation for local government services in distressed times. For example, since 2006, satisfaction with police services has been climbing steadily, reaching an all-time high of nearly 70% in 2010 (Figure 7-6).

Opinions about fire and emergency medical services have shown the same trend, as have opinions about street repair (not shown). In fact, virtually all examined services—trash haul, code enforcement, parks and recreation, library, and services overall—at least held steady in resident opinion over the two years following the economic crisis (not shown). Hypotheses to explain the unanticipated buoyancy of resident opinion abound but none with compelling proof.

- Are residents acknowledging that their local government deserves praise when it tries harder despite the turn of the screws? (The Hurt Dividend)

- Have local governments tried harder to provide top-quality services when the going got tough—and did they succeed? (Call it the "Too Good to Fail" theory)

- Has the press painted such a gloomy picture that residents expected worse than they actually experienced? Have the real problems in places depicted in the news made people in communities with less economic hardship more appreciative of the services they are receiving? Have cuts been more strategic—excising much more fat than muscle—than what the press has led residents to believe was required? (Name it "Oversold Gloom")

- Will the real impact of service cuts only begin to be felt in 2011 and beyond? (The "Hang onto Your Hat" hypothesis)

Conclusion

As the puzzle presented by our findings is contemplated, it is important to remember that these responses have been culled from the broadest cross-section of residents represented in well-conducted citizen surveys. And these residents do not sound like disgruntled citizens who come to public meetings every Tuesday night to gripe about how their local government is letting them down. Most residents in most communities across America are pleased with where they live and with the services their local government provides. That this sentiment of general approval has been (at least so far) sustained through this deep recession may say as much about real service delivery as it does about expectations and community engagement.

Local government managers should read several opportunities into these findings:

- If the Hurt Dividend keeps resident opinion strong about community and local government services because residents are especially grateful for the extraordinary effort when things get tough, manag-

ers could seek to harness that community goodwill by offering more opportunities for residents to participate in local governance and community service.

- If residents are pleased that good work continues through cutbacks caused by lean times because services are ramped up to overdrive, managers could continue to show that they are too good to fail by running lean and letting residents know how much has been and can be accomplished economically, even when the economy rebounds.
- If the media have oversold the gloominess of the downturn, managers could see how the local press can help them harness the goodwill that such pot-stirring creates.
- If the downturn's real impact on service delivery is just around the corner, managers could alert residents about the sacrifices to come and engage them in replacing some services with community labor and sweat.

Whatever the reason for residents' sustained support of local government services, the prospect for the future in any one town, city, or county depends on unique local conditions—for example, a strong economic development plan, new programs to purchase green spaces, better recycling, improved transportation connections. Managers must keep the relatively small investment in their trend line solid so that whatever happens in local government service delivery can be read in the spikes and turns of resident perspective.

NRC researchers will continue to cultivate the growing database of citizen survey opinions to find answers as they become apparent. In the meantime, managers should cash in on that Hurt Dividend.

Notes

1. Associated Press, "Bill Would Allow Indiana Cities to Declare Bankruptcy," (Fort Wayne) *Journal Gazette*, December 27, 2010, journalgazette.net/article/20101227/NEWS07/101229608 (accessed February 18, 2011).

2. Joseph Spector, "Cuomo's Consolidation Plan a Work in Progress," (Binghamton) *Pressconnects.com*, October 25, 2010, pressconnects.com/article/20101025/NEWS01/10250329/Cuomo-s-consolidation-plan-a-work-in-progress (accessed January 20, 2011).

3. Monica Balderrama, "City Manager Denies Huge Police Shortage," *KFOXTV.com*, December 21, 2010, kfoxtv.com/news/26211469/detail.html (accessed January 20, 2011).

4. Mike Wiser, "Winnebago County May Trim Funding for 10 Service Programs," *RRSTAR.COM*, November 22, 2010, rrstar.com/carousel/x1892562439/Winnebago-County-may-trim-funding-for-crime-fighting-programs?photo=0 (accessed January 20, 2011).

5. William Selway, "Defaults by Cities Looming as U.S. Mayors Say Deficits Hinder Debt Payment," *Bloomberg*, January 19, 2011, bloomberg.com/news/2011-01-19/cities-may-default-on-borrowings-amid-financial-strains-u-s-mayors-say.html (accessed January 20, 2011).

8

How Local Governments Are Navigating the Fiscal Crisis: Taking Stock and Looking Forward

Karen Thoreson
Alliance for Innovation

James H. Svara
Arizona State University, Center for Urban Innovation

The impacts of the fiscal crisis that is engulfing local governments in the United States have the potential to fundamentally reshape local governance. For a growing number of cities and counties, the shortfalls are substantially diminishing their resources and their capacity to deliver the range of services they provided previously. In a fiscal crisis, an immediate reaction is often to stop spending wherever possible and impose cross-the-board budget cuts. However, research on previous cutback periods indicates that reactive approaches are often counterproductive.[1] Uniform cuts applied across an organization do not distinguish essential from less important activities or productive from unproductive operations.

In a period of retrenchment, change is unavoidable because the decline in resources means that the government cannot maintain the status quo. Many officials have asserted that "a crisis is a terrible thing to waste," and it is common to hear brave calls to take advantage of trying times to make constructive changes. Pressing need can unleash the creativity of participants in the local government to come up with innovative possibilities. And, in fact, analysis of the conditions that engender award-winning innovation stresses the importance of crisis or challenge as a stimulus to change. In this

SELECTED FINDINGS

New fiscal realities have created an opportunity for local governments to redefine policies and standard operating procedures in innovative ways. Burdened with some of the highest foreclosure rates in the country, Las Vegas created "Stop NV Foreclosures," a program that focuses on preventing foreclosures rather than dealing solely with their aftermath.

Communities are assessing their core service areas and paring back funding for nonessential services. Downers Grove, Illinois, has developed a system for budget prioritization that helps staff, elected officials, and citizens identify and select the community's core services.

Many communities have embraced partnerships to create synergy, cost savings, and a new approach to providing local services. Alachua County, Florida, has entered into a dozen partnerships to leverage financial and human resources for comprehensive open space and land stewardship.

sense, the experience of innovative local governments supports the aphorism that "necessity is the mother of invention." Unfortunately, given what we have learned from previous cutback periods, necessity can simply be the mother of reaction. Often, those governments that handle cutbacks well are those that have made preparations in advance of the crisis or have strong organizational capacity for leadership, analysis, and decision making. Recognizing the value of these factors is important for understanding why some organizations succeed and others decline.

Local Governments in Fiscal Crisis

In the middle of 2009, ICMA conducted a survey of 2,214 city and county administrators for local governments exceeding 2,500 in population. One question asked respondents about the effects of the fiscal crisis on their communities, and their answers ranged across the spectrum as follows (n = 2,116)[2]:

- No impact: 0.5% (10)
- Minimal impact: 17.5% (370)
- Moderate impact: 44.5% (941)
- Significant impact: 30.8% (651)
- Severe impact: 6.8% (144)

Despite some positive signs in the economy, hardly any local governments are escaping any negative consequences, and nearly half are experiencing serious effects. According to the ICMA survey, the degree of impact increases with larger population size, especially in cities. For cities over 100,000 in population, more than three in five are grappling with major budget problems. In counties, the problems are somewhat greater as county size increases; however, the relationship is not as strong. According to the National League of Cities' *City Fiscal Conditions in 2010* report, nearly nine out of ten cities were less able to meet financial needs in both 2009 and 2010 than they were in the past.[3] Because of lags in property tax assessments and collections, declining property values continued to push down property tax receipts in 2010 and are expected to remain flat or decline further in 2011. Sales taxes did not decline as much in 2010 as they did the previous year, but they were still down 5% from 2009.

As a consequence of these conditions, local governments have been challenged to make immediate responses to the crisis; however, the fiscal strain continues, underscoring the need to develop new approaches for the future. As stated in a 2009 article in the *Harvard Business Review*, "It would be profoundly reassuring to view the current economic crisis as simply another rough spell that we need to get through.

Unfortunately, though, today's mix of urgency, high stakes and uncertainty will continue as the norm even after the recession ends."[4] When the Alliance for Innovation issued *Navigating the Fiscal Crisis: Tested Strategies for Local Leaders*, a white paper prepared for ICMA in 2009, it was not yet clear that the navigation challenge was not a quick plunge down icy rapids but rather a protracted effort to stay afloat and maintain a positive course through seas that will continue to be turbulent.[5]

Since the early months of 2009, the Alliance for Innovation has been monitoring how the budget crisis was affecting 11 local governments across the United States and what approaches were being taken to handle budget retrenchment. These governments (shown with their estimated 2009 populations)—Hickory, North Carolina (40,469); Jefferson County, Colorado (536,922); Las Vegas, Nevada (567,641); Overland Park, Kansas (174,907); Phoenix, Arizona (1,601,587); Polk County, Florida (583,403); Prince William County, Virginia (379,166); Rancho Cordova, California (62,939); Rockville, Maryland (62,105); San Antonio, Texas (1,373,668); and Washtenaw County, Michigan (347,563)—all have been members of the Alliance.

The governments vary in the severity of the financial difficulties they face—from Las Vegas and Phoenix, which are experiencing dramatic declines in sales taxes and development-related revenues, to San Antonio and Rockville, which have had only a modest loss of revenue at this point. Some governments have experienced protracted fiscal strain because of the shrinking traditional industrial base in Michigan and North Carolina and the state-imposed cuts in local taxes that preceded the fiscal crisis in Florida. What these governments have in common, however, appears to be a general and long-term commitment to change.

Management Capacity at the Start of the Crisis

Research on previous cutback periods shows that governments with strong management capacity are more likely to respond quickly and adopt proactive rather than reactive approaches.[6] All the local governments being monitored had generally established the policy and management preconditions that would enable them to anticipate a change in economic conditions and make adjustments based on strategic choices. Almost all of them had in place a set of strategies, goals, and priorities before the downturn began. When choices were made about what programs and services to continue or cut, these governments could be guided by goals that were already established rather than set in response to crisis conditions. They were also able to identify changes in financial conditions before those changes were generally obvious.

Hickory and Washtenaw County, for example, had experienced severe declines in 2002–2003 and took advantage of that experience to respond to the current crisis. Jefferson County had developed a five-year forecast in early 2006 that focused on ongoing and one-time revenues and historical costs and recognized a structural deficit that needed to be corrected. Phoenix had detected early signs of revenue decline in late 2006; Las Vegas and Polk County recognized the downturn in 2007, and Las Vegas has been able to track the severity of the crisis. Prince William County, through its five-year budgeting process, noted the steep increases in foreclosures and made adjustments quickly. These governments generally measure performance and can assess relative levels of effectiveness and efficiency. San Antonio has been working for the past three years to evaluate and in some cases eliminate lesser priority or inefficient programs. Many of the governments had taken functions related to development and new construction and had organized them into an enterprise fund that links the number of staff members with the level of activity, and permits "automatic" expansion and contraction of service levels and staffing. Phoenix had accumulated substantial reserves in its property tax collections for repayment of bonds.

From conversations with individual managers and small focus groups, we were able to form some impressions about the contribution of managers. There is an almost paradoxical contrast between the depressing conditions that local governments face and the enthusiasm expressed by city and county managers regarding the challenge before them. "Getting us through this crisis," one manager said, "is why I am a city manager." There is the widely shared view that the most serious fiscal crisis in 80 years gives them the opportunity to demonstrate extraordinary leadership that draws on all their knowledge, values, and skills. Indeed, many managers seem to shine in situations requiring fundamental adjustments. The anecdote presented above exemplifies their interest in reshaping the local government to meet their demanding professional standards.

The jurisdictions that have goals and priorities in place are using them as criteria for making cuts. In 2009 Las Vegas reassigned a department director to head a fundamental service review team (with assistance from an outside consultant). The team identified $150 million in needed cuts over four months, and nonessential services are being modified, consoli-

dated, or in some cases eliminated. Jefferson County plans to be looking at lower-priority programs and determining their ongoing relevance to its mission.[7] Although few cuts have been made so far, the county anticipates that programs with less priority will be downsized or eliminated in 2011. San Antonio has been working for the past three years to evaluate and, where warranted, eliminate lower-priority or inefficient programs; through that work, the city has eliminated $12.6 million in budget expenditures to date. In contrast, Phoenix has used its "Renewing Phoenix" project undertaken in 2008 to improve performance measurement as guide to its budget response, which resulted in budget cuts of $291 million and the elimination of over 1,500 positions in programs that were judged to be less important and underperforming.

Specific Actions by Monitored Cities and Counties

Beyond these budget-balancing efforts, the communities we monitored have undertaken a range of actions to change the scope of their services and the way they provide them. Their actions have been divided into three broad categories: innovations and improvements in current practices, organizational redesign, and new partnerships (see Table 8–1). Many of the actions span the categories. For example, Prince William County developed a new priority-based budgeting system that incorporates organizational redesign and ensures that the five-year budget is balanced every year. The county executive says that looking long term creates discipline in the staff and elected officials to look at how to pay for services and infrastructure in good times and bad. Partnering is enhanced by holding a "Budget Congress" where representatives of all key sectors of the county listen to all new budget requests and make recommendations to the county board on what to fund. This allows each sector to understand how cuts or additions may affect how they offer services.

It is worth noting the lessons that have been learned from communities that have long been engaged in budget balancing. Both Washtenaw County and Hickory mentioned a sort of "budget-cutting fatigue." Having been at the reduction game for nearly a decade, they both noted that employees, elected officials, and the community are tired of the relentless budget tightening. Hickory said that as they looked to create more shared services, some community members were asserting that they didn't want to do with less anymore! A different view was provided by Rockville, which experienced perhaps the

Table 8-1 Specific Actions by Alliance-Monitored Local Governments

Government	Innovation and improvement	Organizational design and process	Partnerships
Hickory hickorygov.com	– Is applying learned lessons from an earlier recession.	– Has eliminated, combined, or reduced services.	– Is looking at contracting some services that are currently being performed in-house and vice versa.
Jefferson County co.jefferson.co.us	– Has designed "Budgeting for Priorities" to align budgets with citizen-led priorities. – Is focusing on long-term strategies to deliver services at lower cost.	– Has co-located county department data centers. – Is reducing 58 county facilities to fewer strategically located buildings.	– Has partnered with another metro county to develop a shared data recovery center.
Las Vegas lasvegasnevada.gov	– Is installing a content management system to help improve efficiencies in Municipal Court. – Has modified nonmandated services in accordance with results from a fundamental service review. – Is developing IT solutions for "gaps" in service delivery. – Has undertaken initiative to reduce foreclosures.	– Has consolidated public information and graphic arts into a new Office of Communications. – Has implemented a leisure call center. – Has reorganized and consolidated departments and investigated outsourcing.	– Is working with the University of Las Vegas to involve the citizens in priority setting. – Has collaborated with other area cities.
Overland Park opkansas.org	– Is focusing on sustaining services rather than on increasing the financial burden on citizens.	– Is looking for a long-term structural fix, not short-term revenue generators.	– Has developed a partnership with a contractor to use recycled materials from the city's roads in road projects; one project alone saved the city $70,000.
Phoenix phoenix.gov	– Has instituted an annual IT planning process that reviews technology solutions citywide, doing more training electronically. – Has created an Innovations and Efficiency team that identified $10 million in operating revenue/savings beyond $291 million in other budget cuts.	– Has consolidated two departments and five functions into other departments. – Is revising standards for personnel span of control (number of people supervised).	– Is eliminating duplication through partnerships with the private sector (e.g., after-school programs are being taken over by nonprofits). – Has requested 3% giveback from vendors and received $750 thousand. – Is expanding volunteer opportunities, including trained citizen graffiti busters.

least impact of the financial crisis of any community monitored. Although the city was never in desperate straits, its elected officials and leadership nevertheless perceived that the crisis provided them with an opportunity to correct past actions and put the community on an even stronger financial foothold.

Some examples of new approaches from the monitored cities and counties as well as from other governments are highlighted in the sections that follow.

Innovation and Improvement

Innovation can be defined as the creation of a new process, approach, or program that achieves better results than what had been in place previously.

Innovation had been taking place in local governments prior to the current budget crisis; however, the depth of the new fiscal realities has allowed local governments to redefine policies and standard operating procedures in ways that might not have been politi-

Table 8-1 Specific Actions by Alliance-Monitored Local Governments

Government	Innovation and improvement	Organizational design and process	Partnerships
Polk County polk-county.net	– Has implemented a new budgeting system: Budgeting for Outcomes. – Is investigating different technologies, such as an audit of all departments to identify efficiency/cost-savings opportunities.	– Has implemented Better, Faster, Cheaper (an efficiency process) and created SHINE (an employee suggestion program). – Has reduced transit routes. – Has started a neighborhood grants program.	– Is partnering with the public for plant donation. – Has established My Region to connect Orlando and Tampa. – Has set up schools for facility sharing, community colleges for job training, and 17 municipalities to address water and safety needs.
Prince William County co.prince-william.va.us	– Has developed a cross-departmental group to advise the county executive. – Has divided into teams to develop criteria budget cuts/additions and rank priorities against the criteria.	– Has restructured its human services and building departments. – Is using a five-year balanced operating budget, which encourages long-range planning and restraint.	– Has partnered with lending institutions to create an employee home purchase program.
Rancho Cordova cityofranchocordova.org	– Has set up a "Money Matters" committee to focus on enhancing services in the downturn economy.	– Has taken advantage of the slowdown to look at refining processes, plan for new revenue streams, and plan for enhanced services.	– Has established a grants cabinet to bring departments and nonprofits together to look at how to leverage each other's information to be more grant competitive.
Rockville rockvillemd.gov	– Has increased transactions through the city website.	– Has implemented a talent management system. – Has combined all communication systems in the city manager's office.	– Is seeking a new operator for the city-owned golf course.
San Antonio sanantonio.gov	– Is continuing its evaluation of lesser-priority programs, which has so far resulted in a savings of $12.6 million.	– Is continually evaluating its programs to find efficiencies and redirect funds from lower to higher priorities. – Is reviewing its long-term personnel costs.	– Has developed a partnership with Goodwill, a nonprofit organization, to provide preventive health education at existing Goodwill facilities.
Washtenaw County ewashtenaw.org	– Has negotiated new labor contracts and preserved 250 jobs. – Has leveraged $6 million in new revenues.	– Has saved time and money with document imagery.	– Has partnered with Ann Arbor to share technology and with Ann Arbor SPARK (its business accelerator), along with universities, private sector, and other communities, to promote economic development and innovation.

cally possible before. Furthermore, despite budget limitations, local governments continue to innovate in other areas, as evidenced by case studies submitted to the Alliance for Innovation in 2009 and 2010. Some examples of these innovations are as follows.

- Jefferson County, Polk County, and Prince William County, as well as Downers Grove, Illinois, have developed new budgeting systems that place greater focus on prioritization, outcome measurement, and long-term perspective.

- Las Vegas, suffering from some of the highest foreclosure rates in the country, has created "Stop NV Foreclosures," a new program that focuses effort on preventing foreclosures rather than dealing solely with the aftermath of residents losing their homes.

- Phoenix has included $10 million worth of savings in its fiscal year (FY) 2011 operating budget that would come from innovations and efficiencies identified during the course of the year. By

December 2010, a team consisting of city staff and citizens came up with more than $10 million in general fund savings and more than $25 million in savings to all funds by eliminating positions, consolidating departments and functions, revising some transit services, rebidding some contracts, and realizing nearly $800,000 in "givebacks" from 100 private sector business partners who agreed to reduce contract fees.

- Johnson City, Tennessee, has revamped its economic development approach in a program called "Will This Float?" Focusing inward on the talent of local entrepreneurs, it has paired those emerging businesses with venture capital investment firms looking for new ideas.

- Novi, Michigan, has established a joint Public Safety Administration Team that unifies the police and fire service under one administrator while allowing each department to still retain its mission independence. This change has allowed for cost savings, significantly greater collaboration and improved databases, and systems more focused on results in this Detroit suburb.

Organizational Design and Process

Many communities have responded to the crisis by rethinking their general or strategic plan. Others have looked internally to how they could redesign fundamental processes to improve performance. An important feature in these efforts has been the involvement of a diverse set of actors.

- Polk County uses a "managing for results" approach that focuses on the delivery of seven classifications of services, from basic needs to recreation and cultural arts.[8] The county establishes what citizens' expectations for service delivery are and then measures on a quarterly basis how it is doing in meeting those expectations.

- Speak UP Winnipeg, Manitoba, has designed and implemented its first community planning process. To develop a collaborative vision, the city has connected directly with over 42,000 Winnipeggers: its website has had over 8.5 million hits, over 26,000 visitors, and over 1,650 posted blog comments. At a cost of $3.2 million, the 25-year development plan is uniquely suited this large Canadian city. As this *Year Book* goes to press, the plan is still awaiting provincial approval.

- "Durham First" in Durham, North Carolina, has brought a new focus to its staff through an emphasis on a "culture of service." The program highlights the benefits of being a public servant and the rewards of providing service to the community and to the organization.

- Philadelphia, Pennsylvania, has established public service areas in its most vulnerable neighborhoods. Working with local residents who set the agenda for change and have a say in service delivery, the city is changing the way it interacts with its neighborhoods and citizens.

- Downers Grove has developed a system for "budget prioritization" that helps staff, elected officials, and citizens identify and select the community's core services. That process has guided a challenging budget process and helped set a tone for service delivery in future years.

- Wellington, Florida, has established a safe neighborhood initiative along with the Palm Beach County Sheriff's Office, which provides police service under contract. The initiative has mobilized the entire city organization to refocus city resources on reaching citizens and children in vulnerable neighborhoods. Police services are provided through a contract with the Palm Beach County Sheriff's Office. Through this focus the city has achieved measured results, such as a 25% drop in serious crime, including drug cases and burglaries, over the previous year. There has also been an increased number of reports from residents to code compliance officers where vandalism or code violations have taken place. Before the Safe Neighborhood program was implemented, 90% of the calls were reactive responses to trouble. By the end of 2009, that volume was down to 25%, meaning that three-quarters of the deputies' calls were proactive stops to check on residents or area businesses.

Partnerships

Developing new partnerships includes engaging diverse stakeholders to join in efforts that create synergy, cost savings, and a new approach to providing local services.

- Phoenix and Polk County both have embraced the opportunity to work with citizens through robust volunteer programs.

- San Antonio has developed a partnership with Goodwill, a nonprofit organization, to provide preventive health education at existing Goodwill facilities and job training to the unemployed and underemployed.[9]

- Vista Grande Joint Use Library in Casa Grande, Arizona, has developed an improved, high-tech, and cost-saving facility that both the city and the school district use to the benefit of all local citizens.

- Alachua County, Florida, has converted its conservationist principles into a dozen partnerships that leverage financial and human resources for comprehensive open space and land stewardship.

Looking to the Future

The fiscal crisis is producing change and rethinking, but substantial innovation is only beginning. There are impediments to mixing creativity and crisis, particularly in the initial period of downturn. Resources are limited for investing in innovation, and a lot of time and attention is being given to making reductions rather than improvements. At the same time, however, the sustained crisis is forcing local governments to go beyond immediate actions that produce savings in one budget year but cannot be repeated or sustained. We do not yet know what the full extent of change in practices will be. This is the point at which innovation may be more evident as the rebuilding process begins. During final interviews with our 11 communities, officials were asked to look to the future and describe what they expect the "new normal" will look like. Here are insights from their comments.

There will be much greater focus on and discipline related to core priorities.
Each local government spoke to this in its own way. Most plan to continue a focus on core services—those that reflect the revised priorities of citizens and officials. They are also looking to build capacity through reserves and financial modeling systems to ensure that they are better able to weather any future crisis without having to cut into core services or the resources needed to provide them. Rancho Cordova, California, quickly responded to the downturn by eliminating nonessential services and reducing contract staff in areas where requests for services had dropped. Las Vegas established an essential service review that identified core services and corresponding cuts in programs that did not address those needs. Communities that were not monitored through the two-year-long project are also stepping up.

Growth for our community or region will probably not be same again—maybe ever.
A number of local managers noted that as the community grew in good times, their organizations grew dramatically as well and were able to add increments to program funding with little annual review. These governments also expanded their infrastructure to attract new growth. But changing economic con-

ditions and demographics are expected to mean a decline in growth, and any new growth is more likely to be accommodated through in-fill development. New investments are not expected soon, but the most frequently mentioned areas for new investments are sustainability, economic development, and technology.

Community expectations will need to shift.
Many managers said that "we can't be or have everything" anymore. For decades local governments have been using tax revenues to subsidize services that might not be considered public goods. Now, however, citizens should expect to pay closer to the full cost for specialized services that benefit an individual (e.g., recreation classes, fairground use, some library services, parking meters) rather than the whole community (e.g., streets, public safety, elections). Moreover, citizens can no longer look to government to solve their problems, nor should government view citizens as passive consumers of services. Increasingly, service needs and community problems must be addressed through a partnership between government, community organizations, and citizens. This new approach is a major theme in the white paper on citizen engagement recently released by the Alliance.[10]

Service production and delivery will need to change.
As a consequence of these changed expectation, service delivery will continue to change. Some governments are stressing a "right-sourcing" approach, critically reexamining the mix of services delivered internally and through outsourcing. Many local governments are exploring how to better involve citizens in the delivery of public services. A shift from a government-centered model to coproduction with citizens is anticipated. Neighborhoods will shift from a dependent to an interdependent state. The approaches include increasing opportunities for volunteerism; encouraging neighborhoods to raise funds to support nearby parks and other amenities; and generally including residents in decision-making roles in areas that affect their quality of life. In general, this trend could greatly affect how local governments operate in the future.

Conclusion

It appears that the overall response to the current fiscal crisis has been more proactive and strategic than it was in earlier retrenchment periods. In the past, most governments simply hunkered down and made across-the-board cuts without making distinctions between programs. Today, local governments are making both general cuts and targeted reductions. Guided by existing priorities, over three in five local governments throughout the country with significant or severe budget reductions have made targeted cuts, and about half have made cuts to all departments.[11] In many of the monitored communities that made budget adjustments guided by existing priorities, the next step is to reexamine the priorities themselves and fundamentally rethink how the local government functions.

The crisis has prompted deep reflection on what the role of local government will be in the future. It has not been a temporary downturn followed by a return to previous conditions. The duration and severity of the crisis have raised questions about how government is financed, what services it provides, and how it interacts with citizens and other organizations in addressing community needs. The new reality has set the stage for true discourse among officials and citizens on the future of communities and the local governments that serve them.

Notes

1. Charles H. Levine, "More on Cut-back Management: Hard Questions for Hard Times," *Public Administration Review* 39, no. 2 (1979): 179–183.

2. Gerald J. Miller, "Weathering the Local Government Fiscal Crisis: Short-Term Measures or Permanent Change?" *The Municipal Year Book 2010* (Washington, D.C.: ICMA, 2010), 34.

3. Christopher W. Hoene and Michael A. Pagano, *City Fiscal Conditions in 2010* (Washington, D.C.: National League of Cities, October 2010), nlc.org/ASSETS/AE26793318A645C795C9CD11DAB3B39B/RB_CityFiscalConditions2010.pdf (accessed December 2, 2010).

4. Ronald Heifetz, Alexander Grashow, and Marty Linsky, "Leadership in a (Permanent) Crisis," *Harvard Business Review* (July/August 2009), coffou.com/bm ~ doc/leadership-in-a-permanent-crisis.pdf (accessed December 2, 2010).

5. Gerald J. Miller and James H. Svara, eds., *Navigating the Fiscal Crisis: Tested Strategies for Local Leaders* (white paper prepared for ICMA, Arizona State University, January 2009), icma.org/en/icma/priorities/public_policy/policy_papers (accessed December 2, 2010).

6. Robert J. O'Neill Jr., "Excelling in Times of Fiscal Distress," *Governing* (October 1, 2008), governing.com/columns/mgmt-insights/Excelling-in-Times-of.html (accessed December 2, 2010); James H. Svara, "Innovation and Constructive Change in Cutback Management: A Compendium of Research and Commentary by Local Government Leaders" (background paper for *Navigating the Fiscal Crisis*, see note 5).

7. Jefferson County has determined that a low-priority activity such as the fairground can continue as it is entirely self-supporting; see Scott Collins, Brandon Hanlon, and Ed Scholz, "Faltering Economy: Time to Thoughtfully Challenge the Status Quo," *PM Magazine* 91 (June 2009): 6–9.

8. For more information on this program, see Karen Thoreson and James H. Svara, "Award-Winning Local Government Innovations, 2009," in *The Municipal Year Book 2010* (Washington, D.C.: ICMA, 2010), 43.

9. For more information on this program, see Thoreson and Svara, "Award-Winning Local Government Innovations, 2009," 39.

10. James H. Svara and Janet Denhart, eds., *Connected Communities: Local Governments as a Partner in Citizen Engagement and Community Building* (white paper prepared for the Alliance for Innovation, Arizona State University, October 15, 2010), transformgov.org/Documents/Document/Document/301763 (accessed December 2, 2010).

11. Miller, "Weathering the Local Government Fiscal Crisis," 36; James H. Svara, "Local Government Leadership in the Fiscal Crisis in the United States of America," *International Journal of Policy Studies* 1 (July 2010): 18.

9

Police and Fire Personnel, Salaries, and Expenditures for 2010

Evelina R. Moulder
ICMA

Unlike 2009, when it appeared that police and fire departments were shielded from budget cuts, 2010 brought financial challenges of such severity to local governments that police and fire departments saw their budgets reduced just like those of other local government departments. In response, some police departments are reducing the number of civilian staff, and others are telling residents to file online reports for petty crimes in order to allow the department to focus on violent crimes. Fire departments, too, are finding ways to cope with budget cuts in personnel and expenditures for equipment.

The statistics in this annual article are not intended to be used for benchmarking, which requires that many factors be considered to identify localities of similar characteristics, such as population density, vulnerability to natural disasters, and the like. Rather, these statistics are meant to provide a general picture of police and fire personnel and expenditures for each year.

Methodology

The data in this research were collected from responses to ICMA's annual *Police and Fire Personnel, Salaries, and Expenditures* survey, which was mailed in February 2010 to 3,286 municipalities with populations of 10,000 or more (Table 9–1). A second survey was sent to those local governments that did not respond to the first. Respondents had a choice of completing and submitting the survey on the Web or by mail. A total

SELECTED FINDINGS

The average entrance salaries are $43,432 for police and $40,470 for fire personnel. The average maximum salaries for police and fire personnel are $61,478 and $55,244, respectively.

The average maximum salary including longevity pay for police officers is $65,553. These salaries vary significantly by geographic division: East South-Central cities show the lowest average maximums while Mid-Atlantic and Pacific Coast cities show the highest. One possible explanation is the cost of living: median home prices in the central United States are much lower than they are on the East and West Coasts.

Per capita average overtime expenditures were $12.67 for police and $9.78 for fire departments.

The average per capita total departmental expenditures 2010 were $282.22 for police and $177.25 for fire departments.

of 1,235 jurisdictions submitted surveys for an overall response rate of 38%, which is almost identical to last year's response rate.

The survey response patterns are presented in Table 9–1 by population group, geographic region,

Table 9-1 Survey Response

Classification	No. of municipalities[1] surveyed (A)	Respondents No.	Respondents % of (A)
Total	3,286	1,235	38
Population group			
Over 1,000,000	9	2	22
500,000-1,000,000	3	7	30
250,000-499,999	36	9	25
100,000-249,999	179	69	39
50,000-99,999	419	152	36
25,000-49,999	784	298	38
10,000-24,999	1,836	698	38
Geographic region			
Northeast	892	226	25
North-Central	922	369	40
South	846	373	44
West	626	267	43
Geographic division			
New England	352	96	27
Mid-Atlantic	540	130	24
East North-Central	675	242	36
West North-Central	248	127	51
South Atlantic	387	194	50
East South-Central	169	48	28
West South-Central	289	131	45
Mountain	161	67	42
Pacific Coast	465	200	43
Metro status			
Central	539	204	38
Suburban	2,127	775	36
Independent	620	256	41

1   For a definition of terms, please see "Inside the *Year Book*," xi.

geographic division, and metropolitan status. There is variation in the response patterns by population size, with a low of 22% in cities with over 1,000,000 population (two cities—Phoenix and San Antonio—responded in this population group) and a high of 39% in cities with a population of 100,000–249,999. The patterns by geographic division show that Mid-Atlantic and New England jurisdictions were the least likely to complete the questionnaire (24% and 27%, respectively), while South Atlantic and West North-Central jurisdictions were the most likely to do so (50% and 51%, respectively). There is slight variation by metropolitan status.

Cities that reported a public safety department (consolidated police and fire)

Calexico, CA	Mexico, MO
Ceres, CA	Sikeston, MO
Sunnyvale, CA	West Plains, MO
Longmont, CO	Kinston, NC
Greenacres, FL	Morganton, NC
Alpharetta, GA	Brook Park, OH
Bainbridge, GA	Grants Pass, OR
East Grand Rapids, MI	Cayce, SC
Escanaba, MI	North Augusta, SC
Farmington, MI	Spartanburg, SC
Grand Haven, MI	Mitchell, SD
Novi, MI	East Ridge, TN
Gladstone, MO	Ashwaubenon, WI
Maryville, MO	

Administration

Respondents were asked several questions about service provision and delivery. Virtually all the jurisdictions responding to the 2010 survey (96%) indicated that they provide police services, and 85% reported that they provide fire services (not shown)—figures that have remained almost identical for several years. Twenty-seven jurisdictions reported having a public safety department. To be counted among these respondents, a city had to report "public safety department" as the type of service for both police and fire (see sidebar above).

These data on cities that provide police and fire services do not necessarily mean that all these cities actually deliver each service: 4% of jurisdictions reported contracting with another government for police service delivery (Figure 9–1). The highest percentage of cities reporting this arrangement is in the Pacific Coast division (20%) (not shown). Among the 48 cities that do not provide police services, 44 answered the question about how the services are provided, and of those, the majority (31), all of which are under 250,000 in population, reported that the county provides the service (not shown). Five cities reported a regional police service; none reported a special district.

Of the cities that provide fire protection services, the majority (65%) reported having a full-time paid

Figure 9-1 Type of Service, 2010

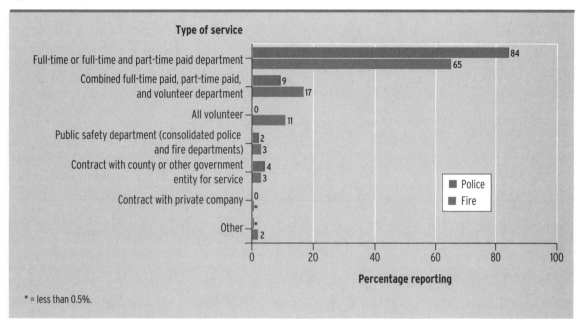

* = less than 0.5%.

or a full-time and part-time paid fire department, 17 % reported a combination of paid and volunteer fire personnel, 11 % reported an all-volunteer fire department, and the remaining cities said they contract out for such services or provide them in some other way (Figure 9-1). Among the 181 cities that do not provide fire services, 174 provided information on how the services are provided, and of those, 51 % reported that services are provided by a special district, and 29 % indicated that the county provides the service (not shown). Regional fire services were reported by 8 %.

Personnel

The average size of the full-time paid workforce for both police and fire departments is presented in Table 9-2. The data include both uniformed and civilian, or nonuniformed, personnel. The average number of total police department employees, 114, represents a decrease over the average number reported in 2009, which was 128. The average number of fire personnel is 76, compared with 79 in 2009. As with all averages in this article, these fluctuate depending on which cities report information each year. Using the average number of personnel per capita normalizes the data. The average number of full-time paid police personnel per 1,000 population is 2.73; that of fire personnel is 1.71.

The average numbers of full-time police personnel by population category in 2010 differ somewhat from

the 2009 figures. Because only Phoenix responded in 2009, the averages for cities over 1,000,000 should not be compared; however, cities in the 500,000–1,000,000 population group show an average of 1,868 police personnel in 2009, compared with 1,931 police employees in 2010. In 2009, only eight cities responded in that population group; in 2010 five cities reported. If the seven cities over 500,000 are excluded, the per capita police personnel figures vary somewhat between a high of 2.81 for the population group 10,000–24,999 and a low of 2.53 for the group 50,000–99,999.

The patterns for fire departments are similar to those for police departments (Table 9-2). Cities in the population group of 500,000–1,000,000 show an average of 1,105 fire employees in 2010, compared with 996 in 2009. Continuing down in population, the average for communities in the 10,000–24,999 population group is 28, identical to the average in 2009.

With the exception of cities in the 500,000–1,000,000 population group, per capita figures per 1,000 population show slightly higher numbers of full-time paid fire personnel among cities under 100,000, from a high of 1.74 for the population group 10,000–24,999 to a low of 1.58 for the population group 100,000–249,999.

The cross-sectional patterns by geographic division indicate that municipalities in the Mountain division have the highest average number of full-time police employees (223) and that those in the New England division have the lowest (50), followed

Table 9-2 Full-Time Paid Personnel, 2010

Classification	Police			Fire		
	No. of cities reporting	Mean	Per capita per 1,000 population	No. of cities reporting	Mean	Per capita per 1,000 population
Total	1,047	114	2.73	850	76	1.71
Population group						
Over 1,000,000	2	3,870	3.09	2	1,912	1.55
500,000–1,000,000	5	1,931	3.34	5	1,105	1.89
250,000–499,999	8	977	2.79	7	579	1.60
100,000–249,999	58	396	2.63	55	240	1.58
50,000–99,999	120	172	2.53	111	110	1.63
25,000–49,999	250	92	2.64	214	61	1.73
10,000–24,999	604	45	2.81	456	28	1.74
Geographic division						
New England	83	50	2.31	76	43	1.69
Mid-Atlantic	106	51	2.19	55	34	1.19
East North-Central	204	68	2.33	176	49	1.57
West North-Central	117	84	2.35	92	52	1.17
South Atlantic	173	140	3.83	142	92	2.39
East South-Central	41	201	3.39	41	119	2.63
West South-Central	125	191	3.01	118	124	1.86
Mountain	59	223	3.14	45	146	1.68
Pacific Coast	139	117	2.30	105	67	1.30
Metro status						
Central	184	322	2.86	176	200	1.87
Suburban	627	76	2.67	468	47	1.63
Independent	236	52	2.78	206	35	1.77

closely by those in the Mid-Atlantic division (51) (Table 9–2)—patterns similar to those in 2009. Regarding full-time paid fire employees, the highest average number is again in the Mountain division (146), and the lowest is in the Mid-Atlantic division (34). For both the police and fire departments, the South Atlantic and East-South Central divisions show the highest average numbers of full-time paid personnel per 1,000 population; for police, the lowest number of full-time paid personnel per 1,000 population is in the Mid-Atlantic division, while for fire, the lowest number is in the West North-Central division, followed closely by the Mid-Atlantic division.

Not surprisingly, metropolitan status patterns indicate that central cities have larger police and fire departments than either independent or suburban cities. In 2010, central cities averaged 322 full-time paid police department personnel, compared with 76 and 52 for suburban and independent communities,

respectively (Table 9–2). The figures for full-time paid fire department personnel show a similar pattern, as the central cities show an average of 200, compared with 47 for suburban cities and 35 for independent cities. These differences, of course, reflect population differences in the communities served and are consistent with the patterns reported in previous surveys. The per capita figures per 1,000 population show the highest per capita full-time paid police and fire department personnel in central and independent jurisdictions.

Figure 9–2 shows the changes over ten years in the average number of full-time employees per 1,000 population for both services.

Table 9–3 presents the average numbers of full-time uniformed, or sworn, personnel in police and fire departments as of January 1, 2010. Among reporting cities, these numbers are 88 for police departments and 74 for fire departments, lower than the 2009

Figure 9-2   Police and Fire Trends in Employees per 1,000 Population, 2000–2010

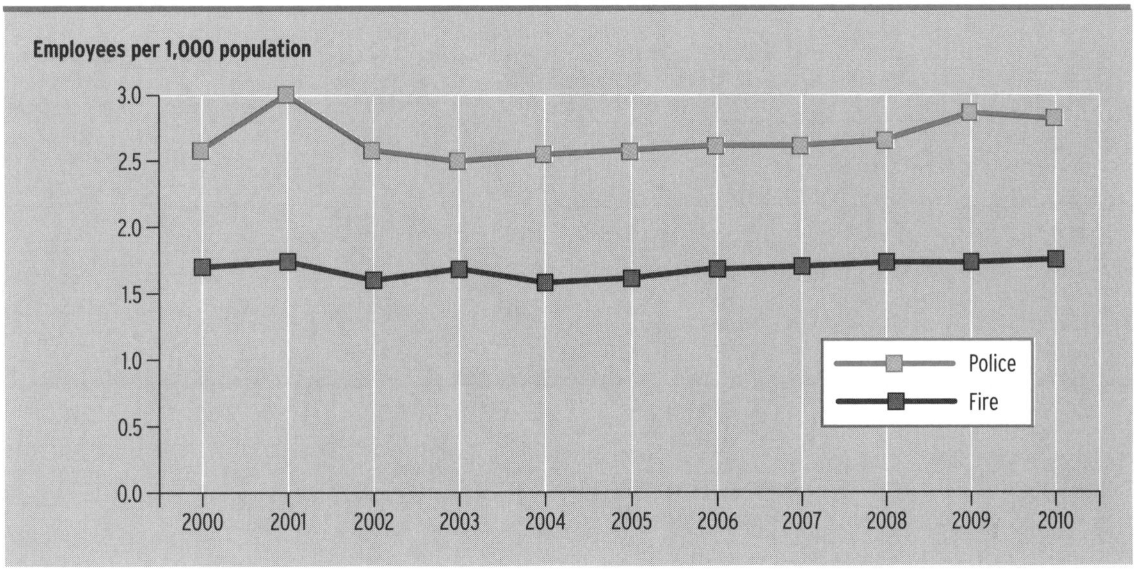

Employees per 1,000 population

Table 9-3   Uniformed Sworn Personnel, 2010

	Police			Fire		
Classification	No. of cities reporting	Mean	Per capita per 1,000 population	No. of cities reporting	Mean	Per capita per 1,000 population
Total	1,044	88	2.12	797	74	1.64
Population group						
Over 1,000,000	2	2,944	2.36	2	1,660	1.35
500,000–1,000,000	5	1,543	2.67	5	1,014	1.73
250,000–499,999	9	746	2.15	8	532	1.50
100,000–249,999	60	294	1.94	55	217	1.42
50,000–99,999	120	126	1.86	106	102	1.53
25,000–49,999	250	70	2.02	207	58	1.65
10,000–24,999	598	36	2.24	414	28	1.71
Geographic division						
New England	84	41	1.90	68	44	1.75
Mid-Atlantic	99	45	1.92	41	41	1.33
East North-Central	204	56	1.85	163	51	1.51
West North-Central	117	67	1.87	80	51	1.13
South Atlantic	171	108	2.98	139	86	2.24
East South-Central	42	160	2.70	41	111	2.48
West South-Central	125	148	2.24	117	118	1.76
Mountain	62	159	2.30	46	120	1.41
Pacific Coast	140	81	1.61	102	60	1.14
Metro status						
Central	185	253	2.22	175	186	1.74
Suburban	627	57	2.06	427	46	1.57
Independent	232	41	2.23	195	34	1.71

Table 9-4   Minimum Crew per Fire Apparatus, 2010

Classification	Pumpers		Ladders		Rescue units	
	No. of cities reporting	Average minimum crew	No. of cities reporting	Average minimum crew	No. of cities reporting	Average minimum crew
Total	598	3.1	552	3.0	453	2.4
Population group						
Over 1,000,000	2	4.0	2	4.0	1	2.0
500,000-1,000,000	4	4.0	4	3.8	3	2.7
250,000-499,999	8	3.6	8	3.5	7	3.0
100,000-249,999	48	3.4	48	3.3	40	2.5
50,000-99,999	92	3.1	92	3.1	79	2.3
25,000-49,999	165	3.0	158	2.9	122	2.2
10,000-24,999	279	3.1	240	2.9	201	2.6
Geographic division						
New England	32	2.8	29	2.5	28	2.2
Mid-Atlantic	42	3.6	39	3.3	30	3.1
East North-Central	100	3.0	91	2.8	84	2.4
West North-Central	68	3.4	63	3.1	51	2.7
South Atlantic	113	3.0	106	2.8	77	2.3
East South-Central	31	3.0	30	2.8	24	2.4
West South-Central	86	3.2	79	2.9	68	2.4
Mountain	34	3.5	33	3.5	21	2.1
Pacific Coast	92	2.9	82	3.2	70	2.3
Metro status						
Central	148	3.2	144	3.0	116	2.4
Suburban	329	3.1	298	3.0	260	2.4
Independent	121	3.0	110	2.8	77	2.6

averages (128 and 79, respectively). For the two cities reporting with over 1,000,000 in population, the average number of sworn police personnel reported in 2010 is 2,944. Predictably, the remaining averages are consistently correlated with the population size of the responding jurisdictions: the police department averages range from 1,543 for cities of 500,000–1,000,000 to 36 for cities of 10,000–24,999. The figures per 1,000 population show a high of 2.67 for the 500,000–1,000,000 population group and a low of 1.86 for cities of 50,000–99,999.

The East South-Central and Mountain divisions show the highest average numbers of sworn full-time police personnel (160 and 159, respectively), while the New England and Mid-Atlantic divisions show the lowest (41 and 45, respectively) (Table 9–3). When per capita per 1,000 population figures are reviewed, the South Atlantic (2.98) and East South-Central (2.70) divisions are the highest, and the Pacific Coast division is the lowest (1.61), which was also the case in 2009. For fire personnel, the Mountain division again shows the highest average number of uniformed per-

sonnel per capita (120), followed closely by the West South-Central division (118), while the Mid-Atlantic and New England divisions again show the lowest (41 and 44, respectively). When per capita per 1,000 population figures are reviewed, the East South-Central division shows the highest average (2.48) and the West North-Central shows the lowest (1.13), as was seen in 2009. The differences by metropolitan status show that independent and central cities have higher per capita numbers of uniformed personnel in both services than do suburban communities.

Staffing Requirements for Fire Personnel

All reporting jurisdictions with a population of 250,000 and over reported minimum staffing requirements, as did 81% of reporting jurisdictions overall (not shown). The responses by geographic division indicate that the majority of jurisdictions in all areas of the country have a minimum requirement, and that more than 90% of cities in the South Atlantic, Pacific Coast, East

Table 9-5   Police Officers' Annual Base Salary, 2010

Classification	Entrance salary					Maximum salary					No. of years to reach maximum	
	No. of cities reporting	Mean ($)	First quartile ($)	Median ($)	Third quartile ($)	No. of cities reporting	Mean ($)	First quartile ($)	Median ($)	Third quartile ($)	No. of cities reporting	Mean
Total	1,072	43,432	35,683	42,224	49,417	1,040	61,478	50,955	59,640	69,870	865	8
Population group												
Over 1,000,000	2	44,920	41,630	44,920	48,210	2	66,260	63,190	66,260	69,330	2	15
500,000-1,000,000	5	46,059	42,102	47,878	48,838	5	63,585	54,729	54,747	72,321	5	12
250,000-499,999	9	47,333	41,550	42,927	52,994	9	70,957	63,383	65,360	74,360	8	7
100,000-249,999	59	50,322	38,683	49,629	57,476	59	70,848	62,226	68,391	79,774	54	9
50,000-99,999	122	47,646	40,598	46,319	54,198	122	66,139	58,235	65,795	75,240	98	8
25,000-49,999	256	45,267	36,876	44,140	51,298	251	62,440	51,859	59,760	70,936	216	7
10,000-24,999	619	41,103	33,987	40,450	46,636	592	58,998	48,249	56,410	67,206	482	7
Geographic division												
New England	85	44,246	39,728	43,868	47,271	80	56,221	50,871	55,016	59,666	79	8
Mid-Atlantic	110	45,481	39,100	45,361	50,943	107	78,298	67,850	76,627	89,884	109	6
East North-Central	211	44,860	39,060	44,648	50,705	206	61,223	52,828	61,152	69,452	199	6
West North-Central	119	39,625	34,816	39,864	44,942	113	54,175	46,342	54,630	63,125	95	7
South Atlantic	174	36,084	31,481	34,620	39,975	167	56,687	48,207	55,000	65,346	80	12
East South-Central	43	30,480	27,380	30,740	33,242	40	45,907	39,918	45,841	50,440	32	12
West South-Central	129	40,092	34,196	40,003	45,859	126	53,424	44,380	54,394	62,980	97	10
Mountain	61	42,138	36,982	41,494	46,829	61	60,277	51,574	59,845	67,056	42	9
Pacific Coast	140	59,163	51,652	57,703	64,949	140	75,831	66,178	74,434	82,080	132	5
Metro status												
Central	188	42,923	34,638	41,157	48,118	186	60,477	51,388	59,234	66,792	153	9
Suburban	641	46,025	38,901	44,990	51,804	621	66,071	55,180	64,875	74,619	532	7
Independent	243	36,985	31,220	35,696	41,568	233	50,035	42,016	48,336	55,896	180	8

South-Central, and West South-Central divisions have requirements or policies advising minimum staffing per shift. This pattern is similar to that reported in previous surveys, as are the differences by metropolitan status, which range from a low of 77% for suburban cities to a high of 93% for central cities.

The average minimum staffing for apparatus—pumpers, ladders, and other equipment—is presented in Table 9–4. For pumpers, ladders, and rescue units, the average minimum crew is generally higher among larger cities.

Hours Worked per Shift

Several questions were asked regarding the average number of hours worked per week and per shift for both services. The results, which are not displayed, are as expected. Approximately 76% of jurisdictions reported that their police department employees work 40 hours a week, and 16% reported a 42-hour workweek. Fire departments had more varied responses to the workweek question: 43% indicated that their

workweek is 56 hours, and only 9% reported a 40-hour workweek. Twenty-six percent reported a 50- to 54-hour workweek in 2010.

The average number of hours worked per shift also varies between the services. Thirty-nine percent of the cities indicated that their police officers work an 8-hour shift, and 56% reported 10- or 12-hour shifts (not shown). Fire departments, on the other hand, are most likely to have 24-hour shifts (79%), virtually unchanged from 2009.

Salary and Longevity Pay

Tables 9–5 through 9–8 present various salary and longevity pay data for full-time police officers and firefighters.

Minimum and Maximum Salaries

Tables 9–5 and 9–6 present detailed entrance and maximum salary data for police officers and firefighters, respectively, as well as the average number of years required for each to reach the maximum. In

Table 9-6 Firefighters' Annual Base Salary, 2010

Classification	Entrance salary					Maximum salary					No. of years to reach maximum	
	No. of cities reporting	Mean ($)	First quartile ($)	Median ($)	Third quartile ($)	No. of cities reporting	Mean ($)	First quartile ($)	Median ($)	Third quartile ($)	No. of cities reporting	Mean
Total	776	40,470	33,005	39,000	46,268	764	55,244	46,338	53,594	63,094	622	8
Population group												
Over 1,000,000	2	46,708	46,661	46,708	46,754	2	60,522	57,801	60,522	63,242	2	12
500,000–1,000,000	5	43,121	40,027	45,014	47,986	5	65,194	57,775	61,235	77,602	5	9
250,000–499,999	8	41,087	35,913	37,818	44,680	8	64,920	55,076	58,297	73,184	7	8
100,000–249,999	53	45,034	36,000	42,486	50,778	53	62,713	52,486	62,055	68,392	47	8
50,000–99,999	101	44,758	37,871	42,666	50,641	101	60,901	52,000	61,510	69,310	82	7
25,000–49,999	201	41,968	34,162	40,365	47,533	201	56,719	48,430	55,014	63,456	175	7
10,000–24,999	406	37,990	30,944	36,968	43,962	394	51,688	42,682	50,627	59,600	304	8
Geographic division												
New England	69	40,382	36,573	40,325	44,005	65	52,057	46,936	51,034	55,735	60	8
Mid-Atlantic	41	41,337	35,000	39,727	45,136	44	59,512	50,663	57,947	78,560	43	7
East North-Central	166	43,167	37,544	42,750	48,280	161	57,496	49,008	56,800	65,620	155	6
West North-Central	73	37,353	32,162	36,442	43,225	73	49,815	44,904	50,116	55,053	62	8
South Atlantic	134	32,435	28,399	31,742	35,295	131	52,737	43,688	50,520	57,085	57	12
East South-Central	37	29,355	25,813	28,986	32,864	35	43,879	39,512	44,294	49,842	26	12
West South-Central	116	38,158	32,507	38,156	44,931	114	48,894	40,393	50,136	58,488	89	8
Mountain	42	39,039	35,566	39,255	43,404	43	54,490	49,777	53,560	61,643	29	9
Pacific Coast	98	56,455	49,443	53,870	61,175	98	70,917	62,915	69,732	80,067	101	5
Metro status												
Central	174	39,728	33,192	38,298	45,906	172	55,365	47,655	53,786	62,008	143	8
Suburban	404	43,926	36,044	42,620	49,682	398	60,018	50,550	58,636	67,995	331	7
Independent	198	34,069	28,580	32,840	38,946	194	45,344	39,866	45,216	52,044	148	8

addition to the measures of central tendency (mean and median) for the salary data, the first and third quartiles are included to indicate the degree of dispersion. The annual base salaries are the entrance salaries paid to sworn police officers or firefighters within their first 12 months of employment. Each reported amount excludes uniform allowances, holiday pay, hazardous duty pay, and any other form of additional compensation. The maximum is the highest annual base salary paid to uniformed personnel who do not hold any promotional rank.

The median entrance salary for police personnel is $42,224 and the mean is $43,432 (Table 9–5). The median maximum salary for police is $59,640 and the mean is $61,478. The entrance salary for firefighters tends to be lower than that for police, with a median of $39,000 and a mean of $40,470 (Table 9–6). The maximum fire salary median and mean are $53,594 and $55,244, respectively. For both police and fire, the mean is higher than the median salary. This means that some higher salaries are positively skewing the mean.

The highest average entrance salaries for both police personnel and firefighters are found in suburban cities and the Pacific Coast division. The highest average maximum salaries for both groups of personnel are also found in suburban cities; geographically, however, the highest average maximum salary for firefighters is again in the Pacific Coast division while that for police personnel is in the Mid-Atlantic division, followed closely by the Pacific Coast division. The lowest average entrance and maximum salaries for both police personnel and firefighters are found in independent cities and in the East South-Central division. For both services, the difference between the highest and lowest average entrance salaries among the geographic divisions is substantial: $28,683 for police and $27,100 for fire. The difference between the highest and lowest average maximum salaries among the geographic divisions for police is $32,391, compared with $27,038 for firefighters.

For both police and fire services, an average of eight years of service is required to reach the maximum salary.

Table 9-7 Longevity Pay for Police Officers, 2010

Classification	No. of cities reporting (A)	Yes No.	Yes % of (A)	No No.	No % of (A)	No. of cities reporting	Mean ($)	First quartile ($)	Median ($)	Third quartile ($)	No. of cities reporting	Mean
	Personnel can receive longevity pay					Maximum salary including longevity pay					No. of years of service to receive longevity pay	
Total	722	549	76	173	24	503	65,553	53,097	62,858	74,870	511	6
Population group												
Over 1,000,000	2	2	100	0	0	2	73,684	72,313	73,684	75,055	2	4
500,000-1,000,000	6	4	67	2	33	4	64,431	55,376	59,131	68,187	4	4
250,000-499,999	4	2	50	2	50	2	65,080	64,428	65,080	65,731	3	7
100,000-249,999	39	29	74	10	26	28	73,971	64,899	69,860	75,210	26	7
50,000-99,999	78	52	67	26	33	52	67,805	58,297	66,032	82,026	51	6
25,000-49,999	186	144	77	42	23	136	66,957	54,195	63,700	76,690	130	7
10,000-24,999	407	316	78	91	22	279	63,566	50,540	60,627	71,803	295	6
Geographic division												
New England	71	51	72	20	28	50	60,373	52,432	58,848	62,114	47	8
Mid-Atlantic	107	97	91	10	9	81	84,512	66,693	80,742	98,482	90	5
East North-Central	169	130	77	39	23	123	62,042	53,947	62,858	70,822	124	6
West North-Central	64	44	69	20	31	42	58,794	50,800	57,786	69,454	45	7
South Atlantic	76	56	74	20	26	50	58,285	49,007	56,464	71,986	49	7
East South-Central	21	14	67	7	33	14	45,564	40,402	44,248	51,921	13	6
West South-Central	118	88	75	30	25	81	56,661	49,618	57,240	65,150	83	3
Mountain	27	13	48	14	52	10	61,754	53,422	58,356	71,562	11	6
Pacific Coast	69	56	81	13	19	52	81,722	73,427	80,386	86,140	49	10
Metro status												
Central	130	90	69	40	31	91	61,458	53,696	58,984	70,298	83	6
Suburban	442	352	80	90	20	312	70,843	59,382	68,712	79,901	325	7
Independent	150	107	71	43	29	100	52,777	45,555	49,500	55,925	103	5

Longevity Pay

Longevity pay is defined as compensation beyond the regular maximum salary based on number of years of service. Longevity serves as an economic incentive to decrease employee turnover and reward those employees who have already achieved the maximum salary and now have limited opportunities for promotion. Longevity pay can be administered in several ways—a flat dollar amount, a percentage of the base salary, a percentage of the maximum pay, or a step increase in the basic salary plan.

Tables 9–7 and 9–8 show a range of longevity pay data for police and firefighter personnel, respectively. The tables cover whether personnel can receive longevity pay, the maximum salary they can receive including longevity pay, and the average number of years of service that is required for them to receive longevity pay.

Seventy-six percent of all police departments reporting have a system that awards longevity pay to their personnel (Table 9–7). The Mid-Atlantic and Pacific Coast divisions show the highest percentages of cities with longevity pay for police personnel (91% and 81%, respectively).

The average maximum salary including longevity pay for police officers is $65,553. The figures range from a low of $63,566 for cities with populations of 10,000–24,999 to a high of $73,971 for cities with a population of 100,000–249,999. Geographic divisions show a clear disparity in this regard. Once again, cities in the East South-Central division show the lowest average maximum at $45,564, while the highest average maximums are $84,512 for Mid-Atlantic and $81,722 for Pacific Coast jurisdictions. Cost of living is certainly a factor to consider. The median home prices in the central United States are much lower than they are on the East and West Coasts. Again, suburban cities have a higher average maximum salary with longevity pay ($70,843) than either central ($61,458) or independent ($52,777) cities.

Table 9-8 Longevity Pay for Firefighters, 2010

Classification	No. of cities reporting (A)	Yes No.	Yes % of (A)	No No.	No % of (A)	No. of cities reporting	Mean ($)	First quartile ($)	Median ($)	Third quartile ($)	No. of cities reporting	Mean
Total	812	453	56	359	44	422	54,644	46,974	54,958	65,934	484	6
Population group												
Over 1,000,000	2	2	100	0	0	2	67,479	66,237	67,479	68,721	2	4
500,000-1,000,000	5	5	100	0	0	5	57,379	52,741	64,874	78,838	5	3
250,000-499,999	7	3	43	4	57	2	59,775	58,946	59,775	60,604	6	6
100,000-249,999	57	35	61	22	39	30	62,642	53,466	62,840	69,972	30	5
50,000-99,999	95	54	57	41	43	55	56,507	52,970	60,122	71,983	64	5
25,000-49,999	206	129	63	77	37	123	57,827	50,842	56,469	68,516	134	7
10,000-24,999	440	225	51	215	49	205	50,822	43,282	50,970	60,882	243	5
Geographic division												
New England	67	50	75	17	25	46	50,048	47,601	52,250	56,736	49	7
Mid-Atlantic	63	33	52	30	48	36	61,038	51,451	60,772	84,038	39	6
East North-Central	163	118	72	45	28	114	54,731	48,575	57,848	66,312	127	6
West North-Central	86	31	36	55	64	25	52,551	50,516	52,888	55,516	39	6
South Atlantic	137	54	39	83	61	46	51,753	43,731	53,318	63,746	48	6
East South-Central	37	16	43	21	57	15	40,794	36,900	42,173	50,619	16	6
West South-Central	99	86	87	13	13	86	50,019	42,200	52,488	60,492	106	2
Mountain	47	15	32	32	68	12	53,740	48,062	54,169	62,936	19	6
Pacific Coast	113	50	44	63	56	42	73,050	69,243	75,020	82,514	41	10
Metro status												
Central	163	102	63	61	37	99	54,058	50,074	55,215	63,160	110	6
Suburban	451	243	54	208	46	223	58,561	50,622	60,142	71,330	259	6
Independent	198	108	55	90	46	100	46,488	41,578	47,800	52,935	115	5

The longevity pay patterns for firefighters (Table 9–8) show that 56% of jurisdictions reported longevity pay for fire personnel, including 87% of jurisdictions in the West South-Central division (the high) and 32% of those in the Mountain division (the low). Central jurisdictions (63%) are ahead of suburban (54%) and independent (55%) jurisdictions in offering longevity pay for firefighters.

The average maximum salary with longevity pay for firefighters is $54,644. Among population groups, the two cities with populations over 1,000,000 show the highest average maximum salary with longevity pay ($67,479). Geographically, Pacific Coast jurisdictions show the highest average maximum salary with longevity pay ($73,050), and East South-Central communities again show the lowest ($40,794). Suburban communities show a higher average maximum salary ($58,561) than either central ($54,058) or independent ($46,488) cities.

Overall, the length of service required for police

and firefighters to receive longevity pay is six years for both, which is identical to the number reported every year since 2006. However, the number of years varies somewhat within the classification categories. In the Pacific Coast division, for example, both groups of personnel serve a well-above-average number of years (10) to qualify for longevity pay.

Expenditures

Respondents were asked to provide expenditure (not budget) figures for their police and fire departments' most recently completed fiscal year. The items include salaries and wages for all department personnel, contributions for employee benefits, capital outlays, and all other departmental expenditures. Average expenditures are presented in Tables 9–9 through 9–16. Per capita expenditures are shown in addition to average expenditures. Again, per capita presentations are useful because they normalize the information.

Table 9-9 Expenditures for Salaries and Wages (Civilian and Uniformed), 2010

	Police			Fire		
Classification	No. of cities reporting	Mean ($)	Per capita ($)	No. of cities reporting	Mean ($)	Per capita ($)
Total	960	7,790,826	182.54	778	5,378,251	109.12
Population group						
Over 1,000,000	2	258,216,912	206.56	2	141,596,270	114.80
500,000-1,000,000	4	122,386,757	206.61	4	83,393,611	140.77
250,000-499,999	9	65,961,108	194.36	8	40,879,633	117.28
100,000-249,999	57	27,369,446	184.90	52	17,621,386	117.75
50,000-99,999	110	11,787,463	172.97	101	8,115,469	121.55
25,000-49,999	222	6,279,546	174.55	192	4,234,279	119.06
10,000-24,999	556	2,929,539	186.92	419	1,650,403	100.01
Geographic division						
New England	9	3,445,888	159.63	74	2,840,192	110.40
Mid-Atlantic	106	4,047,668	180.27	45	2,934,674	95.09
East North-Central	195	5,452,632	172.25	169	3,842,993	108.98
West North-Central	98	5,521,558	127.17	77	3,339,674	62.05
South Atlantic	154	7,580,762	200.06	123	5,059,793	125.10
East South-Central	39	10,391,760	149.70	38	6,694,341	122.76
West South-Central	116	12,355,732	241.48	112	8,063,751	107.38
Mountain	50	17,774,673	197.77	43	11,516,663	111.48
Pacific Coast	123	10,396,948	186.31	97	6,807,502	127.64
Metro status						
Central	172	20,662,551	170.75	161	13,972,602	120.01
Suburban	581	5,803,902	201.21	431	3,670,215	112.88
Independent	207	2,672,304	139.91	186	1,896,921	90.98

Salaries and Wages

Part of ICMA's process of reviewing survey results is to design logic checks that will identify problematic values. One logic check is that total expenditures for salaries and wages must be greater than the minimum salary for police (or fire) sworn personnel multiplied by the number of sworn personnel reported. For those jurisdictions reporting total expenditures for salaries and wages below that amount, the total salary and wage expenditures amount was removed.

Table 9-9 shows that the average per capita expenditure for civilian and uniformed police personnel in 2010 was $182.54, an increase from the 2009 average of $166.40. As population decreases, average per capita expenditures also generally decrease. So, too, do average salary and wage expenditures for police: from $258,216,912 for the two cities with populations of over 1,000,000 to $2,929,539 for cities of 10,000-24,999 in population. The average expenditure decrease is more pronounced than the average per capita decrease among population groups, which

is to be expected because, again, per capita amounts normalize the data.

Overall, the spread of average per capita salary and wage expenditures is greater for police departments than for fire departments. The average per capita police expenditures show a low of $172.97 in cities of 50,000–99,999 in population and highs of $206.61 in cities of 500,000–1,000,000 in population and of $206.56 in the two cities with over 1,000,000 in population (Table 9-9). For firefighters, the average per capita expenditures range from a low of $100.01 in cities with populations of 10,000–24,999 to a high of $140.77 in cities with populations of 500,000–1,000,000.

Geographically, South Atlantic and West South-Central jurisdictions show the highest average per capita salary and wage expenditures for police personnel ($200.06 and $241.48, respectively), and Pacific Coast jurisdictions show the highest for firefighters ($127.64). Cities in the West North-Central division show the lowest for both police ($127.17) and fire ($62.05) personnel.

Table 9-10 Total Municipal Contributions to Social Security and State/City-Administered Employee Retirement Systems, 2010

Classification	Police			Fire		
	No. of cities reporting	Mean ($)	Per capita ($)	No. of cities reporting	Mean ($)	Per capita ($)
Total	919	1,618,144	35.06	744	1,124,851	23.45
Population group						
Over 1,000,000	2	58,714,960	46.96	2	30,491,446	24.69
500,000-1,000,000	4	17,963,958	30.70	3	10,267,879	17.26
250,000-499,999	9	11,770,219	34.33	8	9,179,955	27.41
100,000-249,999	56	6,502,031	44.06	51	3,745,437	25.32
50,000-99,999	106	2,482,697	36.10	97	1,772,371	26.69
25,000-49,999	213	1,345,537	38.10	184	934,075	26.53
10,000-24,999	529	525,478	32.68	399	342,997	20.96
Geographic division						
New England	50	588,890	26.08	45	526,381	17.70
Mid-Atlantic	95	742,590	34.00	42	566,177	19.92
East North-Central	186	1,104,732	34.05	161	986,771	28.12
West North-Central	104	959,901	22.16	86	613,952	11.82
South Atlantic	155	1,782,156	43.68	128	1,209,768	28.63
East South-Central	39	1,390,085	27.78	37	805,949	22.64
West South-Central	118	2,130,622	28.79	113	1,446,293	19.22
Mountain	52	3,435,277	34.83	41	1,924,517	18.37
Pacific Coast	120	2,677,325	49.90	91	1,656,548	31.21
Metro status						
Central	167	4,363,535	35.47	160	2,756,802	25.18
Suburban	546	1,186,591	37.96	396	813,463	25.32
Independent	206	536,339	27.04	188	391,859	18.03

Social Security and Retirement Benefits

The average expenditures for municipal contributions to federal social security and other employee retirement programs are reported in Table 9–10. These expenditures are for both uniformed and civilian personnel. The table shows combined retirement and social security contributions because some states opt out of social security programs for local government employees, relying instead on an employee-sponsored retirement program. Zeros have been removed from the calculations because although zero is a legitimate answer, it skews the averages.

The average per capita expenditure for employee social security and retirement benefits for police in 2010 ($35.06) is up from the 2009 amount ($33.35). Among the population groups, if the two cities over 1,000,000 are excluded, the highest average police per capita expenditure for social security and retirement ($44.06) is in the 100,000–249,999 population group. Geographically, the highest average police department per capita expenditure for these benefits is found in

the Pacific Coast division ($49.90); the lowest is in the West North-Central division ($22.16). Suburban cities show a slightly higher average per capita municipal contribution ($37.96) than central cities ($35.47); independent cities show a lower amount ($27.04).

The average per capita expenditure for social security and retirement benefits for fire departments in 2010 was $23.45 (Table 9–10), compared with $21.75 in 2009. The per capita amounts fluctuate among the population groups. Among the geographic divisions, the highest average fire department per capita expenditure for social security and retirement benefits is again in the Pacific Coast cities ($31.21), and the lowest is again in the West North-Central ($11.82) cities. Suburban cities show the highest average per capita expenditure at $25.32, followed closely by central cities at $25.18.

Health, Hospitalization, Disability, and Life Insurance

Table 9–11 shows the average total municipal contributions for health, hospitalization, disability, and life

Table 9-11   Total Municipal Contributions for Health, Hospitalization, Disability, and Life Insurance Programs, 2010

	Police			Fire		
Classification	No. of cities reporting	Mean ($)	Per capita ($)	No. of cities reporting	Mean ($)	Per capita ($)
Total	886	1,476,774	30.46	723	876,072	18.54
Population group						
Over 1,000,000	1	45,384,000	34.35	2	25,102,117	20.51
500,000-1,000,000	4	64,517,770	102.26	3	11,082,282	18.35
250,000-499,999	9	9,995,934	29.73	8	5,986,046	16.92
100,000-249,999	57	4,400,521	29.97	52	2,788,827	19.07
50,000-99,999	102	1,964,676	28.57	92	1,263,833	18.78
25,000-49,999	207	1,052,720	29.96	182	704,772	20.04
10,000-24,999	506	485,897	30.53	384	292,970	17.72
Geographic division						
New England	45	657,214	29.52	40	625,428	22.45
Mid-Atlantic	87	746,537	36.40	41	521,634	20.06
East North-Central	178	988,081	31.38	154	731,359	20.52
West North-Central	101	871,283	21.60	84	549,013	11.38
South Atlantic	154	1,188,669	32.05	125	788,805	20.63
East South-Central	38	6,614,151	32.54	35	1,007,655	19.64
West South-Central	114	1,333,255	23.23	113	1,082,145	14.02
Mountain	51	2,404,942	29.94	39	1,639,675	17.11
Pacific Coast	118	2,042,244	37.08	92	1,175,558	22.29
Metro status						
Central	164	4,303,106	29.78	158	2,142,641	19.08
Suburban	519	947,526	31.66	382	606,921	19.23
Independent	203	546,535	27.92	183	344,366	16.63

insurance programs. The mean per capita expenditures for 2010 increased to $30.46 for police and to $18.54 for fire. In 2009, they were $28.09 for police and $17.82 for fire.

Total Personnel Expenditures

Table 9–12 shows the total personnel expenditures for civilian and uniformed employees for both police and fire services. These data represent total salaries and wages; contributions for federal social security and other retirement programs; and contributions to health, hospitalization, disability, and life insurance programs. To be included in this table, the jurisdiction had to provide each of these expenditures. Those who reported an amount of zero were excluded from the table. Again, although zero is a legitimate amount, it negatively skews the average.

For fire services in particular, the workforce composition affects personnel expenditures. Departments that rely heavily on volunteers have significantly lower personnel expenditures than those that use paid staff.

The mean per capita personnel expenditure amounts are $242.38 for police and $147.86 for fire. For police departments, these amounts fluctuate among population groups, although in general the per capita figures are lower among smaller population groups. Among the geographic divisions, the high for police is in the West South-Central division ($292.59), followed by the South Atlantic division ($274.33); the low is in the West North-Central division ($169.71).

For fire departments, the mean per capita personnel expenditures also vary among population groups. Geographically, the average per capita high is seen in the Pacific Coast division ($177.81), followed closely by the South Atlantic division ($173.84), and the low is again seen in the West North-Central division ($85.06). The highest average per capita personnel expenditure for police departments is found in suburban cities ($263.20); for fire, the highest is in central cities ($162.60). For both services, independent cities have the lowest average per capita personnel expenditures.

Table 9-12 Total Personnel Expenditures, 2010

	Police			Fire		
Classification	No. of cities reporting	Mean ($)	Per capita ($)	No. of cities reporting	Mean ($)	Per capita ($)
Total	960	10,651,886	242.38	778	7,239,347	147.86
Population group						
Over 1,000,000	2	339,623,872	270.70	2	197,189,833	160.01
500,000-1,000,000	4	204,868,485	339.57	4	99,406,231	167.47
250,000-499,999	9	87,727,262	258.42	8	56,045,634	161.60
100,000-249,999	57	38,025,169	257.41	52	23,969,755	160.78
50,000-99,999	110	15,938,156	233.18	101	10,909,488	163.47
25,000-49,999	222	8,475,970	236.59	192	5,785,740	163.18
10,000-24,999	556	3,840,371	243.92	419	2,226,002	134.97
Geographic division						
New England	79	4,192,966	192.96	74	3,498,358	133.30
Mid-Atlantic	106	5,323,137	240.45	45	3,929,039	131.49
East North-Central	195	7,346,348	230.96	169	5,422,177	153.62
West North-Central	98	7,398,755	169.71	77	4,590,536	85.06
South Atlantic	154	10,476,124	274.33	123	7,014,056	173.84
East South-Central	39	18,226,403	209.19	38	8,407,183	162.89
West South-Central	116	15,787,527	292.59	112	10,607,479	140.58
Mountain	50	23,662,645	258.50	43	14,825,972	143.74
Pacific Coast	123	14,911,051	268.44	97	9,473,723	177.81
Metro status						
Central	172	28,924,217	232.74	161	18,727,694	162.60
Suburban	581	7,719,069	263.20	431	4,945,551	152.60
Independent	207	3,700,801	191.99	186	2,610,327	124.13

Overtime Expenditures

At the request of some local governments, a new survey question was added on overtime expenditures (Table 9–13). Per capita average overtime expenditures for police for 2010 were $12.67 and for fire, $9.78. Overtime expenditures for fire personnel show more variation than those for police among population groups, and both services show noticeable variation among the geographic divisions.

As with all police and fire expenditures, it is important to consider population density and other factors before making definitive comparisons. A community with high manufacturing activity may pose a higher risk for fire, resulting in more overtime, and high levels of gang activity may influence the need for police overtime. In addition, for some communities, paying overtime is less costly than hiring additional personnel.

Capital Outlays

Table 9–14 (see page 100) shows departmental expenditures for capital outlays. These outlays include the purchase and replacement of equipment, the purchase of land and existing structures, and construction. The amounts include the capital expenditures within individual departmental budgets as well as those expenditures included in citywide capital budgets designated for departmental programs or equipment.

Total capital outlay expenditures may fluctuate dramatically from one year to the next for both police and fire departments. This is because the cost of individual capital projects varies widely among communities as well as within the same community over time. Whereas the number of employees, which relates to population size, determines personnel expenditures, fire equipment such as pumpers will cost the same regardless of the size of the community. Thus, the per capita cost for the pumpers will necessarily be higher among cities with fewer people.

The 2010 average municipal capital outlay expenditures per capita were $11.56 for police, a decrease from the $12.35 shown in 2009, and $11.38 for fire, which is below the 2009 figure of $12.64. For police, the highest average capital outlay expenditures per

Table 9-13 Total Overtime Expenditures, 2010

	Police			Fire		
Classification	No. of cities reporting	Mean ($)	Per capita ($)	No. of cities reporting	Mean ($)	Per capita ($)
Total	956	540,442	12.67	724	485,639	9.78
Population group						
Over 1,000,000	2	15,994,681	12.94	2	13,465,136	11.49
500,000-1,000,000	4	7,151,347	11.95	4	7,970,966	14.04
250,000-499,999	9	4,227,715	12.57	8	2,710,897	8.41
100,000-249,999	58	2,013,198	13.79	53	1,363,753	9.35
50,000-99,999	113	820,428	11.98	100	709,288	10.58
25,000-49,999	220	410,697	11.70	187	379,802	10.64
10,000-24,999	550	214,893	13.09	370	153,705	9.17
Geographic division						
New England	75	348,149	15.93	60	434,909	17.32
Mid-Atlantic	99	272,354	11.93	37	257,948	8.50
East North-Central	191	372,694	12.92	155	287,406	8.50
West North-Central	103	300,237	7.05	72	179,025	4.53
South Atlantic	154	524,198	15.56	124	303,038	7.50
East South-Central	37	753,142	10.61	34	425,083	6.78
West South-Central	117	688,910	8.78	110	581,156	6.35
Mountain	53	979,226	12.21	39	1,007,183	10.15
Pacific Coast	127	947,917	16.37	93	1,110,640	19.67
Metro status						
Central	171	1,397,147	12.06	165	1,074,888	9.15
Suburban	580	421,575	14.26	388	379,670	11.01
Independent	205	162,131	8.67	171	157,510	7.60

capita are in the two cities with populations over 1,000,000 ($16.55) and the cities in the East South-Central division ($22.89). For fire services, the average capital outlays per capita are also highest in the cities with populations over 1,000,000 ($15.91) and cities in the East South-Central division ($19.66). For police services, the lowest average capital outlays per capita are in New England and West North-Central division cities ($5.99 and $6.78, respectively) and for fire, the lowest is in the Mountain division ($7.50)

Although the average capital outlay expenditures continue to decrease, it is not possible to know whether that is because there have been fewer needs for these types of expenditures or because the fiscal crisis influenced spending.

Other Expenditures

Table 9–15 (see page 101) presents the data for all other departmental expenditures not accounted for in the previous tables. These include ongoing maintenance, utilities, fuel, supplies, and other miscellaneous items. The average per capita expenditures in 2010 were $36.51 for police, a decrease from the $41.30 reported in 2009, and $23.90 for fire, which is virtually identical to the 2009 average.

Total Departmental Expenditures

Table 9–16 (see page 102) shows the combined personnel, capital outlay, and all other departmental expenditures. The average per capita figures for 2010 are $282.22 and $177.25 for police and fire, respectively—increases over the $269.63 reported for police personnel and over the $164.34 reported for fire personnel in 2009.

Total expenditures are not included for those localities in which the sum of expenditures reported (salaries and wages, employee benefit contributions, capital outlay, and other expenses) differed from the amount reported for total expenditures by more than $100. Most of the variations were by thousands of dollars. This same logic has been applied each year for the analysis.

Not all cities include the same expenditures in their budgets. Of the 755 jurisdictions providing

Table 9-14 Municipal Expenditures for Capital Outlays, 2010

	Police			Fire		
Classification	No. of cities reporting	Mean ($)	Per capita ($)	No. of cities reporting	Mean ($)	Per capita ($)
Total	850	467,372	11.56	660	455,611	11.38
Population group						
Over 1,000,000	2	21,549,466	16.55	2	20,967,782	15.91
500,000-1,000,000	4	1,500,989	2.85	4	438,192	0.79
250,000-499,999	8	4,194,825	10.88	7	3,425,781	8.65
100,000-249,999	53	901,834	6.15	49	945,871	6.78
50,000-99,999	96	901,532	12.54	88	687,164	10.37
25,000-49,999	200	461,269	11.90	161	333,751	9.56
10,000-24,999	487	180,712	11.88	349	207,686	13.27
Geographic division						
New England	63	121,927	5.99	55	217,476	10.09
Mid-Atlantic	81	196,828	9.07	43	206,408	9.47
East North-Central	172	332,058	13.48	139	299,560	11.38
West North-Central	92	321,665	6.78	71	475,936	9.46
South Atlantic	147	445,918	13.69	105	490,041	13.98
East South-Central	37	711,472	22.89	30	404,676	19.66
West South-Central	106	754,635	11.00	96	581,817	11.45
Mountain	47	1,226,722	12.49	38	1,453,114	7.50
Pacific Coast	105	546,790	11.07	83	358,662	10.27
Metro status						
Central	157	1,065,263	8.67	144	958,501	7.83
Suburban	503	388,467	12.84	361	364,496	13.00
Independent	190	182,216	10.57	155	200,620	10.90

information about services included in the fire department budget, 53% cited ambulance personnel and 54% cited ambulance equipment (not shown). Emergency medical technicians (EMTs) were included by 91%, and EMT equipment was included by 92%. This does not necessarily mean, however, that these are the only jurisdictions that provide EMT and ambulance services; these are just the cities that reported having these services in the fire department budget.

Conclusion

This report has examined the cross-sectional and longitudinal patterns found in the responses to ICMA's annual *Police and Fire Personnel, Salaries, and Expenditures* survey. Most of the changes over time in police and fire employment and expenditures have been small, incremental shifts. It is not uncommon for one year to show increases and the next to show decreases in average expenditures.

Although using per capita figures instead of absolute numbers reduces the skew of the data, any analysis of the reported changes must control for population size of the responding jurisdictions. Another influential factor is a significant difference in the number reporting in any population group. Any major increase or decrease in that number can affect the average.

Table 9-15 All Other Department Expenditures, 2010

	Police			Fire		
Classification	No. of cities reporting	Mean ($)	Per capita ($)	No. of cities reporting	Mean ($)	Per capita ($)
Total	929	1,657,698	36.51	783	1,073,743	23.90
Population group						
Over 1,000,000	2	43,661,880	35.19	2	27,437,834	22.49
500,000-1,000,000	4	20,269,379	35.55	4	11,850,530	20.28
250,000-499,999	9	12,811,659	39.69	8	5,365,129	16.79
100,000-249,999	57	6,362,494	42.17	53	3,454,030	23.59
50,000-99,999	109	2,880,073	42.52	101	1,952,063	29.58
25,000-49,999	215	1,353,381	38.56	185	810,331	23.25
10,000-24,999	533	541,705	33.81	430	384,673	23.06
Geographic division						
New England	74	408,345	19.60	67	459,009	18.76
Mid-Atlantic	90	401,258	18.00	61	410,086	18.04
East North-Central	184	1,044,059	30.03	162	695,532	21.62
West North-Central	103	967,115	25.63	86	517,890	16.57
South Atlantic	157	1,915,401	52.27	126	1,223,437	30.05
East South-Central	37	2,037,695	33.60	36	1,002,276	18.87
West South-Central	113	2,164,260	32.71	109	1,449,612	22.59
Mountain	51	3,305,413	44.78	39	2,257,110	24.97
Pacific Coast	120	3,272,510	60.47	97	1,974,098	36.38
Metro status						
Central	163	4,646,188	41.15	156	2,765,575	27.52
Suburban	562	1,166,549	36.41	441	763,019	24.30
Independent	204	622,905	33.09	186	391,504	19.92

Table 9-16   Total Department Expenditures, 2010

	Police			Fire		
Classification	No. of cities reporting	Mean ($)	Per capita ($)	No. of cities reporting	Mean ($)	Per capita ($)
Total	645	11,257,952	282.22	556	8,267,946	177.25
Population group						
Over 1,000,000	0	0	0	1	214,209,902	187.14
500,000-1,000,000	2	192,471,866	325.92	4	123,419,827	212.21
250,000-499,999	3	102,355,433	311.94	3	67,456,959	196.58
100,000-249,999	40	46,443,678	300.78	38	27,414,387	183.81
50,000-99,999	76	20,074,588	290.31	64	13,457,558	202.40
25,000-49,999	148	10,149,189	279.72	133	7,130,774	199.59
10,000-24,999	376	4,478,387	279.13	313	2,668,672	161.15
Geographic division						
New England	56	5,024,183	223.30	54	4,764,238	174.25
Mid-Atlantic	67	6,344,126	279.24	48	3,533,323	124.51
East North-Central	123	7,908,124	263.07	114	6,216,203	177.83
West North-Central	66	6,076,190	199.99	56	3,789,612	113.90
South Atlantic	114	13,564,847	347.31	86	8,524,077	211.62
East South-Central	27	7,757,313	274.63	28	14,432,641	190.25
West South-Central	80	17,925,926	255.73	81	14,487,888	178.18
Mountain	31	17,992,647	322.14	24	9,267,452	183.62
Pacific Coast	81	17,698,206	343.30	65	11,017,258	217.63
Metro status						
Central	114	26,593,243	272.33	107	21,944,326	184.56
Suburban	388	9,134,888	299.40	314	5,735,213	183.71
Independent	143	4,793,097	243.50	135	3,319,098	156.41

Directories

1

U.S., Canadian, and International Organizations Serving Local Governments

Directory 1 in this section of the *Year Book* provides the names and websites of U.S. state municipal leagues; provincial and territorial associations and unions in Canada; state agencies for community affairs; provincial and territorial agencies for local affairs in Canada; U.S. municipal management associations; international municipal management associations; state associations of counties; and U.S. councils of governments recognized by ICMA. In all cases, where there is no website available, we have provided the name of the president/permanent officer/executive director and all contact information for that individual.

U.S. State Municipal Leagues

Directory 1-1 shows 49 state leagues of municipalities serving 49 states. (Hawaii does not have a league.) Information, which was obtained from the National League of Cities (nlc.org), includes league address and website. State municipal leagues provide a wide range of research, consulting, training, publications, and legislative representation services for their clients.

Provincial and Territorial Associations and Unions in Canada

Directory 1-2 shows the websites of the 16 associations and unions serving the 12 provinces and territories of Canada. Information was obtained from the Federation of Canadian Municipalities (fcm.org).

State Agencies for Community Affairs

Directory 1-3 shows the addresses and websites of 47 agencies for community affairs in the United States, as well as that for Puerto Rico. Information was obtained from the Council of State Community Development Agencies (coscda.org). These agencies of state governments offer a variety of research, financial information, and coordination services for cities and other local governments.

Provincial and Territorial Agencies for Local Affairs in Canada

Directory 1-4 shows the addresses, phone numbers, fax numbers, and websites of the agencies for local affairs serving the 12 provinces and territories of Canada. Information was obtained from the Ontario Ministry of Municipal Affairs and Housing (mah.gov.on.ca/).

U.S. Municipal Management Associations

Directory 1-5, with information obtained from ICMA files, shows the websites of municipal management associations serving 48 of the United States. (The states of Wyoming, Idaho, Montana, North Dakota, and South Dakota are served by the Great Open Spaces City Management Association; Idaho and South Dakota are also served by their own associations; and neither Hawaii nor Louisiana has an association.)

International Municipal Management Associations

Directory 1–6, with information obtained from ICMA files, shows the websites (where available) of municipal management associations serving Canada and 21 other countries.

U.S. State Associations of Counties

Directory 1–7 shows the websites for 53 county associations serving 47 states, as obtained from the National Association of Counties (naco.org). (Two associations serve the states of Arizona, South Dakota, Washington, and West Virginia; three associations serve the state of Illinois; and three states—Connecticut, Rhode Island, and Vermont—do not have associations.) Like their municipal league counterparts, these associations provide a wide range of research, training, consulting, publications, and legislative representation services.

U.S. Councils of Governments Recognized by ICMA

Directory 1–8, with information obtained from ICMA files, gives the websites for 96 councils of governments recognized by ICMA.

Other Local Government Directories

The names of municipal officials not reported in the *Year Book* are available in many states through directories published by state municipal leagues, state municipal management associations, and state associations of counties. Names and websites of these leagues and associations are shown in Directories 1–1, 1–5, and 1–7. In some states, the secretary of state, the state agency for community affairs (Directory 1–3), or another state agency publishes a directory that includes municipal and county officials. In addition, several directories with national coverage are published for health officers, welfare workers, housing and urban renewal officials, and other professional groups.

Directory 1-1   U.S. State Municipal Leagues

Shown below are the state municipal leagues of municipalities serving 49 states. For each league the directory provides the address and website so that readers can go directly to the site to find additional information.

Alabama
Alabama League of Municipalities
535 Adams Avenue
Montgomery 36104
alalm.org

Alaska
Alaska Municipal League
217 Second Street, Suite 200
Juneau 99801
akml.org

Arizona
League of Arizona Cities and Towns
1820 West Washington Street
Phoenix 85007
azleague.org

Arkansas
Arkansas Municipal League
301 North Second Street
Box 38
North Little Rock 72115
arml.org

California
League of California Cities
1400 K Street, Suite 400
Sacramento 95814
cacities.org

Colorado
Colorado Municipal League
1144 Sherman Street
Denver 80203
cml.org

Connecticut
Connecticut Conference of Municipalities
900 Chapel Street, 9th Floor
New Haven 06510-2807
ccm-ct.org

Delaware
Delaware League of Local Governments
P.O. Box 484
Dover 19903-0484
dllg.org/about.html

Florida
Florida League of Cities
301 South Bronough Street, Suite 300
Tallahassee 32301
flcities.com

Georgia
Georgia Municipal Association
201 Pryor Street, S.W.
Atlanta 30303
gmanet.com/home

Idaho
Association of Idaho Cities
3100 South Vista Avenue, Suite 310
Boise 83705
idahocities.org

Illinois
Illinois Municipal League
500 East Capitol Avenue
Springfield 62701
iml.org

Indiana

Indiana Association of Cities and Towns
200 South Meridian Street, Suite 340
Indianapolis 46225
citiesandtowns.org

Iowa

Iowa League of Cities
317 Sixth Avenue, Suite 800
Des Moines 50309-4111
iowaleague.org

Kansas

League of Kansas Municipalities
300 S.W. Eighth Avenue
Topeka 66603
lkm.org

Kentucky

Kentucky League of Cities
100 East Vine Street, Suite 800
Lexington 40507
klc.org

Louisiana

Louisiana Municipal Association
700 North 10th Street
Baton Rouge 70802
lamunis.org

Maine

Maine Municipal Association
60 Community Drive
Augusta 04330
memun.org

Maryland

Maryland Municipal League
1212 West Street
Annapolis 21401
mdmunicipal.org

Massachusetts

Massachusetts Municipal Association
One Winthrop Square
Boston 02110
mma.org

Michigan

Michigan Municipal League
1675 Green Road
Ann Arbor 48105
mml.org

Minnesota

League of Minnesota Cities
145 University Avenue West
St. Paul 55103-2044
lmnc.org

Mississippi

Mississippi Municipal League
600 East Amite Street, Suite 104
Jackson 39201
mmlonline.com

Missouri

Missouri Municipal League
1727 Southridge Drive
Jefferson City 65109
mocities.com

Montana

Montana League of Cities and Towns
208 North Montana Avenue, Suite 106
Helena 59601
mlct.org

Nebraska

League of Nebraska Municipalities
1335 L Street
Lincoln 68508
lonm.org

Nevada

Nevada League of Cities and Municipalities
310 South Curry Street
Carson City 89703
nvleague.org

New Hampshire

New Hampshire Local Government Center
25 Triangle Park Drive
Concord 03301
nhlgc.org/LGCWebsite/index.asp

New Jersey

New Jersey State League of Municipalities
222 West State Street
Trenton 08608
njslom.com

New Mexico

New Mexico Municipal League
1229 Paseo de Peralta
Santa Fe 87501
nmml.org

New York

New York State Conference of Mayors and Municipal Officials
119 Washington Avenue
Albany 12210
nycom.org

North Carolina

North Carolina League of Municipalities
215 North Dawson Street
Raleigh 27603
nclm.org

North Dakota

North Dakota League of Cities
410 East Front Avenue
Bismarck 58504
ndlc.org

Ohio

Ohio Municipal League
175 South Third Street, Suite 510
Columbus 43215
omlohio.org

Oklahoma

Oklahoma Municipal League
201 N.E. 23rd Street
Oklahoma City 73105
oml.org

Oregon

League of Oregon Cities
1201 Court Street, N.E., Suite 200
Salem 97301
orcities.org

Pennsylvania

Pennsylvania League of Cities and Municipalities
414 North Second Street
Harrisburg 17101
plcm.org

Rhode Island

Rhode Island League of Cities and Towns
One State Street, Suite 502
Providence 02908
rileague.org

South Carolina

Municipal Association of South Carolina
1411 Gervais Street
Columbia 29211
masc.sc

South Dakota

South Dakota Municipal League
208 Island Drive
Fort Pierre 57532
sdmunicipalleague.org

Tennessee

Tennessee Municipal League
226 Capitol Boulevard, Suite 710
Nashville 37219
tml1.org

Texas

Texas Municipal League
1821 Rutherford Lane, Suite 400
Austin 78754
tml.org

Utah

Utah League of Cities and Towns
50 South 600 East, Suite 150
Salt Lake City 84102
ulct.org

Vermont

Vermont League of Cities and Towns
89 Main Street, Suite 4
Montpelier 05602-2948
vlct.org

Virginia

Virginia Municipal League
13 East Franklin Street
Richmond 23219
vml.org

Washington

Association of Washington Cities
1076 Franklin Street, S.E.
Olympia 98501
awcnet.org

West Virginia

West Virginia Municipal League
2020 Kanawha Boulevard East
Charleston 25311
wvml.org

Wisconsin

League of Wisconsin Municipalities
122 West Washington Avenue, Suite 300
Madison 53703-2715
lwm-info.org

Wyoming

Wyoming Association of Municipalities
315 West 27th Street
Cheyenne 82001
wyomuni.org

Directory 1–2 Provincial and Territorial Associations and Unions in Canada

Shown below are the associations and unions serving the provinces and territories of Canada. For each association the directory provides the website so that readers can go directly to the site to find additional information. Where there is no website available, we have provided the names of the president and permanent officer, along with all contact information for the latter.

Alberta

Alberta Association of Municipal Districts and Counties
aamdc.com

Alberta Urban Municipalities Association
munilink.net/live/

British Columbia

Union of British Columbia Municipalities
civicnet.bc.ca/ubcm

Manitoba

Association of Manitoba Municipalities
amm.mb.ca

New Brunswick

Association Francophone des Municipalités du Nouveau-Brunswick
afmnb.org

Cities of New Brunswick Association
Joel Richardson, president
Sandra Mark, executive director
P.O. Box 1421, Station A
Fredericton E3B 5E3
506-357-4242 (phone)
506-357-4243 (fax)
cities@rogers.com

Newfoundland and Labrador

Newfoundland and Labrador Federation of Municipalities
municipalitiesnl.ca

Northwest Territories

Northwest Territories Association of Communities
nwtac.com

Nova Scotia

Union of Nova Scotia Municipalities
unsm.ca

Ontario

Association of Municipalities of Ontario
amo.on.ca

Federation of Canadian Municipalities
fcm.ca

Prince Edward Island

Federation of Prince Edward Island Municipalities
fpeim.ca

Québec

Union des Municipalités du Québec
umq.qc.ca

Saskatchewan

Saskatchewan Association of Rural Municipalities
sarm.ca/

Saskatchewan Urban Municipalities Association
suma.org

Yukon

Association of Yukon Communities
ayc.yk.ca

Directory 1-3 State Agencies for Community Affairs

Shown below are the agencies for community affairs for 46 states and Puerto Rico. For each agency the directory provides the address and website so that readers can go directly to the site to find additional information.

Alabama

Department of Economic and Community Affairs
401 Adams Avenue
Montgomery 36104
adeca.state.al.us

Alaska

Department of Commerce, Community and Economic Development
P.O. Box 110800
Juneau 99811-0800
dced.state.ak.us

Arizona

Arizona Commerce Authority
1700 West Washington, Suite 600
Phoenix 85007
azcommerce.com

Arkansas

Economic Development Commission
900 West Capitol Avenue
Little Rock 72201
1800arkansas.com

California

Department of Housing and Community Development
1800 Third Street
Sacramento 95811-6942
hcd.ca.gov

Colorado

Department of Local Affairs
1313 Sherman Street, Suite 500
Denver 80203
dola.state.co.us

Connecticut

Department of Economic and Community Development
505 Hudson Street
Hartford 06106-7106
ct.gov/ecd/site/default.asp

Delaware

Delaware State Housing Authority
18 The Green
Dover 19901
destatehousing.com/

Florida

Department of Community Affairs
2555 Shumard Oak Boulevard
Tallahassee 32399-2100
dca.state.fl.us

Georgia

Department of Community Affairs
60 Executive Park South, N.E.
Atlanta 30329
dca.state.ga.us

Idaho

Idaho Department of Commerce
700 West State Street
Boise 83720-0093
commerce.idaho.gov

Illinois

Illinois Department of Commerce and Economic Opportunity
500 East Monroe
Springfield 62701
commerce.state.il.us/dceo

Indiana

Indiana Housing and Community Development Authority
30 South Meridian Street, Suite 1000
Indianapolis 46204
in.gov/ihfa

Iowa

Iowa Department of Economic Development
200 East Grand Avenue
Des Moines 50309
iowalifechanging.com

Kansas

Department of Commerce
Division of Community Development
1000 S.W. Jackson Street, Suite 100
Topeka 66612
kansascommerce.com/index.aspx?NID=98

Kentucky

Department for Local Government
Division of Grants
1024 Capital Center Drive, Suite 340
Frankfort 40601
dlg.ky.gov/grants/

Louisiana

Office of Community Development
Division of Administration
1201 North Third Street
Claiborne Building, Suite 7-270
Baton Rouge 70802
doa.louisiana.gov/cdbg/cdbg.htm

Maine

**Maine Department of Economic and
Community Development**
59 State House Station
Augusta 04333-0059
econdevmaine.com

Maryland

**Department of Housing and Community
Development**
100 Community Place
Crownsville 21032
dhcd.state.md.us

Michigan

**Michigan Economic Development
Corporation**
300 North Washington Square
Lansing 48913
medc.michigan.org

Minnesota

**Department of Employment and
Economic Development**
First National Bank Building
332 Minnesota Street, Suite E-200
St. Paul 55101-1351
positivelyminnesota.com/

Mississippi

Mississippi Development Authority
501 North West Street
Jackson 39201
Mississippi.org

Missouri

Department of Economic Development
301 West High Street
P.O. Box 1157
Jefferson City 65102
ded.mo.gov

Montana

Department of Commerce
Local Government Assistance Division
301 South Park
P.O. Box 200501
Helena 59620-0501
commerce.mt.gov/

Nebraska

**Nebraska Department of Economic
Development**
301 Centennial Mall South
P.O. Box 94666
Lincoln 68509-4666
neded.org

Nevada

**Nevada Commission on Economic
Development**
808 West Nye Lane
Carson City 89703
diversifynevada.com/

New Hampshire

Office of Energy and Planning
4 Chenell Drive
Concord 03301-8501
nh.gov/oep

New Jersey

Department of Community Affairs
101 South Broad Street
P.O. Box 800
Trenton 08625-0800
state.nj.us/dca

New Mexico

**Department of Finance and
Administration**
Local Government Division
Bataan Memorial Building, Suites 201-203
Santa Fe 87501
local.nmdfa.state.nm.us

New York

**New York State Division of Housing and
Community Renewal**
Hampton Plaza, 38-40 State Street
Albany 12207
nysdhcr.gov/index.htm

North Carolina

Department of Commerce
301 North Wilmington Street
Raleigh 27601-1058
nccommerce.com/en

North Dakota

Department of Commerce
Division of Community Services
1600 East Century Avenue, Suite 2
P.O. Box 2057
Bismarck 58503-2057
state.nd.us/dcs

Ohio

Department of Development
77 South High Street
Columbus 43216-1001
odod.state.oh.us

Oklahoma

Department of Commerce
900 North Stiles Avenue
Oklahoma City 73104
okcommerce.gov

Oregon

Business Oregon
775 Summer Street, N.E., Suite 200
Salem 97301-1280
oregon4biz.com/

Pennsylvania

**Department of Community and
Economic Development**
Commonwealth Keystone Building
400 North Street, 4th Floor
Harrisburg 17120-0225
newpa.com/default.aspx?id=223

Puerto Rico

**Office of the Commissioner of Municipal
Affairs**
P.O. Box 70167
San Juan 00936-8167
ocam.gobierno.pr

Rhode Island

**Rhode Island Housing Resources
Commission**
One Capitol Hill, 3rd Floor
Providence 02908
hrc.ri.gov/index.php

South Carolina

Department of Commerce
1201 Main Street, Suite 1600
Columbia 29201-3200
sccommerce.com

South Dakota

Department of Tourism and State Development
711 East Wells Avenue
Pierre 57501-3369
tsd.sd.gov/index.asp

Tennessee

Tennessee Housing Development Agency
404 James Robertson Parkway, Suite 1200
Nashville 37243-0900
state.tn.us/thda

Texas

Texas Department of Housing and Community Affairs
221 East 11th Street
P.O. Box 13941
Austin 78701-2401
tdhca.state.tx.us

Utah

Utah Governor's Office of Economic Development
324 South State Street, Suite 500
Salt Lake City 84111
goed.utah.gov

Utah Department of Community and Culture
324 South State Street, Suite 500
Salt Lake City 84111
community.utah.gov

Vermont

Vermont Department of Housing and Community Affairs
National Life Building, 6th Floor
One National Life Drive
Montpelier 05620
dhca.state.vt.us/

Virginia

Virginia Department of Housing and Community Development
Main Street Centre
600 East Main Street, Suite 300
Richmond 23219
dhcd.virginia.gov

Washington

Department of Commerce
1011 Plum Street S.E.
P.O. Box 42525
Olympia 98504-2525
cted.wa.gov

West Virginia

West Virginia Department of Commerce
Capitol Complex, Building 6, Room 525
1900 Kanawha Boulevard East
Charleston 25305-0311
wvcommerce.org/business/business
_external/default.aspx

Wisconsin

Wisconsin Department of Commerce
201 West Washington Avenue
Madison 53703
commerce.state.wi.us

Directory 1-4   Provincial and Territorial Agencies for Local Affairs in Canada

Shown below are the agencies for local affairs serving the provinces and territories of Canada. For each agency the directory provides the address and website for the ministry so that readers can go directly to the site to find additional information.

Alberta

Alberta Municipal Affairs
Communications Branch
Commerce Place, 18th Floor
10155-102 Street
Edmonton T5J 4L4
municipalaffairs.gov.ab.ca

British Columbia

Ministry of Community, Sport and Cultural Development
P.O. Box 9490
Station Provincial Government
Victoria V8W 9N7
gov.bc.ca/cserv/index.html

Manitoba

Manitoba Aboriginal and Northern Affairs
344-450 Broadway
Winnipeg R3C 0V8
gov.mb.ca/ana

New Brunswick

Aboriginal Affairs Secretariat
Kings Place
P.O. Box 6000
Fredericton E3B 5H1
www2.gnb.ca/content/gnb/en/
departments/aboriginal_affairs.html

Newfoundland and Labrador

Department of Municipal Affairs
Confederation Building, 4th Floor (West Block)
P.O. Box 8700
St. John's A1B 4J6
ma.gov.nl.ca/ma

Northwest Territories

Department of Education, Culture and Employment
P.O. Box 1320
Yellowknife X1A 2L9
ece.gov.nt.ca

Nova Scotia

Service Nova Scotia and Municipal Relations
Mail Room, 8 South, Maritime Centre
1505 Barrington Street
Halifax B3J 3K5
gov.ns.ca/snsmr/

Ontario

Ministry of Municipal Affairs and Housing
777 Bay Street, 17th Floor
Toronto M5G 2E5
mah.gov.on.ca/

Prince Edward Island

Department of Finance and Municipal Affairs
Shaw Building, Second Floor South
95 Rochford Street
P.O. Box 2000
Charlottetown C1A 7N8
gov.pe.ca/finance/index.php3

Québec

Affaires Municipales, Régions et Occupation du territoire
(Ministry of Municipal Affairs, Regions and Land Occupancy)
mamrot.gouv.qc.ca/

Saskatchewan

Public Service Commission
2350 Albert Street
Regina S4P 4A6
psc.gov.sk.ca

Yukon

Department of Community Services
Yukon Government Administration Building
2071 Second Avenue
P.O. Box 2703
Whitehorse Y1A 1B2
community.gov.yk.ca/

Directory 1–5   U.S. Municipal Management Associations

Shown below are the 48 municipal management associations in the United States. For each association the directory provides the website so that readers can go directly to the site to find additional information. Where there is no website available, we have provided the name, address, and all contact information for the association president (current as of January 15, 2011).

Alabama

Alabama City/County Management Association
accma-online.org/

Alaska

Alaska Municipal Management Association
akml.org/amma.html

Arizona

Arizona City/County Management Association
azmanagement.org/

Arkansas

Arkansas City/County Management Association
Bryan Day (until June 2011)
Assistant City Manager
Little Rock City Hall
500 West Markham, Room 203
Little Rock 72201
bday@littlerock.org
501-371-4510 (phone)
501-371-4498 (fax)

California

City Manager's Department, League of California Cities
cacities.org

Cal-ICMA
icma.org/en/ca/home

Colorado

Colorado City and County Management Association
cml.org/cccma.aspx

Connecticut

Connecticut Town and City Management Association
cttcma.govoffice3.com/

Delaware

City Management Association of Delaware
Rebecca Greene (through October 2011)
Town Manager
Town of Felton
P.O. Box 329
Felton 19943
rgreene@townoffelton.com
302-284-9365 (phone)
302-284-3449 (fax)

Florida

Florida City and County Management Association
fccma.org/

Georgia

Georgia City-County Management Association
gccma.com

Idaho

Idaho City/County Management Association
Ben Marchant
City Administrator
City of Jerome
152 East Avenue A
Jerome 83338
bmarchant@ci.jerome.id.us
208-324-8169 (phone)

Illinois

Illinois City/County Management Association
ilcma.org/

Indiana

Indiana Municipal Management Association
citiesandtowns.org/topic/subtopic
.php?fDD=4-50

Iowa

Iowa City/County Management Association
Iacma.net

Kansas

Kansas Association of City/County Management
kacm.us/

Kentucky

Kentucky City/County Management Association
kccma.org/

Maine

Maine Town and City Management Association
mtcma.org

Maryland

Maryland City County Management Association
icma.org/en/md/home

Massachusetts

Massachusetts Municipal Management Association
massmanagers.org/Pages/index

Michigan

Michigan Local Government Management Association
mlgma.org

Minnesota

Minnesota City/County Management Association
mncma.org

Mississippi

Mississippi City and County Management Association
Mary Ann Hess (through May 2011)
Finance Director/City Clerk
City of Laurel
P.O. Box 647
Laurel 39441-0647
maryannhess@laurelms.com
601-428-6430 (phone)
601-428-6415 (fax)

Missouri

Missouri City/County Management Association
momanagers.org

Montana

See Wyoming

Nebraska

Nebraska City/County Management Association
nebraskacma.org

Nevada

Local Government Managers Association of Nevada
nevadalogman.org/

New Hampshire

New Hampshire Municipal Management Association
nhmunicipal.org

New Jersey

New Jersey Municipal Management Association
njmma.org/

New Mexico

New Mexico City Management Association
Timothy P. Dodge (through September 2011)
City Manager
City of Las Vegas
1700 North Grand Avenue
Las Vegas 87701-4731
tdodge@ci.las-vegas.nm.us
505-454-1401 (phone)
505-425-7335 (fax)

New York

New York State City/County Management Association
nyscma.govoffice.com/

North Carolina

North Carolina City and County Management Association
ncmanagers.org/

North Dakota

See Wyoming

Ohio

Ohio City/County Management Association
ocmaohio.org/

Oklahoma

City Management Association of Oklahoma
cmao-ok.org/

Oregon

Oregon City/County Management Association
occma.org

Pennsylvania

Association for Pennsylvania Municipal Management
apmm.net

Rhode Island

Rhode Island City and Town Management Association
Richard M. Brown, ICMA-CM (through September 2011)
City Manager
City of East Providence
145 Taunton Avenue
East Providence 02914-4530
rbrown@cityofeastprov.com
401-435-7520 (phone)
401-438-1719 (fax)

South Carolina

South Carolina City and County Management Association
scccma.org/

South Dakota

South Dakota City Management Association
sdmunicipalleague.org (Go to "Affiliate Organizations" and then to "City Management")

Tennessee

Tennessee City Management Association
tncma.org/

Texas

Texas City Management Association
tcma.org/

Utah

Utah City Management Association
ucma-utah.org/

Vermont

Vermont Town and City Management Association
Dennis C. McCarthy (through June 2011)
Town Administrator
Town of Winhall
P.O. Box 420
Bondville 05262-0420
wintownhall@comcast.net
802-297-2119 (phone)
802-297-2177 (fax)

Virginia

Virginia Local Government Management Association
vlgma.org

Washington

Washington City/County Management Association
wccma.org

West Virginia

West Virginia City Management Association
wvmanagers.org/

Wisconsin

Wisconsin City/County Management Association
wcma-wi.org

Wyoming, Idaho, Montana, North Dakota, and South Dakota

Great Open Spaces City Management Association
Leon R. Schochenmaier (through April 2011)
City Administrator
City of Pierre
222 East Dakota
Pierre, SD 57006-0270
leon.schochenmaier@ci.pierre.sd.us
605-773-7341 (phone)
605-773-7406 (fax)

Directory 1-6   International Municipal Management Associations

Shown below are the names of 22 international municipal management associations. For each association the directory provides the website so that readers can go directly to the site to find additional information. Where there is no website available, we have provided the name, address, and all contact information for the president of the association (current as of January 15, 2011).

Australia

Local Government Managers Australia (LGMA)
lgma.org.au

Canada

Canadian Association of Municipal Administrators (CAMA)
camacam.ca

Denmark

National Association of Chief Executives in Danish Municipalities (KOMDIR)
komdir.dk

Georgia, Republic of

Municipal Service Providers' Association (Georgia)
mspa.ge/

Hungary

Partnership of Hungarian Local Government Associations
Dr. Levente Magyar
Co-President
Pf. 484
Budapest 1538
polhivjb@mail.datanet.hu
36-1-225-8510
36-1-225-8511

India

City Managers' Association, Gujarat
cmag-india.com

City Managers' Association, Karnataka (CMAK)
cmakarnataka.com/

City Managers' Association, Orissa
cmao.nic.in

Indonesia

All-Indonesia Association of City Government (APEKSI)
apeksi.or.id

Ireland

County and City Managers' Association
Anne O'Keeffe
Director
Office for Local Authority Management
County and City Manager's Association
Floor 2, Cumberland House
Fenian Street
Dublin 2
anneokeeffe15@gmail.com
353-94-90-24444

Israel

Union of Local Authorities in Israel (ULAI)
http://www.masham.org.il/English/Pages/default.aspx

Mexico

Mexican Association of Municipalities (AMMAC)
ammac.org.mx

Nepal

Municipal Association of Nepal (MuAN)
muannepal.org.np/

Netherlands

Dutch City Managers Association
gemeentesecretaris.nl

New Zealand

New Zealand Society of Local Government Managers
solgm.org.nz

Norway

Norwegian Forum of Municipal Executives
Finn Brevig
Executive Director
Norsk Radmannsforum
Box 354
2001 Lillestrom
f.c.brevig@radmann.no
477-785-0100

Russia

Russian National Congress of Municipalities
fz131.minregion.ru/main/main*root

Slovakia

Slovak City Managers' Association
apums.sk

South Africa

Institute for Local Government Management of South Africa
ilgm.co.za

South Korea

Korean Urban Management Association
kruma.org

Spain

L'Union des Dirigeants Territoriaux de l'Europe (U.Di.T.E.)
udite.eu

Sri Lanka

Federation of Sri Lankan Local Government Authorities (FSLGA)
fslga.wordpress.com/

Sweden

Association of Swedish City Managers
Anna Sandborgh
Chair
Karlstads kommun
Kommunledningskontoret
651 84 Karlstad
anna.sandborgh@karlstad.se
46-5-429-5102

United Kingdom

Society of Local Authority Chief Executives (SOLACE)
solace.org.uk

Viet Nam

Association of Cities of Viet Nam
acvn.vn

Directory 1-7   U.S. State Associations of Counties

Shown below are the 53 state associations of counties in the United States. For each association the directory provides the address and website so that readers can go directly to the site to find additional information. Where there is no website available, we have provided the name and phone number for the executive director (current as of January 15, 2011).

Alabama

Association of County Commissions of Alabama
100 North Jackson Street
Montgomery 36104
acca-online.org

Alaska

Alaska Municipal League
217 Second Street, Suite 200
Juneau 99801
akml.org

Arizona

Arizona Association of Counties
1910 West Jefferson, Suite 1
Phoenix 85009
azcounties.org

County Supervisors Association of Arizona
1905 West Washington Street, Suite 100
Phoenix 85009
countysupervisors.org

Arkansas

Association of Arkansas Counties
1415 West Third Street
Little Rock 72201
arcounties.org

California

California State Association of Counties
1100 K Street, Suite 101
Sacramento 95814
csac.counties.org

Colorado

Colorado Counties, Inc.
800 Grant Street, Suite 500
Denver 80203
ccionline.org

Delaware

Delaware Association of Counties
12 North Washington Avenue
Lewes 19958-1806
dacounties.org/

Florida

Florida Association of Counties
P.O. Box 549
Tallahassee 32302
fl-counties.com

Georgia

Association County Commissioners of Georgia
50 Hurt Plaza, Suite 1000
Atlanta 30303
accg.org

Hawaii

Hawaii State Association of Counties
4396 Rice Street, Suite 206
Lihue 96766
hawaii-county.com/

Idaho

Idaho Association of Counties
700 West Washington
P.O. Box 1623
Boise 83701
idcounties.org

Illinois

Illinois Association of County Board Members
413 West Monroe Street, 2nd Floor
Springfield 62704
ilcounty.org/

Metro Counties of Illinois
1303 Brandywine Road
Libertyville 60048-3000
Dwight Magalis, executive director
847-816-0889

United Counties Council of Illinois
217 East Monroe Street, Suite 101
Springfield 62701
unitedcounties.com/default.asp

Indiana

Association of Indiana Counties
101 West Ohio Street, Suite 1575
Indianapolis 46204
indianacounties.org

Iowa

Iowa State Association of Counties
501 S.W. Seventh Street, Suite Q
Des Moines 50309-4540
iowacounties.org

Kansas

Kansas Association of Counties
300 S.W. Eighth Street, 3rd Floor
Topeka 66603
kansascounties.org

Kentucky

Kentucky Association of Counties
400 Englewood Drive
Frankfort 40601
kaco.org

Louisiana

Police Jury Association of Louisiana
707 North Seventh Street
Baton Rouge 70802
lpgov.org

Maine

Maine County Commissioners Association
11 Columbia Street
Augusta 04330
mainecounties.org/commissioners.html

Maryland

Maryland Association of Counties
169 Conduit Street
Annapolis 21401
mdcounties.org

Massachusetts

Massachusetts Association of County Commissioners
614 High Street
Dedham 02027-0310
Peter Collins, executive director
781-461-6105

Michigan

Michigan Association of Counties
935 North Washington Avenue
Lansing 48906
micounties.org

Minnesota

Association of Minnesota Counties
125 Charles Avenue
St. Paul 55103-2108
mncounties.org

Mississippi

Mississippi Association of Supervisors
793 North President Street
Jackson 39202
masnetwork.org

Missouri

Missouri Association of Counties
516 East Capitol Avenue
P.O. Box 234
Jefferson City 65102-0234
mocounties.com

Montana

Montana Association of Counties
2715 Skyway Drive
Helena 59602-1213
maco.cog.mt.us

Nebraska

Nebraska Association of County Officials
625 South 14th Street
Lincoln 68508
nacone.org

Nevada

Nevada Association of Counties
201 South Roop Street, Suite 101
Carson City 89701
nvnaco.org

New Hampshire

New Hampshire Association of Counties
Bow Brook Place
46 Donovan Street, Suite 2
Concord 03301-2624
nhcounties.org

New Jersey

New Jersey Association of Counties
150 West State Street
Trenton 08608
njac.org

New Mexico

New Mexico Association of Counties
613 Old Santa Fe Trail
Santa Fe 87505
nmcounties.org

New York

New York State Association of Counties
540 Broadway, 5th Floor
Albany 12207
nysac.org

North Carolina

North Carolina Association of County Commissioners
215 North Dawson Street
Raleigh 27603
ncacc.org

North Dakota

North Dakota Association of Counties
1661 Capitol Way
P.O. Box 877
Bismarck 58502-0877
ndaco.org

Ohio

County Commissioners Association of Ohio
209 East State Street
Columbus 43215-4309
ccao.org

Oklahoma

Association of County Commissioners of Oklahoma City
429 N.E. 50th Street
Oklahoma City 73105
okacco.com

Oregon

Association of Oregon Counties
P.O. Box 12729
Salem 97309
aocweb.org

Pennsylvania

County Commissioners Association of Pennsylvania
P.O. Box 60769
Harrisburg 17106-0769
pacounties.org

South Carolina

South Carolina Association of Counties
1919 Thurmond Mall
Columbia 29201
sccounties.org

South Dakota

South Dakota Association of County Officials
300 East Capitol Avenue, Suite 2
Pierre 57501
sdcounties.org

South Dakota Association of County Commissioners
222 East Capitol Avenue, Suite 1
Pierre 57501
sdcc.govoffice2.com

Tennessee

Tennessee County Services Association
226 Capitol Boulevard, Suite 700
Nashville 37219-1896
tncounties.org

Texas

Texas Association of Counties
1210 San Antonio Street
Austin 78701
county.org

Utah

Utah Association of Counties
5397 South Vine Street
Salt Lake City 84107
uacnet.org

Virginia

Virginia Association of Counties
1207 East Main Street, Suite 300
Richmond 23219-3627
vaco.org

Washington

Washington Association of County Officials
206 Tenth Avenue, S.E.
Olympia 98501
wacounties.org/waco

Washington State Association of Counties
206 Tenth Avenue, S.E.
Olympia 98501
wacounties.org/wsac

West Virginia

County Commissioners' Association of West Virginia
2309 Washington Street, East
Charleston 25311
polsci.wvu.edu/wv

West Virginia Association of Counties
2211 Washington Street East
Charleston 25311-2118
wvcounties.org

Wisconsin

Wisconsin Counties Association
22 East Mifflin Street, Suite 900
Madison 53703
wicounties.org

Wyoming

Wyoming County Commissioners Association
409 West 24th Street
P.O. Box 86
Cheyenne 82003
wyo-wcca.org

Directory 1-8 U.S. Councils of Governments Recognized by ICMA

Shown below are the names and websites of the 96 U.S. councils of government recognized by ICMA state associations of counties in the United States. Where there is no website available, we have provided the phone number for the council office.

ALABAMA-4

Central Alabama Regional Planning and Development Commission
carpdc.com

East Alabama Regional Planning & Development Commission
earpdc.org

Regional Planning Commission of Greater Birmingham
rpcgb.org

South Central Alabama Development Commission
scadc.state.al.us

ARIZONA-2

Maricopa Association of Governments
azmag.gov

Pima Association of Governments
pagnet.org

ARKANSAS-3

Metroplan
metroplan.org

Northwest Arkansas Regional Planning Commission
nwarpc.org

White River Planning & Development District
wrpdd.org

CALIFORNIA-9

Association of Bay Area Governments
abag.ca.gov

Council of Fresno County Governments
fresnocog.org

Sacramento Area Council of Governments
sacog.org

San Bernardino Associated Governments
sanbag.ca.gov

San Diego Association of Governments
sandag.cog.ca.us

Santa Barbara County Association of Governments
sbcag.org/

Southern California Association of Governments
scag.ca.gov

Stanislaus Area Association of Governments
stancog.org

Western Riverside Council of Governments
wrcog.ca.us

COLORADO-1

Denver Regional Council of Governments
drcog.org

DISTRICT OF COLUMBIA-1

Metropolitan Washington Council of Governments
mwcog.org

FLORIDA-2

Solid Waste Authority of Palm Beach County
swa.org

Tampa Bay Regional Planning Council
tbrpc.org/

GEORGIA-3

Atlanta Regional Commission
atlantaregional.com

Middle Georgia Regional Development Center
mgrdc.org

Southeast Georgia Regional Development Center
segardc.org

IDAHO-1

Panhandle Area Council
pacni.org/pachome.htm

ILLINOIS-9

Bi-State Regional Commission
bistateonline.org

Champaign County Regional Planning Commission
ccrpc.org

DuPage Mayors and Managers Conference
dmmc-cog.org

Lake County Municipal League
lakecountyleague.org

North Central Illinois Council of Governments
ncicg.org

Northwest Municipal Conference
nwmc-cog.org

South Central Illinois Regional Planning and Development Commission
little-egypt.com/scirpdc

Southwestern Illinois Metropolitan and Regional Planning Commission
618-344-4250

Tri-County Regional Planning Commission
tricountyrpc.org/about/index.htm

IOWA-1

Midas Council of Governments
midascog.net

KENTUCKY-4

Barren River Area Development District
bradd.org

Big Sandy Area Development District
bigsandy.org

Lincoln Trail Area Development District
ltadd.org

Northern Kentucky Area Development District
nkadd.org

MARYLAND-2

Baltimore Metropolitan Council
baltometro.org

Tri-County Council For Southern Maryland
tccsmd.org

MICHIGAN-1

Southeast Michigan Council of Governments
semcog.org

MISSISSIPPI-1

Central Mississippi Planning & Development District
cmpdd.org

MISSOURI-3

East-West Gateway Coordinating Council
ewgateway.org

Mid-America Regional Council
marc.org

South Central Ozark Council of Governments
users.townsqr.com/scocog

NEW MEXICO-2

Middle Rio Grande Council of Governments
mrcog-nm.gov

Southwest New Mexico Council of Governments
nmlocalgov.net/southwestern

NEW YORK-1

Capital District Regional Planning Commission
cdrpc.org/index.shtml

NORTH CAROLINA-5

Centralina Council of Governments
centralina.org

Lumber River Council of Governments
lrcog.dst.nc.us

Piedmont Triad Council of Governments
ptcog.org

Region L-Upper Coastal Plain Council of Governments
ucpcog.org

Region P-Eastern Carolina Council of Governments
eccog.org

OHIO-4

Miami Valley Regional Planning Commission
mvrpc.org

Ohio-Kentucky-Indiana Regional Council of Governments
oki.org

Ohio Mid-Eastern Governments Association
omegadistrict.org

Toledo Metropolitan Area Council of Governments
tmacog.org/

OKLAHOMA-2

Association of Central Oklahoma Governments
acogok.org

Central Oklahoma Economic Development District
coedd.org

OREGON-4

Lane Council of Governments
lcog.org

Mid-Columbia Economic Development District
mcedd.org

Mid-Willamette Valley Council of Governments
mwvcog.org

Oregon Cascades West Council of Governments
ocwcog.org/cog_ga1.htm

SOUTH CAROLINA-3

Central Midlands Council of Governments
centralmidlands.org

South Carolina Appalachian Council of Governments
scacog.org

Upper Savannah Council of Governments
uppersavannah.com

SOUTH DAKOTA-2

Northeast Council of Governments
abe.midco.net/necog

Planning and Development District III
districtiii.org/land.htm

TEXAS-15

Alamo Area Council of Governments
aacog.dst.tx.us

Ark-Tex Council of Governments
atcog.org/

Capital Area Planning Council
capco.state.tx.us

Central Texas Council of Governments
ctcog.org

Coastal Bend Council of Governments
cbcog98.org

Concho Valley Council of Governments
cvcog.org

Deep East Texas Council of Governments
detcog.org

Heart of Texas Council of Governments
hotcog.org

Houston-Galveston Area Council
h-gac.com/

Nortex Regional Planning Commission
nortexrpc.org

North Central Texas Council of Governments
nctcog.org

Panhandle Regional Planning Commission
prpc.cog.tx.us

South Plains Association of Governments
spag.org

Texoma Council of Governments
texoma.cog.tx.us

West Central Texas Council of Governments
txregionalcouncil.org/regions/wctcog.htm

UTAH-1

Five County Association of Governments
fcaog.state.ut.us

VIRGINIA-5

Crater Planning District Commission
craterpdc.state.va.us

Hampton Roads Planning District Commission
hrpdc.org

Northern Neck Planning District Commission
nnpdc.org

Northern Virginia Planning District Commission
novaregion.org

West Piedmont Planning District Commission
wppdc.org

WASHINGTON-1

Benton-Franklin Regional Council
wa.gov/bfcog

WEST VIRGINIA-3

Bel-O-Mar Regional Council
belomar.org

Mid-Ohio Valley Regional Council
movrc.org

Region One Planning & Development Council
regiononepdc.org

WISCONSIN-1

East Central Wisconsin Regional Planning Commission
eastcentralrpc.org

2

Professional, Special Assistance, and Educational Organizations Serving Local and State Governments

This article briefly describes 81 organizations that provide services of particular importance to cities, counties, and other local and state governments. Most of the organizations are membership groups for school administrators, health officers, city planners, city managers, public works directors, city attorneys, and other administrators who are appointed rather than elected. Several are general service and representational organizations for states, cities, counties, and administrators and citizens. Some organizations provide distinctive research, technological, consulting, and educational programs on a cost-of-service basis and have been established to meet specific needs of state and local governments. The others support educational activities and conduct research in urban affairs or government administration, thereby indirectly strengthening professionalism in government administration.

The assistance available through the secretariats of these national organizations provides an excellent method of obtaining expert advice and actual information on specific problems. The information secured in this way enables local and state officials to improve administrative practices, organization, and methods and thus improve the quality of services rendered. Many of these organizations also are active in raising the professional standards of their members through in-service training, special conferences and seminars, and other kinds of professional development.

Research on current problems is a continuing activity of many of these groups, and all issue a variety of publications ranging from newsletters and occasional bulletins to diversified books, monographs, research papers, conference proceedings, and regular and special reports.

These organizations provide many of the services that in other countries would be the responsibility of the national government. They arrange annual conferences, answer inquiries, provide in-service training and other kinds of professional development, provide placement services for members, and develop service and cost standards for various activities. Most of the organizations listed have individual memberships, and several also have agency or institutional memberships. Some of these organizations have service memberships that may be based on the population of the jurisdiction, the annual revenue of the jurisdiction or agency, or other criteria that roughly measure the costs of providing service. In addition to these kinds of membership fees, some of the organizations provide specialized consulting, training, and information services both by annual subscription and by charges for specific projects.

Listing of Organizations

Academy for State and Local Government

444 North Capitol Street, N.W., Suite 309
Washington, D.C. 20001-1512
202-434-4850

Chief consult: Richard Ruda

Publication list: Available on request

Purpose: To coordinate cooperative efforts among federal, state, and local governments; the private sector; and the country's research community in addressing key issues facing state and local governments. Also serves as a policy center for joint projects and programs of ICMA and the Council of State Governments, National Association of Counties, National Conference of State Legislatures, National Governors Association, National League of Cities, and U.S. Conference of Mayors. The State and Local Legal Center, an arm of the academy, is devoted to the interests of state and local governments in the Supreme Court. Established 1971.

Airports Council International–North America (ACI-NA)

1775 K Street, N.W., Suite 500
Washington, D.C. 20006
202-293-8500; fax: 202-331-1362

Website: aci-na.org

President: Greg Principato

Major publications: *Airport Highlights*; studies, surveys, reports

Purpose: To promote sound policies dealing with the financing, construction, management, operations, and development of airports; to provide reference and resource facilities and information for airport operators; and to act as the "voice" of airports to governmental agencies, officials, and the public on problems and solutions concerning airport operations. Established 1948.

American Association of Airport Executives (AAAE)

601 Madison Street, Suite 400
Alexandria, Virginia 22314
703-824-0500; fax: 703-820-1395

Website: aaae.org

President: Charles M. Barclay

Major publications: *Airport Report; Airport Magazine; Airport Report Express*

Purpose: To assist airport managers in performing their complex and diverse responsibilities through an airport management reference library; a consulting service; publications containing technical, administrative, legal, and operational information; an electronic bulletin board system; a professional accreditation program for airport executives; and Aviation News and Training Network, a private satellite broadcast network for airport employee training and news. Established 1928.

American Association of Port Authorities (AAPA)

1010 Duke Street
Alexandria, Virginia 22314-3589
703-684-5700; fax: 703-684-6321

E-mail: info@aapa-ports.org

Website: aapa-ports.org

President: Kurt J. Nagle

Major publications: *Alert Newsletter; AAPA Directory–Seaports of the Americas; Seaport Magazine*

Purpose: To promote the common interests of the port community and provide leadership on trade, transportation, environmental, and other issues related to port development and operations. As the alliance of ports of the Western Hemisphere, AAPA furthers public understanding of the essential role fulfilled by ports within the global transportation system. It also serves as a resource to help members accomplish their professional responsibilities. Established 1912.

American Association of School Administrators (AASA)

801 North Quincy Street, Suite 700
Arlington, Virginia 22203
703-528-0700; fax: 703-841-1543

Website: aasa.org

Executive director: Daniel A. Domenech

Major publications: *The School Administrator;* Critical Issues Series

Purpose: To develop qualified educational leaders and support excellence in educational administration; to initiate and support laws, policies, research, and practices that will improve education; to promote programs and activities that focus on leadership for learning and excellence in education; and to cultivate a climate in which quality education can thrive. Established 1865.

American College of Healthcare Executives (ACHE)

One North Franklin Street, Suite 1700
Chicago, Illinois 60606-3529
312-424-2800; fax: 312-424-0023

Website: ache.org

President/CEO: Thomas C. Dolan, PhD, FACHE, CAE

Major publications: *Journal of Healthcare Management; Healthcare Executive; Frontiers of Health Services Management*; miscellaneous studies and task force, committee, and seminar reports

Purpose: To be the premier professional society for health care executives who are dedicated to improving health care delivery and to advancing health care management excellence. Established 1933.

American Institute of Architects (AIA)

1735 New York Avenue, N.W.
Washington, D.C. 20006
202-626-7300; fax: 202-626-7547
800-242-3837

Website: aia.org

President: Clark Manus

Major publication: *AIArchitect*

Purpose: To organize and unite in fellowship the members of the architectural profession; to promote the aesthetic, scientific, and practical efficiency of the profession; to advance the science and art of planning and building by advancing the standards of architectural education, training, and practice; to coordinate the efforts of the building industry and the profession of architecture to ensure the advancement of living standards for people through improved environment; and to make the profession of architecture one of ever-increasing service to society. Established 1857.

American Library Association (ALA)

50 East Huron Street
Chicago, Illinois 60611
312-944-6780; fax: 312-440-9374
800-545-2433
Also at 1615 New Hampshire Avenue, N.W.
Washington, D.C. 20009-2520
202-628-8410; fax: 202-628-8419
800-941-8478

Website: www.ala.org

Executive director: Keith Michael Fiels

Major publications: *American Libraries; Booklist; Book Links*

Purpose: To assist libraries and librarians in promoting and improving library service and librarianship. Established 1876.

American Planning Association (APA), and its professional institute, the American Institute of Certified Planners (AICP)

1030 15th Street, N.W.
Washington, D.C. 20005-1503
202-872-0611; fax: 202-872-0643
Also at 205 North Michigan Avenue, Suite 1200
Chicago, Illinois 60601
312-431-9100; fax: 312-786-6700

Website: planning.org

Executive director/CEO: W. Paul Farmer, FAICP

Major publications: *Journal of the APA; Planning; Planning and Environmental Law; Zoning Practice; The Commissioner; Practicing Planner; Interact; APA Advocate*; Planning Advisory Service (PAS) Reports

Purpose: To encourage planning that will meet the needs of people and society more effectively. APA is a nonprofit public interest and research organization representing 43,000 practicing planners, officials, and citizens involved with urban and rural planning issues. Sixty-five percent of its members work for state and local government agencies and are involved, on a day-to-day basis, in formulating planning policies and preparing land-use regulations. AICP is APA's professional institute, providing recognized leadership nationwide in the certification of professional planners, ethics, professional development, planning education, and the standards of planning practice. APA resulted from a consolidation of the American Institute of Planners, founded in 1917, and the American Society of Planning Officials, established in 1934.

American Public Gas Association (APGA)

201 Massachusetts Avenue, N.E., Suite C-4
Washington, D.C. 20002
202-464-2742; fax: 202-464-0246

E-mail: bkalisch@apga.org

Website: apga.org

President/CEO: Bert Kalisch

Major publications: *Public Gas News* (bi-weekly newsletter); *Publicly Owned Natural Gas System Directory* (annual); *The Source* (quarterly magazine)

Purpose: To be an advocate for publicly owned natural gas distribution systems, and effectively educate and communicate with members to promote safety, awareness, performance, and competitiveness. Established 1961.

American Public Health Association (APHA)

800 I Street, N.W.
Washington, D.C. 20001-3710
202-777-2742; fax: 202-777-2534

Website: apha.org

Executive director: Georges Benjamin, MD

Major publications: *American Journal of Public Health*; The Nation's Health

Purpose: To protect the health of the public through the maintenance of standards for scientific procedures, legislative education, and practical application of innovative health programs. Established 1872.

American Public Human Services Association (APHSA)

1133 19th Street, N.W., Suite 400
Washington, D.C. 20036
202-682-0100; fax: 202-289-6555

Website: aphsa.org

Executive director: Tracy Wareing

Major publications: *Policy and Practice* magazine; *Public Human Services Directory; This Week in Health; This Week in Washington; W-Memo; Working for Tomorrow*

Purpose: To develop and promote policies and practices that improve the health and well-being of families, children, and adults. Established 1930.

American Public Power Association (APPA)

1875 Connecticut Avenue, N.W., Suite 1200
Washington, D.C. 20009
202-467-2900; fax: 202-467-2910

Website: appanet.org

President/CEO: Mark Crisson

Major publications: *Public Power* (bimonthly magazine); *Public Power Weekly* (newsletter); *Public Power Daily*

Purpose: To promote the efficiency and benefits of publicly owned electric systems; to achieve cooperation among public systems; to protect the interests of publicly owned utilities; and to provide service in the fields of management and operation, energy conservation, consumer services, public relations, engineering, design, construction, research, and accounting practice. APPA represents more than 2,000 community-owned electric utilities and provides services in the areas of government relations, engineering and operations, accounting and finance, energy research and development, management, customer relations, and public communications. The association represents public power interests before Congress, federal agencies, and the courts; provides educational programs and energy planning services in technical and management areas; and collects, analyzes, and disseminates information on public power and the electric utility industry. APPA publishes a weekly newsletter, bimonthly magazine, and many specialized publications; funds energy research and development projects; recognizes utilities and individuals for excellence in management and operations; and serves as a resource for federal, state, and local policy makers and officials, news reporters, public interest and other organizations, and the general public on public power and energy issues. Established 1940.

American Public Transportation Association (APTA)

1666 K Street, N.W., Suite 1100
Washington, D.C. 20006
202-496-4800; fax: 202-496-4324

Website: apta.com

President: William W. Millar

Major publications: *Passenger Transport; Public Transportation Fact Book*

Purpose: To represent the operators of and suppliers to public transit; to provide a medium for discussion, exchange of experiences, and comparative study of industry affairs; and to research and investigate methods to improve public transit. The association also assists public transit entities with special issues, and collects and makes available public transit-related data and information. Established 1882.

American Public Works Association (APWA)

2345 Grand Boulevard, Suite 700
Kansas City, Missouri 64108-2625
816-472-6100; fax: 816-472-1610
Also at 1275 K Street, N.W., Suite 750
Washington, D.C. 20005-4083
202-408-9541; fax: 202-408-9542

Website: apwa.net

Executive director: Peter B. King

Major publications: *APWA Reporter* (12 issues), research reports, technical publications and manuals

Purpose: To develop and support the people, agencies, and organizations that plan, build, maintain, and improve our communities. Established 1894.

American Society for Public Administration (ASPA)

1301 Pennsylvania Avenue, N.W., Suite 840
Washington, D.C. 20004
202-393-7878; fax: 202-638-4952

Website: aspanet.org

Executive director: Antoinette A. Samuel

Major publications: *Public Administration Review; PA Times*

Purpose: To improve the management of public service at all levels of government; to advocate on behalf of public service; to advance the science, processes, and art of public administration; and to disseminate information and facilitate the exchange of knowledge among persons interested in the practice or teaching of public administration. Established 1939.

American Water Works Association (AWWA)

6666 West Quincy Avenue
Denver, Colorado 80235
303-794-7711; fax: 303-347-0804

Website: awwa.org

Executive director: David B. LaFrance

Major publications: *AWWA Journal; MainStream; OpFlow; WaterWeek*

Purpose: To promote public health and welfare in the provision of drinking water of unquestionable and sufficient quality. Founded 1881.

Association of Public-Safety Communications Officials–
International, Inc.

351 North Williamson Boulevard
Daytona Beach, Florida 32114-1112
386-322-2500; fax: 386-322-2501
Also at 1426 Prince Street
Alexandria, Virginia 22314-2815
571-312-4400; fax: 571-312-4419

Website: apcointl.org

Executive director: George S. Rice Jr.

Major publications: *APCO BULLETIN; The Journal of Public Safety Communications; Public Safety Operating Procedures Manual;* APCO training courses

Purpose: To promote the development and progress of public safety telecommunications through research, planning, and training; to promote cooperation among public safety agencies; to perform frequency coordination for radio services administered by the Federal Communications Commission; and to act as a liaison with federal regulatory bodies. Established 1935.

Association of Public Treasurers (APT)

962 Wayne Avenue, Suite 910
Silver Spring, Maryland 20910
301-495-5560; fax: 301-495-5561

Website: aptusc.org

Executive director: Lindsey Dively

Major publications: *Technical Topics; Treasury Notes*

Purpose: To enhance local treasury management by providing educational training, technical assistance, legislative services, and a forum for treasurers to exchange ideas and develop policy papers and positions. Established 1965.

Canadian Association of Municipal Administrators (CAMA)

P.O. Box 128, Station A
Fredericton, New Brunswick E3B 4Y2
866-771-2262; fax: 506-460-2134

Website: camacam.ca

Executive director: Jennifer Goodine

Purpose: To achieve greater communication and cooperation among municipal managers across Canada, and to focus the talents of its members on the preservation and advancement of municipal government by enhancing the quality of municipal management in Canada. Established 1972.

Center for State and Local Government Excellence (SLGE)

777 North Capitol Street, N.E., Suite 500
Washington, D.C. 20002-4201
202-682-6100; fax: 202-962-3604

Website: slge.org

Executive director: Elizabeth Kellar

Major publications: Research reports: "The Funding of State and Local Pensions: 2009–2013," "How Local Governments Are Addressing Retiree Health Care Funding," "Out of Balance? Comparing Public and Private Sector Compensation Over 20 Years," "The Great

Recession and the State and Local Workforce"; other research and case studies on public sector pensions and retiree health, online polls, public opinion surveys, competitive employment practices, health care reform, and workforce demographics.

Purpose: To help state and local governments become knowledgeable and competitive employers so that they can attract and retain talented, committed, and well-prepared individuals to public service. Research areas are workforce analysis and implications of changing demographics, competitive employment practices, compensation analysis, state and local government retirement plans, post-employment and retiree health care benefits, and financial wellness and retirement planning. Established 2006.

Council of State Community Development Agencies (COSCDA)

1825 K Street, Suite 515
Washington, D.C. 20006
202-293-5820; fax: 202-293-2820

Website: coscda.org

Executive director: Dianne Taylor

Major publications: *The National Line; StateLine; Member Update; Annual Report*

Purpose: To promote the value and importance of state involvement in community development, economic development, affordable housing, and homelessness programs. For over 30 years, COSCDA has positioned itself as the premier national association charged with advocating and enhancing the leadership role of states in these issue areas, which it accomplishes through information sharing and a variety of technical assistance programs. COSCDA seeks to support, facilitate, and communicate states' priorities to its membership, as well as to elected and appointed officials and to state and federal policy makers. Its Training Academy offers basic and advanced courses on community development block grants and an introductory course on housing programs. COSCDA also holds an annual training conference in the fall and a program managers' conference in the spring. Established 1974.

Council of State Governments (CSG)

2760 Research Park Drive
P.O. Box 11910
Lexington, Kentucky 40511
859-244-8000; fax: 859-244-8001

Website: csg.org

Executive director/CEO: David Adkins

Major publications: *Book of the States; Capitol Ideas* magazine; *CSG State Directories*

Purpose: To prepare states for the future by interpreting changing national and international trends and conditions; to promote the sovereignty of the states and their role in the American federal system; to advocate multistate problem solving and partnerships; and to build leadership skills to improve decision making. CSG is a multibranch and regionally focused association of the states, U.S. territories, and commonwealths. Established 1933.

Federation of Canadian Municipalities (FCM)

24 Clarence Street
Ottawa, Ontario K1N 5P3
613-241-5221; fax: 613-241-7440

E-mail: ceo@fcm.ca

Website: fcm.ca

CEO: Brock Carlton

Major publications: *Forum* (national magazine); *Crossroads: The Newsletter for FCM International*

Purpose: To represent the interests of all municipalities on policy and program matters within federal jurisdictions. Policy and program priorities are determined by FCM's board of directors, standing committees, and task forces. Issues include payments in lieu of taxes, goods and service taxes, economic development, municipal infrastructure, environment, transportation, community safety and crime prevention, quality-of-life social indicators, housing, race relations, and international trade and aid. FCM members include Canada's largest cities, small urban and rural communities, and the 18 major provincial and territorial municipal associations, which together represent more than 20 million Canadians. Established 1937.

Government Finance Officers Association (GFOA)

203 North LaSalle Street, Suite 2700
Chicago, Illinois 60601-1210
312-977-9700; fax: 312-977-4806
Also at 1301 Pennsylvania Avenue, N.W., Suite 309
Washington, D.C. 20004
202-393-8020; fax: 202-393-0780

Website: gfoa.org

Executive director/CEO: Jeffrey L. Esser

Major publications: *GFOA Newsletter; Government Finance Review Magazine; Public Investor; GAAFR Review; Pension & Benefits Update; Governmental Accounting, Auditing, and Financial Reporting; Investing Public Funds; Elected Official's Series*

Purpose: To enhance and promote the professional management of governmental financial resources by identifying, developing, and advancing fiscal strategies, policies, and practices for the public benefit. Established 1906.

Government Management Information Sciences Users Group (GMIS)

P.O. Box 27923
Austin, Texas 78755
512-220-1497; fax: 512-857-7711

Website: gmis.org

GMIS listserv: Headquarters@GMIS.org

Executive director: June Randall

Purpose: To provide a forum for the exchange of ideas, information, and techniques; and to foster enhancements in hardware, software, and communication developments as they relate to government activities. State and local government agencies are members represented by their top computer or information technology professionals. The GMIS Annual Educational Conference promotes sharing of ideas and the latest technology. GMIS sponsors an annual "Professional of the Year" program, pub-lishes a newsletter, and provides organizational support to 19 state chapters. State chapters enable member agencies within a geographical area to develop close relationships and to foster the spirit and intent of GMIS through cooperation, assistance, and mutual support. GMIS is affiliated with KommITS, a sister organization of local governments in Sweden; SOCITM in the United Kingdom; ALGIM in New Zealand; VIAG in The Netherlands; MISA/ASIM in Ontario, Canada; LOLA-International (Linked Organisation of Local Authority ICT Societies); and V-ICT-OR in Belgium. Established 1971.

Governmental Accounting Standards Board (GASB)

401 Merritt 7
P.O. Box 5116
Norwalk, Connecticut 06856-5116
203-847-0700; fax: 203-849-9714

Website: gasb.org

Chairman: Robert Attmore

Major publications: Governmental Accounting Standards Series; Codification of Standards; implementation guides; Suggested Guidelines for Voluntary Reporting; exposure drafts; Preliminary Views documents; *The GASB Report* (monthly newsletter); plain-language user guides

Purpose: To establish and improve standards of financial accounting and reporting for state and local governmental entities. GASB standards guide the preparation of those entities' external financial reports so that users of the reports can obtain the state and local government financial information needed to make economic, social, and political decisions. Interested parties are encouraged to read and comment on discussion documents of proposed standards, which can be downloaded free of charge from the GASB website. Final standards, guides to implementing standards and using government financial reports, and subscriptions to the GASB's publications can be ordered through the website as well. GASB's website also provides up-to-date information about current projects, forms for submitting technical questions and signing up for e-mail news alerts, a section devoted to financial report users, and a link to its Performance Measurement for Government website. The GASB is overseen by the Financial Accounting Foundation's Board of Trustees. Established 1984.

Governmental Research Association (GRA)

P.O. Box 292300
Samford University
Birmingham, Alabama 35229
205-870-2482

Website: graonline.org

Executive director: Steven T. Wray

Major publications: *Directory of Organizations and Individuals Professionally Engaged in Governmental Research and Related Activities* (annual); *GRA Reporter* (quarterly)

Purpose: To promote and coordinate the activities of governmental research agencies; to encourage the development of effective organization and methods for the administration and operation of government; to encourage the development of common standards for the appraisal of results; to facilitate the exchange of ideas and experiences; and to serve as a clearinghouse. Established 1914.

ICMA

777 North Capitol Street, N.E., Suite 500
Washington, D.C. 20002-4201
202-289-4262; fax: 202-962-3500

Website: icma.org

Executive director: Robert J. O'Neill Jr.

Major publications: *Homeland Security: Best Practices for Local Government; Statistics for Public Administration: Practical Uses for Better Decision Making; Economic Development: Strategies for State and Local Practice* (2nd ed.); *Capital Budgeting and Finance: A Guide for Local Governments* (2nd ed.); *Human Resource Management in Local Government: An Essential Guide* (3rd ed.); *Managing Local Government: Cases in Effectiveness; Effective Supervisory Practices* (4th ed.); *Leading Your Community: A Guide for Local Elected Leaders; Budgeting: A Guide for Local Governments; A Revenue Guide for Local Government;* "Green" Books, *The Municipal Year Book, Public Management (PM)* magazine, *In Focus* (formerly *IQ Reports*), *ICMA Newsletter;* self-study courses, training packages

Purpose: To create excellence in local governance by developing and advocating professional management of local government worldwide. ICMA provides member support; publications, data, and information; peer and results-oriented assistance; and training and professional development to more than 9,000 city, town, and county experts and other individuals throughout the world. The management decisions made by ICMA's members affect 185 million individuals living in thousands of communities, from small villages and towns to large metropolitan areas. Established 1914.

ICMA Retirement Corporation (ICMA-RC)

777 North Capitol Street, N.E.
Washington, D.C. 20002
202-962-4600; fax: 202-962-4601
800-669-7400

Website: www.icmarc.org

President/CEO: Joan McCallen

Purpose: To provide retirement plans and related services for more than 920,000 public employees in over 9,000 retirement plans. An independent financial services corporation, ICMA-RC is dedicated to helping build retirement security for public employees by providing investment tools, financial education, and other retirement-related services. The corporation also works to ease the administrative responsibility of local, city, and state governments that offer these benefits to their employees. Established 1972.

Institute of Internal Auditors, Inc., (The IIA)

247 Maitland Avenue
Altamonte Springs, Florida 32701-4201
407-937-1100; fax: 407-937-1101

Website: theiia.org

President: Richard Chambers

Major publications: *Internal Auditor; Tone at the Top* (quarterly corporate governance newsletter)

Purpose: To provide comprehensive professional development and standards for the practice of internal auditing; and to research, disseminate, and promote education in internal auditing and internal control. The IIA offers the Certified Government Auditing Professional (CGAP) to distinguish leaders in public sector auditing. In addition to offering quality assessment services, the IIA performs custom on-site seminars for government auditors and offers educational products that address issues pertaining to government auditing. An international professional association with global headquarters in Altamonte Springs, Florida, The IIA has more than 140,000 members in internal auditing, governance, internal control, information technology audit, education, and security. With representation from more than 165 countries, The IIA is the internal audit profession's global voice, recognized authority, acknowledged leader, chief advocate, and principal educator worldwide. Established 1941.

Institute for Public Administration (IPA)

180 Graham Hall
University of Delaware
Newark, Delaware 19716-7380
302-831-8971; fax: 302-831-3488

Website: ipa.udel.edu

Director: Jerome R. Lewis

Major publications: IPA Reports, available at dspace.udel.edu:8080/dspace/handle/19716/7

Purpose: To address the policy, planning, and management needs of its partners through the integration of applied research, professional development, and the education of tomorrow's leaders. IPA provides direct staff assistance, research, policy analysis, training, and forums while contributing to the scholarly body of knowledge in public administration. Established 1906.

Institute of Transportation Engineers (ITE)

1627 Eye Street, N.W., Suite 600
Washington, D.C. 20006
202-785-0060; fax: 202-785-0609

Website: ite.org

Executive director: Thomas W. Brahms

Major publications: *Trip Generation, Parking Generation; Innovative Bicycle Treatments; Transportation and Land Use Development; Transportation Engineering Handbook; Transportation Planning Handbook; Manual of Transportation Engineering Studies; Traffic Safety Toolbox, A Primer on Traffic Safety; Manual of Uniform Traffic Control Devices, 2009; Traffic Control Devices Handbook; ITE Journal*

Purpose: To promote professional development in the field through education, research, development of public awareness, and exchange of information. Established 1930.

International Association of Assessing Officers (IAAO)

314 West 10th Street
Kansas City, Missouri 64105
816-701-8100; fax: 816-701-8149

Website: iaao.org

Executive director: Lisa J. Daniels

Major publications: *Journal of Property Tax Assessment and Administration; Property Appraisal and Assessment Administration; Property Assessment Valuation* (3rd ed., 2010); *Mass Appraisal of Real Property* (1999); *GIS Guidelines for Assessors* (2nd ed., with URISA, 1999); *Assessment Standards*

Purpose: To provide leadership in accurate property valuation, property tax administration, and property tax policy throughout the world. Established 1934.

International Association of Chiefs of Police (IACP)

515 North Washington Street
Alexandria, Virginia 22314-2357
703-836-6767; fax: 703-836-4543
800-THE IACP

Website: theiacp.org

Executive director: Daniel N. Rosenblatt

Major publications: *Police Chief; Training Keys*

Purpose: To advance the art of police science through the development and dissemination of improved administrative, technical, and operational practices, and to promote the use of such practices in police work. Fosters police cooperation through the exchange of information among police administrators, and encourages all police officers to adhere to high standards of performance and conduct. Established 1893.

International Association of Fire Chiefs (IAFC)

4025 Fair Ridge Drive, Suite 300
Fairfax, Virginia 22033-2868
703-273-0911; fax: 703-273-9363

Website: iafc.org

Executive director/CEO: Mark Light, CAE

Major publication: *On Scene* (twice-monthly newsletter)

Purpose: To enhance the professionalism and capabilities of career and volunteer fire chiefs, chief fire officers, and managers of emergency service organizations throughout the international community through vision, services, information, education, and representation. Established 1873.

International Association of Venue Managers (IAVM) (formerly the International Association of Assembly Managers)

635 Fritz Drive, Suite 100
Coppell, Texas 75019-4442
972-906-7441; fax: 972-906-7418

Website: iaam.org

President/CEO: Dexter King, CFE

Major publications: *Facility Manager; IAVM Guide to Members and Services; IAVM E-News; Venue Safety & Security* magazine

Purpose: To educate, advocate for, and inspire public assembly venue professionals worldwide. Established 1925.

International Code Council

500 New Jersey Avenue, N.W., 6th Floor
Washington, D.C. 20001-2070
888-422-7233; fax: 202-783-2348

Website: iccsafe.org

CEO: Richard P. Weiland

Major publication: *The International Codes*

Purpose: To build safety and fire prevention by developing the codes used to construct residential and commercial buildings, including homes and schools. Most U.S. cities, counties, and states that adopt codes choose the international codes developed by the ICC, a membership association. Established 1994.

International Economic Development Council (IEDC)

734 15th Street, N.W., Suite 900
Washington, D.C. 20005
202-223-7800; fax: 202-223-4745

Website: iedconline.org

President/CEO: Jeffrey A. Finkle, CEcD

Major publications: *Economic Development Journal; Economic Development Now; Federal Directory; Federal Review; Budget Overview*

Purpose: To help economic development professionals improve the quality of life in their communities. With more than 4,000 members, IEDC represents all levels of government, academia, and private industry, providing a broad range of member services that includes research, advisory services, conferences, professional certification, professional development, publications, and legislative tracking. Established 2001.

International Institute of Municipal Clerks (IIMC)

8331 Utica Avenue, Suite 200
Rancho Cucamonga, California 91730
909-944-4162; fax: 909-944-8545
800-251-1639

Website: iimc.com

Executive director: Chris Shalby

Major publications: *IIMC News Digest; The Language of Local Government; Meeting Administration Handbook; Parliamentary Procedures in Local Government; Role Call: Strategy for a Professional Clerk;* "Partners in Democracy" video, case study packets, technical bulletins

Purpose: To promote continuing education and certification through university and college-based institutes, and provide networking solutions, services, and benefits to its members worldwide. Established 1947.

International Municipal Lawyers Association (IMLA)

7910 Woodmont Avenue, Suite 1440
Bethesda, Maryland 20814
202-466-5424; fax: 202-785-0152

E-mail: info@imla.org

Website: imla.org

General counsel/executive director: Chuck Thompson

Major publications: *The IMLA Model Ordinance Service; Municipal Lawyer*

Purpose: To provide continuing legal education events, publications, research, legal advocacy assistance, and excellent networking opportunities for the local government legal community. IMLA is a membership organization of U.S. and Canadian city and county attorneys. Established 1935.

International Public Management Association for Human Resources (IPMA-HR)

1617 Duke Street
Alexandria, Virginia 22314
703-549-7100; fax: 703-684-0948

Website: ipma-hr.org

Executive director: Neil E. Reichenberg

Major publications: *Public Personnel Management; HR Bulletin; IPMA-HR News*

Purpose: To improve service to the public by promoting quality human resource management in the public sector. Established 1973.

League of Women Voters of the United States (LWVUS)

1730 M Street, N.W., Suite 1000
Washington, D.C. 20036-4508
202-429-1965; fax: 202-429-0854

Website: lwv.org

Executive director: Nancy Tate

Major publications: *Choosing the President 2008: A Citizen's Guide to the Electoral Process*; voters' reference guides and brochures in English and Spanish

Purpose: To encourage informed and active participation in government and to influence public policy through education and advocacy. The league's current advocacy priorities are health care reform, climate change, election reform, a fair judiciary, immigration, openness in government, redistricting reform, campaign finance, lobbying, and election reform. The League of Women Voters Education Fund, a separate but complementary organization, provides research and public education services to the public to encourage and enable citizen participation in government. Current public education programs include voter outreach and education, the Vote 411.org website, election reform, judicial independence, and international forms and exchange activities. The league is a nonpartisan political organization. Established 1920.

Maritime Municipal Training and Development Board (MMTDB)

Don Smeltzer Training and Management Consultants
3-644 Portland Street, Suite 516
Dartmouth, Nova Scotia B2W 2M3
902-439-8092; fax: 902-484-6113

E-mail: Don@munisource.org

Website for municipal government information: munisource.org

Executive director: A. Donald Smeltzer

Purpose: To provide quality management, education, and training services to the municipal public sector and to volunteer organizations. Professional contacts are maintained with associates throughout North America and elsewhere, enabling the company to respond to many management and organizational needs. Established 1974.

National Animal Control Association (NACA)

P.O. Box 480851
Kansas City, Missouri 64148-0851
913-768-1319; fax: 913-768-1378

Website: nacanet.org

President: Debbie Dawson

Major publications: *The NACA News; The NACA Training Guide*

Purpose: To provide training for animal control personnel; consultation and guidance for local governments on animal control ordinances, animal shelter design, budget and program planning, and staff training; and public education. Established 1978.

National Association of Counties (NACo)

25 Massachusetts Avenue, N.W., Suite 500
Washington, D.C. 20001-1431
202-393-6226; fax: 202-393-2630

Website: naco.org

Executive director: Larry Naake

Major publications: *County News; NACo e-News*

Purpose: To provide essential services to the nation's 3,068 counties. The only national organization that represents county governments in the United States, NACo advances issues with a unified voice before the federal government; improves the public's understanding of county government, assists counties in finding and sharing innovative solutions through education and research, and provides value-added services to save counties and taxpayers money. Established 1935.

National Association of County and City Health Officials (NACCHO)

1100 17th Street, 7th Floor
Washington, D.C. 20036
202-783-5550; fax: 202-783-1583

Website: naccho.org

Executive director: Robert M. Pestronk, MPH

Major publications: *National Profile of Local Health Departments* (annual); *Public Health Dispatch* (newsletter); *NACCHO Exchange* (quarterly); research briefs and videos

Purpose: To support efforts that protect and improve the health of all people and all communities by promoting national policy, developing resources and programs, seeking health equity, and supporting effective local public health practice and systems. Established 1960s.

National Association for County Community and Economic Development (NACCED)

2025 M Street, N.W., Suite 800
Washington, D.C. 20036-3309
202-367-1149; fax: 202-367-2149

Website: nacced.org

Executive director: John Murphy

Purpose: To help develop the technical capacity of county agencies in administering community development, economic development, and affordable housing programs. Created as an affiliate of the National Association of Counties (NACo), NACCED is a nonprofit national organization that also serves as a voice within NACo to articulate the needs, concerns, and interests of county agencies. Established 1978.

National Association of Development Organizations (NADO)

400 North Capitol Street, N.W., Suite 390
Washington, D.C. 20001
202-624-7806; fax: 202-624-8813

Website: nado.org

Executive director: Matthew Chase

Major publications: *EDFS Reporter; NADO News; Regional Development Digest*

Purpose: To provide training, information, and representation for regional development organizations serving small metropolitan and rural America. Building on nearly four decades of experience, the association offers its members exclusive access to a variety of services and benefits–all of which are crafted to enhance the activities, programs, and prospects of regional development organizations. Established 1970s.

National Association of Housing and Redevelopment Officials (NAHRO)

630 Eye Street, N.W.
Washington, D.C. 20001
202-289-3500; fax: 202-289-8181
877-866-2476

Website: nahro.org

CEO: Saul N. Ramirez

Major publications: *Journal of Housing and Community Development; NAHRO Monitor; Directory of Local Agencies; Commissioners Dictionary; The NAHRO Public Relations Handbook; Commissioners Handbook*

Purpose: To serve as a professional membership organization representing local housing authorities; community development agencies; and professionals in the housing, community development, and redevelopment fields. Divided into eight regions and 43 chapters, NAHRO works to provide decent and affordable housing for low- and moderate-income persons. It provides its 20,000 members with information on federal policy, legislation, regulations, and funding. It also provides professional development and training programs in all phases of agency operations, including management, maintenance, and procurement. In addition, NAHRO sponsors a legislative conference, a summer conference, and a national conference and exhibition every year. Established 1933.

National Association of Regional Councils (NARC)

1666 Connecticut Avenue, N.W., Suite 300
Washington, D.C. 20009-1038
202-986-1032; fax: 202-986-1038

Website: narc.org

Executive director: Fred Abousleman

Purpose: To promote regional approaches and collaboration in addressing diverse development challenges. A nonprofit membership organization, NARC has represented the interests of its members and has advanced regional cooperation through effective interaction and advocacy with Congress, federal officials, and other related agencies and interest groups for more than 40 years. Its member organizations are composed of multiple local government units, such as regional councils and metropolitan planning organizations, that work together to serve American communities, large and small, urban and rural. Among the issues it addresses are transportation, homeland security and regional preparedness, economic and community development, the environment, and a variety of community concerns of interest to member organizations. NARC provides its members with valuable information and research on key national policy issues, federal policy developments, and best practices; in addition, it conducts enriching training sessions, conferences, and workshops. Established 1967.

National Association of Schools of Public Affairs and Administration (NASPAA)

1029 Vermont Avenue, N.W., Suite 1100
Washington, D.C. 20005
202-628-8965; fax: 202-626-4978

E-mail: naspaa@naspaa.org

Websites: naspaa.org; globalmpa.org; and publicservicecareers.org

Executive director: Laurel McFarland

Major publications: *Journal of Public Affairs Education (J-PAE); Newsletter; MPA Accreditation Standards; MPA/MPP Brochure;* peer review and accreditation documents

Purpose: To serve as a national and international center for information about programs and developments in the area of public affairs and administration; to foster goals and standards of educational excellence; to represent members' concerns and interests in the formulation and support of national, state, and local policies for public affairs education and research; and to serve as a specialized accrediting agency for MPA/MPP degrees. Established 1970.

National Association of State Chief Information Officers (NASCIO)

c/o AMR Management Services
201 East Main Street, Suite 1405
Lexington, Kentucky 40507
859-514-9156; fax: 859-514-9166

Website: nascio.org

Executive director: Doug Robinson

Major publications: *State CIO's Top Ten Policy and Technology Priorities for 2010; 2009 Best Practices in the Use of Information Tech-*

nology in State Government Booklet; Resource Guide for State Cyber Security Awareness, Education, and Training Initiatives; Security at the Edge: Protecting Mobile Computing Devices; NASCIO Connections (newsletter)

Purpose: To be the premier network and resource for state chief information officers (CIOs) and a leading advocate for information technology (IT) policy at all levels of government. NASCIO represents state CIOs and IT executives from the states, territories, and the District of Columbia. Its primary state government members are senior officials who have executive-level and statewide responsibility for IT leadership. State officials who are involved in agency-level IT management may participate as state members; representatives from other public sector and nonprofit organizations may participate as associate members. Private sector firms may join as corporate members and participate in the Corporate Leadership Council. Established 1969.

National Association of Towns and Townships (NATaT)

1130 Connecticut Avenue, N.W., Suite 300
Washington, D.C. 20036
202-454-3950; fax: 202-331-1598

Website: natat.org

Federal director: Jennifer Imo

Major publication: *Washington Report*

Purpose: To strengthen the effectiveness of town and township government by educating lawmakers and public policy officials about how small-town governments operate and by advocating policies on their behalf in Washington, D.C. Established 1976.

National Career Development Association (NCDA)

305 North Beech Circle
Broken Arrow, Oklahoma 74012
918-663-7060; fax: 918-663-7058

Website: ncda.org

Executive director: Deneen Pennington

Major publications: *A Counselor's Guide to Career Assessments; The Internet: A Tool for Career Planning; Career Developments magazine*

Purpose: To promote career development of all people throughout the lifespan. A division of the American Counseling Association, NCDA provides services to the public and to professionals involved with or interested in career development; services include professional development activities, publications, research, public information, professional standards, advocacy, and recognition for achievement and service. Established 1913.

National Civic League (NCL)

1889 York Street
Denver, Colorado 80206
303-571-4343; fax: 888-314-6053

E-mail: kristins@ncl.org

Website: ncl.org

Blog: allamericacityaward.com

President: Gloria Rubio-Cortés

Major publications: *The Community Visioning and Strategic Planning Handbook; Model County Charter; National Civic Review; 8th Edition of the Model City Charter; New Civic Index*

Purpose: To strengthen democracy by increasing the capacity of our nation's people to fully participate in and build healthy and prosperous communities across America. NCL facilitates community-wide strategic planning in fiscal sustainability, environmental sustainability, transportation-oriented development, and other issues. We are good at the science of local government, the art of public engagement, and the celebration of the progress that can be achieved when people work together. NCL is the home of the All-America City Award, now in its 62nd year, and of the MetLife Foundation Ambassadors in Education Awards. The year 2011 is the *National Civic Review's* 100th year of publishing; the yearlong theme is "What's Working in American Communities." Established 1894.

National Community Development Association (NCDA)

522 21st Street, N.W., #120
Washington, D.C. 20006
202-293-7587; fax: 202-887-5546

Website: ncdaonline.org

Executive director: Cardell Cooper

Purpose: To serve as a national clearinghouse of ideas for local government officials and federal policy makers on pertinent national issues affecting America's communities. NCDA is a national nonprofit organization comprising more than 550 local governments across the country that administer federally supported community and economic development, housing, and human service programs, including those of the U.S. Department of Housing and Urban Development (HUD), the Community Development Block Grant program, and HOME Investment Partnerships. NCDA provides timely, direct information and technical support to its members in their efforts to secure effective and responsive housing and community development programs. Established 1968.

National Conference of State Legislatures (NCSL)

7700 East First Place
Denver, Colorado 80230
303-364-7700; fax: 303-364-7800
Also at 444 North Capitol Street, N.W., Suite 515
Washington, D.C. 20001-1201
202-624-5400; fax: 202-737-1069

Website: ncsl.org

Executive director: William T. Pound

Major publications: *Capitol to Capitol, Federal Update, State Legislatures*

Purpose: To improve the quality and effectiveness of state legislatures; to ensure that states have a strong, cohesive voice in the federal decision-making process; and to foster interstate communication and cooperation. A bipartisan organization that serves the legislators and staffs of the nation's states, commonwealths, and territories, NCSL provides research, technical assistance, and opportunities for policy makers to exchange ideas on the most pressing state issues. Established 1975.

National Environmental Health Association (NEHA)

720 South Colorado Boulevard, Suite 1000-N
Denver, Colorado 80246
303-756-9090; fax: 303-691-9490
E-mail: staff@neha.org

Website: neha.org

Executive director: Nelson E. Fabian

Major publications: *2009 H1N1 Pandemic Influenza Planning Manual; Microbial Safety of Fresh Produce; Planet Water: Investing in the World's Most Valuable Resource; Environmental Toxicants: Human Exposures and Their Health Effects; Resolving Messy Policy Problems; Journal of Environmental Health*

Purpose: To advance the professional in the environmental field through education, professional meetings, and the dissemination of information. NEHA also publishes information relating to environmental health and protection and promotes professionalism in the field. Established 1937.

National Fire Protection Association (NFPA)

One Batterymarch Park
Quincy, Massachusetts 02169-7471
617-770-3000; fax: 617-770-0700

Website: nfpa.org

President/CEO: James M. Shannon

Major publications: *Fire Protection Handbook; Fire Technology; NFPA Journal; National Electrical Code®; National Fire Codes®; Life Safety Code®; Risk Watch™; Learn Not to Burn® Curriculum*; and textbooks, manuals, training packages, detailed analyses of important fires, and fire officers guides

Purpose: To reduce the worldwide burden of fire and other hazards on the quality of life by providing and advocating scientifically based consensus codes and standards, research, training, and education. Established 1896.

National Governors Association (NGA)

Hall of the States
444 North Capitol Street, Suite 267
Washington, D.C. 20001-1512
202-624-5300; fax: 202-624-5313

Website: nga.org

Executive director: Raymond C. Scheppach

Major publications: *The Fiscal Survey of States; Policy Positions;* reports on a wide range of state issues

Purpose: To act as a liaison between the states and the federal government, and to serve as a clearinghouse for information and ideas on state and national issues. Established 1908.

National Housing Conference (NHC)

1801 K Street, N.W., Suite M-100
Washington, D.C. 20006-1301
202-466-2121; fax: 202-466-2122

Website: nhc.org

President/CEO: Maureen Friar

Major publications: *New Century Housing; NHC at Work; NHC Affordable Housing Policy Review; Washington Wire*

Purpose: To promote better communities and affordable housing for Americans through education and advocacy. Established 1931.

National Institute of Governmental Purchasing (NIGP)

151 Spring Street
Herndon, Virginia 20170-5223
703-736-8900; fax: 703-736-2818
800-FOR NIGP (800-367-6447)

Website: nigp.org

CEO: Rick Grimm, CPPO, CPPB

Major publications: *GoPro: Government Procurement* magazine, a bimonthly publication distributed to NIGP members and procurement professionals; NIGP *Sector Spotlight* edition of *BuyWeekly*, published electronically at the beginning of the month to NIGP members with procurement-related news briefs that affect the procurement community; NIGP's *BuyWeekly*, electronic newsletter, distributed midmonth, a quick overview of current highlights in the profession and at NIGP; and the *NIGP Online Dictionary of Purchasing Terms.*

Purpose: To develop, support, and promote the public procurement profession through premier educational and research programs, professional support, technical services, and advocacy initiatives that have benefited members and constituents since 1944. With over 2,600 member agencies representing over 16,000 professionals across the United States, Canada, and counties outside of North America, NIGP is international in its reach. Its goal is recognition and esteem for the government procurement profession and its dedicated practitioners. NIGP's Learning Central offers traditional face-to-face courses, 24/7 online courses, and no-travel webinars that address current industry issues and trends affecting the way governments do business. All NIGP education experiences qualify toward achieving certification from the Universal Public Procurement Certification Council (UPPCC). NIGP hosts an annual

Forum and Products Exposition, the largest gathering of public procurement officials in North America. It offers members a vast resource library of solicitation and template documents as well as access to the VAULT, an active repository with the latest analysis and sector insights from Research Partner, Aberdeen Group; NIGP MEASURE, an online tool that records and reports procurement-generated savings; and an online supplier directory to quickly find over 2,000 government suppliers in the United States and Canada. It also offers fixed-price NIGP Consulting Services, which evaluate policies and procedures, contract administration, and pcard program practices; establish relevant benchmark measures; and identify best practices. A strategic partnership between Spikes Cavell and NIGP brings a proven spend analysis solution to the U.S. public sector. The NIGP Observatory is a spend-and-supplier management solution that delivers the data, tools, and intelligence required to give procurement the insight it needs to reduce cost, realize cooperative opportunities, improve contract compliance, and drive continuous improvements in spend-and-supplier management. NIGP's technology partner, Periscope Holdings, supports the ongoing development of the NIGP Code and the over 1,400 agencies that already use the code, a universal taxonomy for identifying commodities and services in their procurement systems. NIGP is a cofounding sponsor of U.S. Communities and its affiliate, Canadian Communities, demonstrating its conviction to fully support the practice of cooperative purchasing for the efficiencies it achieves for public entities and the tremendous savings cooperative programs realize for the taxpayer. It is also a cofounding supporter of the UPPCC and its two-level certification program for public procurement personnel. Established 1944.

National League of Cities (NLC)

1301 Pennsylvania Avenue, N.W., Suite 550
Washington, D.C. 20004-1763
202-626-3000; fax: 202-626-3043

Website: nlc.org

Executive director: Donald J. Borut

President: Ronald O. Loveridge, mayor, Riverside, California

Major publications: *Nation's Cities Weekly*, guide books, directories, and research reports

Purpose: To strengthen and promote cities as centers of opportunity, leadership, and governance; to serve as an advocate for its members in Washington in the legislative, administrative, and judicial processes that affect them; to offer training, technical assistance, and information to local government and state league officials to help them improve the quality of local government; and to research and analyze policy issues of importance to cities and towns in America. Established 1924.

National Public Employer Labor Relations Association (NPELRA)

1012 South Coast Highway, Suite M
Oceanside, California 92054
760-433-1686; fax: 760-433-1687

E-mail: info@npelra.org

Website: npelra.org

Executive director: Michael T. Kolb

Purpose: To provide its members with high-quality, progressive labor relations professional development that balances the needs of management, employees, and the public. The premier organization for public sector labor relations and human resource professionals, NPELRA is a network of state and regional affiliates. Its more than 3,000 members around the country represent public employers in a wide range of areas, from employee-management contract negotiations to arbitration under grievance and arbitration procedures. NPELRA also works to promote the interests of public sector management in the judicial and legislative arenas, and to provide opportunities for networking among members by establishing state and regional organizations throughout the country. The governmental agencies represented in NPELRA employ more than 4 million workers in federal, state, and local government.

National Recreation and Park Association (NRPA)

22377 Belmont Ridge Road
Ashburn, Virginia 20148
703-858-0784; fax: 703-858-0794

Website: nrpa.org

CEO: Barbara Tulipane

Major publication: *Parks & Recreation Magazine*

Purpose: To advance parks, recreation, and environmental conservation efforts that enhance the quality of life for all people. Established 1965.

National School Boards Association (NSBA)

1680 Duke Street
Alexandria, Virginia 22314-3493
703-838-6722; fax: 703-683-7590

Website: nsba.org

Executive director: Anne L. Bryant

Major publications: *American School Board Journal*; ASBK.com; *Inquiry and Analysis; Leadership Insider; School Board News*

Purpose: To work with and through all our state associations to advocate for excellence and equity in public education through school board leadership. Established 1940.

Police Executive Research Forum (PERF)

1120 Connecticut Avenue, N.W., Suite 930
Washington, D.C. 20036
202-466-7820; fax: 202-466-7826

Website: policeforum.org

Executive director: Chuck Wexler

Major publication: *Subject to Debate* (monthly newsletter)

Purpose: To improve policing and advance professionalism through research and involvement in public policy debate. PERF is a national membership organization of progressive police executives from the largest city, county, and state law enforcement agencies. Its primary sources of operating revenues are government grants and contracts, and partnerships with private foundations and other organizations. Incorporated 1977.

Police Foundation

1201 Connecticut Avenue, N.W.
Washington, D.C. 20036-2636
202-833-1460; fax: 202-659-9149

E-mail: pfinfo@policefoundation.org

Website: policefoundation.org

President: Hubert Williams

Major publications: *Ideas in American Policing* series; research and technical reports on a wide range of law enforcement and public safety issues

Purpose: To improve policing through research, evaluation, field experimentation, training, technical assistance, technology, and information. Objective, nonpartisan, and nonprofit, the Police Foundation helps national, state, and local governments, both in the United States and abroad, to improve performance, service delivery, accountability, and community satisfaction with police services. The foundation offers a wide range of services and specializations, including research, evaluation, surveys, management and operational reviews, climate and culture assessment, training and technical assistance, early-warning and intervention systems, community police collaboration, accountability and ethics, community policing strategies, performance management, racial profiling/biased policing, professional and leadership development. Motivating all its efforts is the goal of efficient, effective, humane policing that operates within the framework of democratic principles. Established in 1970.

Public Entity Risk Institute (PERI)

11350 Random Hills Road, Suite 210
Fairfax, Virginia 22030
703-352-1846; fax: 703-352-6339

E-mail: ghoetmer@riskinstitute.org

Website: riskinstitute.org

Interim executive director: Claire Lee Reiss

Major publications: *Managing for Long-Term Community Recovery in the Aftermath of Disaster; Ideas from an Emerging Field: Teaching Emergency Management in Higher Education; Emergency Management in Higher Education: Current Practices and Conversations; Emergency Management: The American Experience 1900-2005; Risk Identification and Analysis: A Guide for Small Public Entities;* *Community Leadership in a Risky World; Characteristics of Effective Emergency Management Structures; Are You Ready? What Lawyers Need to Know about Emergency Preparedness and Disaster Recovery; Holistic Disaster Recovery: Ideas for Building Local Sustainability after a Natural Disaster; Surviving Extreme Events: A Guide to Help Small Businesses and Not-for-Profit Organizations Prepare for and Recover from Extreme Events; PERIScope Newsletter*

Purpose: To provide risk management education and training resources for local governments and school districts, small businesses, and nonprofits. PERI is a nonprofit, nonmembership organization. Its website, riskinstitute.org, serves as a resource center and clearinghouse with information on a wide range of topics, including disaster management and hazard mitigation, risk financing and insurance, safety and health, workers' compensation, and technology risks. PERI also offers insuranceformynonprofit.org, a website that provides small and medium-sized nonprofit organizations with a self-help tool to identify their insurance needs and find insurers. PERI's professional staff is available to consult with local governments on risk management planning. Established 1996.

Public Risk Management Association (PRIMA)

500 Montgomery Street, Suite 750
Alexandria, Virginia 22314-1516
703-528-7701; fax: 703-739-0200

E-mail: info@primacentral.org

Website: primacentral.org

Executive director: Lisa Lopinsky

Major publications: *Public Risk Magazine; Public Sector Risk Management Manual; Cost of Risk Evaluation in State and Local Government; 1998 Tort Liability Today: A Guide for State and Local Governments; Shaping a Secure Future* (video)

Purpose: To promote effective risk management in the public interest as an essential component of administration. Established 1978.

Public Technology Institute (PTI)

1301 Pennsylvania Avenue, N.W., Suite 830
Washington, D.C. 20004
202-626-2400; fax: 202-626-2498

E-mail: dbowen@pti.org

Website: pti.org

Executive director: Alan R. Shark

Major publications: *CIO Leadership for Cities & Counties; Local Energy Assurance Planning Guide; Beyond e-Government & e-Democracy: A Global Perspective; Measuring Up 2.0; Performance Is the Best Politics; Roads Less Traveled: ITS for Sustainable Communities; Sustainable Building Technical Manual; Mission Possible: Strong Governance Structures for the Integration of Justice Information Systems; E-Government: Factors Affecting ROI; E-Government: A Strategic Planning Guide for Local Officials; Why Not Do It Ourselves? A Resource Guide for Local Government Officials and Citizens Regarding Public Ownership of Utility Systems; Online* magazine (www.prismonline.org); *Winning Solutions* (annual); numerous case studies on energy and environmental technology development and sustainable management

Purpose: To identify and test technologies and management approaches that help all local governments provide the best possible services to citizens and business communities. With ICMA, NLC, and NACo, PTI works with progressive member cities and counties to (1) make communities "well-connected" by advancing communication capabilities; (2) develop tools and processes for wise decision making; and (3) promote sustainable approaches that ensure a balance between economic development and a clean, quality environment. PTI's member program engages cities and counties as laboratories for research, development, and public enterprise to advance technology applications in telecommunications, energy, the environment, transportation, and public safety. To disseminate member research, PTI provides print and electronic resources, and peer consultation and networking. Through partnerships with private vendors, PTI offers several technology products and services that help local governments save money by bypassing rigorist RFP requirements as they are competitively bid and chosen for superior quality and competitive pricing. PTI's research and development division continues to examine information and Internet technology, public safety, geographic information systems (GIS), energy-conserving technologies, sustainable management, and intelligent transportation systems. Established 1971.

Sister Cities International (SCI)

1301 Pennsylvania Avenue, N.W., Suite 850
Washington, D.C. 20004
202-347-8630; fax: 202-393-6524

E-mail: info@sister-cities.org

Website: sister-cities.org

President/CEO: Patrick Madden

Major publication: *Sister Cities International Membership Directory*

Purpose: To build global cooperation at the municipal level, promote cultural understanding, and stimulate economic development. SCI is a nonprofit citizen diplomacy network that creates and strengthens partnerships between U.S. and international communities. With its international headquarters in Washington, D.C., SCI promotes sustainable development, youth involvement, cultural understanding, and humanitarian assistance. As an international membership organization, SCI officially certifies, represents, and supports partnerships between U.S. cities, counties, and states and similar jurisdictions in other countries to ensure their continued commitment and success. The SCI network represents nearly 2,000 partnerships in 136 countries. Established 1956.

Solid Waste Association of North America (SWANA)

1100 Wayne Avenue, Suite 700
Silver Spring, Maryland 20907-7219
301-585-2898; fax: 301-589-7068
800-467-9262

E-mail: info@swana.org

Website: swana.org

Executive director: John H. Skinner, PhD

Purpose: To advance the practice of environmentally and economically sound municipal solid-waste management in North America. Established 1961.

Special Libraries Association (SLA)

331 South Patrick Street
Alexandria, Virginia 22314-3501
703-647-4900; fax: 703-647-4901

E-mail: sla@sla.org

Website: sla.org

CEO: Janice R. Lachance

Major publication: *Information Outlook*

Purpose: To further the professional growth and success of its membership. The international association representing the interests of thousands of information professionals in 84 countries, SLA offers a variety of programs and services designed to help its members serve their customers more effectively and succeed in an increasingly challenging global information arena. Established 1909.

Universal Public Procurement Certification Council (UPPCC)

151 Spring Street
Herndon, Virginia 20170
800-367-6447; fax: 703-796-9611

E-mail: certification@uppcc.org

Website: uppcc.org

Director: Ann Peshoff, CAE, CMP

Purpose: To identify and establish a standard of competency for the public procurement profession; establish and monitor eligibility requirements of those interested in achieving certification; and further the cause of certification in the public sector. The UPPCC certification programs have been established to meet the requirements of all public procurement personnel in federal, state, and local governments. Certification, which reflects established standards and competencies for those engaged in governmental procurement and attests to the purchaser's ability to obtain maximum value for the taxpayer's dollar, is applicable to all public and governmental organizations, regardless of size. The council offers two credentials: the Certified Professional Public Buyer (CPPB), which applies to individuals who have demonstrated prescribed levels of professional competency as buyers in governmental procurement, and the Certified Public Procurement Officer (CPPO), which applies to similar individuals who also assume managerial functions within their jurisdictions or agencies. As the trend in governmental procurement is for mandatory certification of procurement professionals, these credentials communicate to the taxpayer that the public employee who manages tax dollars has reached a level of education and practical experience within government procurement to be recognized by the UPPCC. Established 1978.

Urban Affairs Association (UAA)

298 Graham Hall
University of Delaware
Newark, Delaware 19716
302-831-1681; fax: 302-831-4225

Website: udel.edu/uaa

Executive director: Dr. Margaret Wilder

Major publications: *Journal of Urban Affairs; Urban Affairs* (a newsletter)

Purpose: To encourage the dissemination of information and research findings about urbanism and urbanization; to support the development of university education, research, and service programs in urban affairs; and to foster the development of urban affairs as a professional and academic field. Established 1969.

Urban Institute (UI)

2100 M Street, N.W.
Washington, D.C. 20037
202-833-7200

Website: urban.org

President: Robert D. Reischauer

Publications: Research papers, policy briefs, events, podcasts, web modules, and books on social and economic issues, including health care, welfare reform, immigration policy, tax reform, prisoner reentry, housing policy, retirement, charitable giving, school accountability, economic development, and community revitalization; all publications available online except books

Purpose: To respond to needs for objective analyses and basic information on the social and economic challenges confronting the nation, and for nonpartisan evaluation of the government policies and programs designed to alleviate such problems. Established 1968.

Urban and Regional Information Systems Association (URISA)

701 Lee Street, Suite 680
Des Plaines, Illinois 60016
847-824-6300; fax: 847-824-6363

Website: urisa.org

Executive director: Wendy Nelson

Major publications: *URISA Journal; The GIS Professional;* Quick Studies, books and compendiums, salary surveys, conference proceedings, videos

Purpose: To promote the effective and ethical use of spatial information and information technologies for the understanding and management of urban and regional systems. URISA is a nonprofit professional, educational, and multidisciplinary association where professionals from all parts of the spatial data community can come together and share concerns and ideas. It is the professional home of choice for public sector GIS and information technology executives throughout the United States, Canada, and other countries worldwide. Established 1963.

U.S. Conference of Mayors (USCM)

1620 Eye Street, N.W.
Washington, D.C. 20006
202-293-7330; fax: 202-293-2352

E-mail: info@usmayors.org

Website: usmayors.org

Executive director/CEO: Tom Cochran

Major publications: *U.S. Mayor; Mayors of America's Principal Cities*

Purpose: To act as the official nonpartisan organization of cities with populations of 30,000 or more; to aid the development of effective national urban policy; to ensure that federal policy meets urban needs; and to provide mayors with leadership and management tools. Each city is represented in the conference by its mayor. Established 1932.

Water Environment Federation (WEF)

601 Wythe Street
Alexandria, Virginia 22314-1994
703-684-2552; fax: 703-684-2492
800-666-0206

Websites: wef.org and weftec.org

Executive director: William Bertera

Major publications: *Water Environment Research; Water Practice; Water Environment and Technology; Operations Forum; Water Environment Regulation Watch; Biosolids Technical Bulletin; Utility Executive Technical Bulletin;* series of Manuals of Practice

Purpose: To develop and disseminate technical information concerning the preservation and enhancement of the global water environment. As an integral component of its mandate, the federation has pledged to act as a source of education to the general public as well as to individuals engaged in the field of water pollution control. Established 1928.

Authors and Contributors

Authors and Contributors

Ann O'M. Bowman holds the Hazel Davis and Robert Kennedy Endowed Chair in the Bush School of Government and Public Service at Texas A&M University and directs the Intergovernmental Dynamics Project. Her research focuses on state and local politics and policy, and on federalism and intergovernmental relations. Recent co-authored works include *State and Local Government* (8th ed.) as well as the following journal articles: "Expanding the Scope of Conflict: Interest Groups and Interstate Compacts," "Second Order Devolution: Data and Doubt," and "Blurring Borders: The Effect of Federal Activism on Interstate Cooperation." She has been president of both the Urban Politics and the Public Policy sections of the American Political Science Association, and she currently serves on the editorial advisory board of *Publius: The Journal of Federalism*. She received her PhD from the University of Florida.

Alan R. Brown is a consultant to the Children's Services Council of Palm Beach County, Florida, in the development of a comprehensive "system of care" for early child development. He also serves as consultant to ICMA in the development of a comprehensive performance and resource management system; to the Human Rights Clinic of HealthRight International (formerly Doctors of the World), an organization working with torture survivors from around the world; and to a number of state and federal agencies. In addition, he has worked collaboratively with other states on joining training and research projects. He served as the principal investigator for the Arizona Prevention Resource Center and as the director of research, planning, and special projects. Prior to his retirement, he was a member of the faculty at Arizona State University for 40 years. He has extensive experience in the management of large and complex projects funded by the U.S. Department of Health and Human Services and the U.S. Department of Justice. He holds a PhD in clinical psychology from the University of Texas at Austin.

Ron Carlee is ICMA's chief operating officer and executive in residence. Prior to joining ICMA in 2009, he had held several positions in Arlington, Virginia, including county manager, director of health and human services, director of parks and recreation, and director of information services. Prior to that, he was assistant to the mayor in Birmingham, Alabama. Dr. Carlee is on the faculty of the Trachtenberg School of Public Policy and Public Administration at the George Washington University, and he is a Fellow in the National Academy for Public Administration. He holds a bachelor's degree from the University of Montevallo, a master's degree from the University of Alabama, and doctorate in public administration from George Mason University.

Gail S. Chadwick is the vice president of PreventionMatters, LLC, a consulting firm. From 1990 to 2007, she directed the Arizona Prevention Resource Center (APRC), a partnership of state agencies that provides information, training, and technical assistance in the areas of prevention and health promotion to Arizona's schools, organizations, and communities. From 1997 to 2007 she also directed the legislatively mandated Arizona Drug and Gang Prevention Resource Center, which provides information and technical assistance specifically on those issues, and compiles the annual inventory of Arizona's substance abuse prevention, education, and treatment programs under the auspices of the governor's Drug and Gang Policy Council. Previously she directed the MESA Network, a collaborative substance abuse prevention project in Mesa, Arizona, and from 1984 to 1990 she was a grant and contract administrator at Arizona State University (ASU). Other professional activities have entailed proposal review, grant writing, and organization development issues (including assessment, team building, and human resources) with various public and private sector organizations. She has served on many boards and commissions in Arizona, including the State Commission for National and Community Service, and has chaired the Education Committee for the Coalition for Tobacco Free Arizona. Ms. Chadwick holds a master's of counseling degree from ASU.

Shannon E. Hayden is a coauthor of *Citizen Surveys: A Comprehensive Guide to Making Them Matter* and a senior research associate at National Research Center, Inc. (NRC), where she has worked since 2000. She helped develop The National Citizen Survey™ and has managed major survey research projects at NRC. In addition to regularly presenting survey results to jurisdictions across the country, she has conducted many trainings on surveying and methodology. She has a master's degree in educational psychology, with a focus on research and evaluation methods.

Richard C. Kearney is professor and director of the School of Public and International Affairs at North Carolina State University. His research and teaching specialties are American federalism, state and local politics, and human resource management and labor relations. He has published widely in professional journals in political science and public administration. His most recent books include *Labor Relations in the Public Sector* (4th ed.) and, as coauthor, *State and Local Government* (6th ed.).

Thomas I Miller is a coauthor of the *Citizen Surveys: A Comprehensive Guide to Making Them Matter.* Since 1994, he has headed his own consulting firm, National Research Center, Inc. (NRC), which conducts survey research for local and state governments and training in performance measurement for the public sector. Dr. Miller conceived The National Citizen Survey™, a turnkey survey that NRC has conducted in partnership with ICMA in more than 40 states. He has worked for local and state government for sixteen years, during most of which he headed a division of

the city government in Boulder, Colorado, charged with conducting policy analysis, survey research, and program evaluation. He has a PhD in research and evaluation methodology and is currently an adjunct associate professor at the University of Colorado.

Evelina R. Moulder, director of ICMA's survey research, is responsible for the development of survey instruments, design of the sample, design of logic checks, quality control, and analysis of survey results. Among the surveys conducted by ICMA under her supervision are economic development, e-government, financing infrastructure, homeland security, labor-management relations, parks and recreation, police and fire personnel and expenditures, service delivery, technology, and SARA Title III. She has also directed several survey projects funded by other organizations. With more than 20 years of experience in local government survey research, Ms. Moulder has collaborated extensively with government agencies, professors, the private sector, and other researchers in survey development, and she has played a key role in ICMA's homeland security and emergency response initiatives, including concept and proposal development.

Robert J. O'Neill Jr. is executive director of ICMA and chair of the Center for State and Local Government Excellence, LLC. Prior to joining ICMA in December 2002, he had been president of the National Academy of Public Administration (NAPA), of which he is a Fellow; county executive of Fairfax, Virginia; city manager of Hampton, Virginia; and director of Management Consulting Services for the Virginia offices of Coopers & Lybrand. Mr. O'Neill holds a bachelor's degree from Old Dominion University and a master's of public administration from the Maxwell School of Citizenship and Public Affairs at Syracuse University; he is also a graduate of The Executive Program of the Colgate Darden Graduate School of Business at the University of Virginia, and was awarded an honorary doctorate of laws from Old Dominion University.

Nadia Rubaii-Barrett is associate professor of public administration in the College of Community and Public Affairs at Binghamton University. She has worked for more than two decades with local government officials and professional associations to address issues of service delivery effectiveness, intergovernmental relations, and the challenges of increasing diversity. In 2001–2002, she was part of a four-member team commissioned by the U.S.-Mexico Border Counties Commission to conduct a study of the effects of illegal immigration on county health and criminal justice systems. She has authored several articles, book chapters, and book-length professional reports, including the 2009 ICMA white paper *Immigration Reform: An Intergovernmental Imperative*. As a recognized expert in the field of immigration research and the challenges of increasing language diversity, she is a regular speaker at state, local, and regional events addressing the topic. She received her BA, MA, and PhD in political science from Binghamton University.

James H. Svara is a professor of public affairs at Arizona State University and the director of the Center for Urban Innovation. He specializes in local government leadership, management, and ethics. He is a Fellow of the National Academy of Public Administration, a member of the board of the Alliance for Innovation, and an honorary member of ICMA, and he has served on the ICMA Strategic Planning Committee. His book *More Than Mayor or Manager: Campaigns to Change Form of Government in America's Large Cities*, coedited with Douglas Watson, was recently published by Georgetown University Press.

Jodi E. Swicegood will graduate from the MPA program at North Carolina State University in August 2011. She has devoted the majority of her career as a graduate student to studying second-order devolution and related issues, and she has presented several papers on the topic at academic conferences. Her goal after graduation is to work in research and development or in a setting where she can continue her passion for applied research. Her academic interests include federalism, intergovernmental relations, and state and local government. She earned her undergraduate degree, also from North Carolina State, in political science with a concentration in international politics and a minor in Spanish.

Karen Thoreson is president/chief operating officer for the Alliance for Innovation. Prior to working for the alliance, she was economic development director for the city of Glendale, Arizona. She also served as assistant city manager of Tucson, overseeing downtown revitalization, and as director of the community services department, which manages the city's affordable housing programs, human services, and neighborhood revitalization. Ms. Thoreson began her career in local government in Boulder, Colorado; has been a trainer and a speaker on public-private partnerships, community revitalization, innovation, and strategic planning; served as national president for the National Association of Housing and Redevelopment Organization from 1999 to 2001; and is currently active in local, state, and national groups. She has a

bachelor's degree from the University of Minnesota and a master's degree in public administration from the University of Northern Colorado.

Lance Till currently serves as systems manager with the Healthy Beginnings Program Division at the Children's Services Council of Palm Beach County, Florida. Currently, he oversees the Healthy Beginnings Program— a system of about 30 programs that aim to increase healthy births, prevent child abuse and neglect, and prepare children to be eager for school. His numerous years of experience conducting evaluations of public health and education programs have culminated in white papers and evaluation reports to local, state, and national agencies. Mr. Till holds a master's degree in health communication from the University of Iowa.

Mildred E. Warner is a professor in the City and Regional Planning Department at Cornell University, where her work is primarily on the role of local government in community development. Her research focuses on devolution, privatization, and their implications for local government service delivery. She also studies economic development and the role of local services. She publishes widely in the public administration, planning, and economic development literature. Dr. Warner received her BA from Oberlin College and her MA and PhD from Cornell.

Lisa Williams-Taylor is director of program planning at the Children's Services Council of Palm Beach County, Florida. She is responsible for policy analysis, strategic planning, and leading the program division with regard to evidence-based programming. She works with a variety of community stakeholders and policy makers as well as with state and national organizations on strategic planning and research initiatives. She presents regularly at national, state, and local conferences and has written over 25 publications. Her professional background is in research and evaluation in the areas of addictions, mental health, and criminal justice. Dr. Williams-Taylor holds master of arts degrees in forensic psychology and criminal justice, and a doctorate in criminal justice.

Lingwen Zheng is a doctoral student in the Department of Economics at Cornell University. She analyzed the three ICMA economic development surveys for her master's thesis in city and regional planning, also from Cornell. Her research primarily focuses on public economics and economic development policies—in particular, the role and functions of governments confronted with poverty, unemployment, and socioeconomic polarization.

Cumulative Index, 2007-2011

The cumulative index comprises the years 2007 through 2011 of *The Municipal Year Book*. Entries prior to 2006 are found in earlier editions.

How to Use This Index. Entries run in chronological order, starting with 2005. The **year** is in **boldface** numerals, followed by a colon (e.g., **07:**); the relevant page numbers follow. Years are separated by semicolons.

The Municipal Year Book 2011
   Volume 78

Composition by
   Charles Mountain, Karl Kaufmann
   ICMA

Printing and binding by
   United Book Press, Inc.
   Baltimore, Maryland